THE DEGREES OF THE SPIRITUAL LIFE

A METHOD OF DIRECTING SOULS ACCORDING TO THEIR PROGRESS IN VIRTUE

by

THE ABBÉ A. SAUDREAU

DIRECTOR OF THE MOTHER-HOUSE OF THE GOOD SHEPHERD AT ANGERS

TRANSLATED FROM THE FRENCH BY

DOM BEDE CAMM, O.S.B.

Permissu Superiorum

IN TWO VOLUMES

VOL.II

LONDON

BURNS OATES & WASHBOURNE LTD.

PUBLISHERS TO THE HOLY SEE

ISBN-10: 1981705236

ISBN-13: 978-1981705238

Nihil Obstat.

DOM PETRUS NUGENT, O.S.B.,

Censor Deputatus

Imprimi Potest.

✝ GULIELMUS,

Episcopus Arindelensis,

Vicarius Generalis

WESTMONASTERII,

Die 28 Junii, 1907

This volume is published by Catholic Castle, which is a subdivision of Castle of Grace, LLC.

www.catholiccastle.com

www.castleofgrace.com

OVERVIEW: THE ARRANGEMENT OF THE WHOLE
PROJECT (by the editor of this 2017 edition).

Abbé Saudreau's *The Degrees of the Spiritual Life* is a very
thorough treatment of his subject and it will help the reader to
have an overview of the whole project.

THE FIRST VOLUME

PRELIMINARY: SINNERS
Two preliminary chapters explain the condition of sinners and
how they can be helped to improve.

THE PURGATIVE WAY
This consists of two books: *The First Degree — Believing
Souls* and then *The Second Degree — Good Christian Souls.*

THE ILLUMINATIVE LIFE
This also consists of two books: *The Third Degree — Devout
Souls*, followed by *The Fourth Degree — Fervour.* The author
deals with the Third Degree in great depth and this particular
book is divided into three parts, each part containing a number
of chapters.

THE SECOND VOLUME

THE UNITIVE LIFE
The second volume consists of three books: *The Fifth Degree
— Perfect Souls, The Sixth Degree — Heroic Souls,* and *The
Seventh Degree — Great Saints.* As with the book on the Third
Degree, the book on the Fifth Degree is divided into three
parts, each containing a number of chapters.

A note about the text: This work is the translation made from
the original French by the Englishman, Dom Bede McCann.
His spellings and grammatical usages have for the most part
been retained.

CONTENTS OF VOLUME II

THE UNITIVE LIFE

PROLOGUE

BOOK V

FIFTH DEGREE — PERFECT SOULS

PART I. — CONTEMPLATIVE PRAYER

CHAPTER I

CHAPTER II

CONTENTS OF VOLUME II

CONTENTS OF VOLUME II

CONTENTS OF VOLUME II

CHAPTER IV
CHARACTERISTICS OF CHARITY IN PERFECT SOULS

CHAPTER V
THE EXTERIOR CONDUCT OF PERFECT SOULS

CHAPTER VI
THE MERITS OF THIS STATE OF PERFECTION: HOW IT DIFFERS FROM THE STATE OF SANCTITY

PART III. — ON THE DIRECTION OF PERFECT SOULS — RULES OF THE CONTEMPLATIVE LIFE

CHAPTER I
ON THE IMPORTANCE OF A KNOWLEDGE OF THE RULES OF THE CONTEMPLATIVE LIFE ON THE PART OF THE DIRECTORS

CHAPTER II
RULES TO BE FOLLOWED IN THE DIRECTION OF CONTEMPLATIVE SOULS

CONTENTS OF VOLUME II

CONTENTS OF VOLUME II

CHAPTER III
ON THE INNER DISPOSITIONS OF HEROIC SOULS

BOOK VII

SEVENTH DEGREE — GREAT SAINTS

CHAPTER I
THE WAY LEADING FROM HEROISM TO PERFECT SANCTITY

CONTENTS OF VOLUME II

CHAPTER II
THE LAST DEGREE OF SANCTITY: THE FINAL AND PERFECT UNION

APPENDICES

NOTE

As to the quotations from the writings of the Saints, it should be noted that pains have been taken to refer to the best English translations available, where such versions are to be had, and not simply to translate the authors' French version. Thus, for St. John of the Cross, the translation of Mr. David Lewis (Baker, 1891) has been used. For St. Teresa's Life I have also used Mr. Lewis's version (Baker, 1904); while the quotations from the Interior Castle have been taken from the excellent new translation by the Benedictines of Stanbrook, who have used the Saint's own autograph (Interior Castle; Baker, 1906). For St. Teresa's other works I have been forced to content myself with Canon Dalton's unsatisfactory version. It is to be hoped that the Stanbrook nuns will soon be able to give us a new translation, and thus complete the work so admirably begun.

Here and there short passages from these Saints have been left in the form given them by the author of this work, a form which is sometimes rather a paraphrase than a strict translation. This has been done for the sake of the context.

As to the French writers who are quoted by the author, such as St. Francis of Sales, Pére Surin, and others, I have made my own translations, and have not gone to any other version. But with regard to the Italian and Spanish authors, I have, as already stated, tried to refer to the best English translations published.

THE TRANSLATOR.

PROLOGUE

THE

DEGREES OF THE SPIRITUAL LIFE

THE UNITIVE LIFE

PROLOGUE

OF THE IMPORTANT PART WHICH CONTEMPLATION PLAYS IN THE UNITIVE LIFE

1. ST. TERESA, having arrived at the fourth mansion of the "Interior Castle," begins immediately to speak of contemplation, and her whole subsequent teaching is on this subject. From this point to the end of the book, descriptions of the various states of contemplative prayer occupy a prominent place, and even form what may be called the woof of the fabric. This mode of procedure seems a very sensible one, and on this account.

With beginners (the first and second degrees) prayer is merely one of the day's exercises, of fixed duration, a transitory and accidental act. They strive painfully after recollection, are obliged to follow a regular method and to apply themselves particularly to meditation. At the conclusion of this exercise they betake themselves to their work, and nothing remains of their prayer but the resolutions which they have made; indeed, they often need the use of various devices to recall these to memory.

Later on (the third and fourth degree), the will being definitely won over to God, the heart is filled with good desires, prayer becomes more affective, requires less conscious effort, and leaves more visible traces on the soul. The sentiments which it has excited in itself rekindle of themselves amidst the day's occupations; the soul's love finds utterance, it offers its desires and petitions to God. These are, as it were, shreds, fragments, of prayer. It can be said, then, with Suarez, that there are two kinds of prayer: the continuous prayer, to which the soul devotes itself to the exclusion of all other occupations; and the interrupted, by which is meant the habit of ejaculatory prayer. For souls at this latter stage prayer is still a special exercise; it is not yet an habitual disposition.

But with the Christians of whom we are about to speak prayer is much more than an accident, however frequent and habitual. It is the *foundation* of their lives. The thought of God does not, doubtless, occupy their minds incessantly, but it is present so often, it dominates all the movements of the soul so powerfully, they are so intimately united with God, that they live truly in His presence, in a perpetual spirit of submission and love, and they thus maintain themselves in the perfect life: *Ambula coram me et esto perfectus.*

Prayer is the exercise of the faculties of the soul turning to God in order to pay Him its dues and to become holier. It is not, however, only in moments devoted to prayer, properly so called, that the perfect soul directs all its inner faculties towards God. At every hour of the day — often, even, while giving itself up to secular occupations — it pays Him tribute, and by its ardent desires and acts of love draws down upon itself graces of sanctification. It is thus that it accomplishes as perfectly as possible the recommendation of the Divine Master — *Oportet semper orare.*

It follows, therefore, that it is impossible to convey an idea of the interior state of perfect souls without first explaining their modes of prayer and the nature of their relations with God.

This is why we shall, with the great Saint who acts as our guide, begin to treat of the unitive life by describing the state of prayer which is appropriate to it. We might even have dealt with contemplation, as she has done, at the fourth stage of the spiritual life, where it begins to occur; but we have preferred the order which we now follow, because contemplative prayer is not the ordinary condition of fervent souls. It is present with them only intermittently, whereas at the fifth degree it becomes much more habitual.

BOOK V

FIFTH DEGREE -PERFECT SOULS

PART I. — CONTEMPLATIVE PRAYER

CHAPTER I

HOW THE PASSAGE FROM THE AFFECTIVE STATE TO THAT OF
CONTEMPLATION IS USUALLY EFFECTED BY A GENTLE
AND GRADUAL TRANSITION

2. IT is commonly supposed (we ourselves, at least, were long under this impression) that between ordinary prayer and contemplation such a wide difference, such a deep gulf, exists, that, in order to bridge them over, to pass from the meditative to the contemplative state, a sudden upwinging flight of the soul is required, an overwhelming gust of grace, an almost miraculous operation of the Holy Spirit.

But what we have just said proves that this is not so; that the path leading to the state of contemplation encounters no such chasms, but rises by a continuous ascent until it attains to this high level of the spiritual life. It will not be amiss, however, to insist still further on this point, and to show what the teaching of the best spiritual writers has been with regard to it.

"At first," says Fénelon, "the most natural method of meditation is to take a book, etc. . . . . Afterwards, little by little, the reflections and reasonings are curtailed; the loving affections, the touching conceptions, the desires, multiply; the heart tastes, nourishes itself, is enflamed, kindles, until a single word suffices to occupy it for hours. And the volume of prayer goes on thus increasing by an ever simpler and more steadfast vision, until there is no longer any need for a multitude of subjects and considerations. The same result follows in our relations with God as in the case of a friendship. At first there are a thousand things to be said to our friend, a thousand questions to ask; but presently all these conversational details exhaust themselves, while the pleasure of the intercourse suffers no diminution. Everything is said, but without words. It is happiness to be together, to feel each other's nearness, to rest on the consciousness of a sweet and pure friendship. We are silent, but with a silence which is understood. We know that there is a complete accord, that the two hearts are as one. Each pours itself out incessantly into the other.

"And thus it is that our intercourse with God in prayer resolves itself into a simple and familiar union which is above all discourse. But this species of prayer must proceed solely from God's operation within us, and nothing could be more rash and dangerous than to attempt to arrive at it of ourselves" (*Avis sur la prière el les principaux exercices de la piété*).

In another of his works the same writer justly remarks that the most discursive meditation and, *a fortiori*, affective prayer, often comprise certain definite acts partaking of the nature, and being, indeed, the first beginnings of contemplation.

From these passages contemplation would seem to follow and to be the natural consequence of the lower forms of prayer. It is true that the Divine intervention is necessary in order to aid the soul in its transit from one state to the other; but here, again, the Sovereign Master follows the rule, which He appears to have laid down for Himself, never to work by sudden and unexpected transformations: *Natura non facit saltus.*

3. Fénelon, on this point, has merely summed up the doctrine of the mystics, who regard this slow, progressive movement as the ordinary process of transition from the lower form of prayer to the contemplative state.

Let us now turn to Balthasar Alvarez. "It is by this method (the ordinary mode of prayer practised by the Jesuits) that, in the absence of any special inspiration from Our Lord, a beginning should be made; for the other manner of prayer has its birth therefrom, because it is by way of meditation that the stillness of contemplation is attained. Those who have exercised themselves in ordinary prayer through meditation and reasoning for several years, may be initiated into this path when they are already advanced and disposed towards it by an interior repose in the presence of God by the way of contemplation.[1] They should always, however, be advised not to discontinue the meditation entirely, but to curtail the discursive reasoning little by little."

4. St. Teresa teaches that such souls as are able to practise the ordinary prayer of recollection, "shutting themselves up in that little heaven of the soul where He dwells who has created the heavens and the earth, accustoming themselves to look at nothing outside it, will speedily slake their thirst at the Fountain of Life."

That is to say (following the figurative language of the Saint), it will taste the delights of contemplation. "They progress," she adds, "rapidly towards this goal." Thus, according to St. Teresa, the way for contemplation is prepared by the prayer of recollection, and sooner or later, if the soul is

---

[1] According to his biographer, Ven. Louis de Ponte, Father Balthasar had to endure a perfect tempest of opposition on this point. Some religious of his Order, otherwise commendable for their zeal, and moved by the best intentions, made a violent attack upon his spirituality. They found fault with his doctrine with regard to the Prayer of Quiet, and his undertaking to teach this way of prayer to those whom he regarded as being called thereto by God. They saw here the error of the Illuminati and the Quietists, and a contempt for the method of prayer as taught by St. Ignatius. The Father had no difficulty in exculpating himself, and in proving that his teaching was orthodox and well founded. It should be remembered that Father Balthasar Alvarez, who was held in such high esteem by Bossuet, was one of St. Teresa's most enlightened guides. Our Blessed Lord Himself bore testimony to the Saint as to the high perfection of this admirable religious.

faithful, it will pass from the one to the other. "Accustomed," she says again, "to a state of entire recollection, the soul will soon, God willing, partake of the peace of perfect contemplation" *(Way of Perfection,* xxviii.).

5. Now hear St. Francis of Sales. "Behold the Queen of Saba, Theotimus, considering in detail all the wisdom of Solomon — in his speech, in the beauty of his house, the magnificence of his table, the dwelling-places of his servants. . . . She was smitten with an ardent admiration which transformed her meditation into contemplation. . . . The sight of so many marvels kindled an intense love in her heart, and this in its turn produced a new longing to see ever more and more, and to bask in the presence of him in whom they were manifested. In like manner we begin by reflecting on the goodness of God in order to excite in us the will to love Him; but *the love being once formed in our hearts,* we dwell on this same goodness for the satisfaction of our own devotion, which is insatiate in its desire always to see the beloved object. In fact, meditation is the mother of love, while contemplation is the daughter" *(Treatise on the Love of God,* iv. 3).

Thus, according to the holy Doctor, love, by dint of meditation, gains strength in our hearts, and, growing continually, gives birth finally to contemplation.

6. St. John of the Cross is no less explicit. "In the commencement of this state this loving knowledge is, as it were, imperceptible, because it is then wont to be, in the first place, most subtle and delicate, and, as it were, unfelt; and because, in the second place, the soul, having been accustomed to meditation, which is more cognizable by the sense, does not perceive, and, as it were, does not feel, this new condition, which is not subject to sense, but purely spiritual. This is the more especially when, through not understanding his condition, the spiritual man will not allow himself to rest therein, but will strive after that which is cognizable by sense. This striving, notwithstanding the abundance of loving interior peace, robs him of the sense and enjoyment of it; but the more the soul is

disposed for this tranquillity, the more will it grow therein continually, and the more conscious it will be of this general loving knowledge of God, which is sweeter to it than all besides, because it brings with it peace and rest, sweetness and delight without trouble" *(Ascent of Mount Carmel,* Book II., chap, xiii., pp. 120, 121).

Further on *(Ascent of Mount Carmel,* Book II., chap, xiii.) he again teaches that it will often at first be necessary to resort again to meditation, because during the progressive stage there is, he says, a blending of the two methods;[2] but little by little the habit of contemplation is perfected, and at last the point is reached when the consciousness of this sweet and peaceful knowledge is enjoyed whenever we begin to pray, without any need of meditation.[3]

7. Father Libermann describes this gradual and progressive movement, which ends in contemplative prayer, with equal clearness. According to him, the generous soul, thanks to the sensible sweetness which God communicates to it from the outset, finds itself little by little in an habitual state of prayer. If

---

[2] The Meditative Way and the Contemplative Way.

[3] Certain mystical writers have even wished to define the duration of this transition stage which we term "affective prayer." Bona, following Gelenius, believes that not more than one year usually elapses before the affective soul is raised, if faithful, to the contemplative state. "*In hoc statu aspirationis* (affective prayer) *vix ultra annum devotus exercitator detinebitur, ut Gelenius observat; solet enim eo spatio emenso ad firmum intuitum contemplationis transpire*" (*Via comp.*, chap. ix.). "It is not easy," says Thomas of Jesus, "to determine the length of time which must be devoted to the purgative and the illuminative ways. It must depend, on the one hand, upon the exertions of each individual soul, and on the other upon the cooperating grace of God. As a general rule, however, it may be said that a novice, for instance, who during the whole of his noviciate has exercised himself in the purgative way with great humility, fervour, and compunction, as also in the illuminative way by the imitation of the virtues of Jesus Christ, must be regarded as being up to a certain point ripe for contemplation. We say 'as a general rule,' for it may be sooner with some subjects and later with others" (*The Better Part*; or, *The Contemplative Life*, i., § 5).

it is faithful, if it renounces these joys in order to unite itself with God, then the Divine operations become more interior. . . . "Towards the end of this stage the soul is no longer in such transports, it is less eager, less active, it gravitates incessantly towards God, but less violently. It remains for a certain length of time in this intermediate stage, always advancing towards contemplation. It purifies itself, strips itself ever more of the things of sense, confirms itself in the desire to unite itself with God and to please Him, and tends directly towards Him. It is thus that it progresses by degrees, until it arrives at Divine contemplation" *(Oraison d'Affection,* chap, vi., p. 185).

In one of his letters he enunciates the same doctrine. "The impressions received by the soul in affective prayer become ever more and more pure, more and more intellectual, until prayer becomes pure contemplation. This is achieved by degrees, in proportion as the soul detaches itself from all earthly and sensible things and from itself" *(Lettre* 258).

8. If we read and weigh these extracts attentively it will be seen that all the authors quoted are in agreement on this point. Setting aside cases of very rare and unmerited privilege, the ascent of the soul towards contemplation follows a slow and regular progress. The phenomena of contemplation are hardly distinguishable in their beginnings from those of the ordinary prayer which has prepared and led up to them. Little by little they are accentuated, they become more frequent, and at last the moment arrives when contemplation is fully formed and beyond question.

CHAPTER II

THE NEW METHOD WHEREBY GRACE OPERATES UPON THE
PERFECT SOUL

§ 1. *The Human and the Ultra-Human Methods.*

9. WE in no way intend, by what we have just said, to draw the
conclusion that meditation must necessarily at some given
moment bring forth contemplation as the fruit of our own
effort.

That some souls may thus, merely by the force of their own
intelligence, arrive at the contemplation of truth, and that a
purely active contemplation in this sense exists, we do not
deny; but we believe it to be exceedingly rare, and that such
acts of contemplation, where they occur at all, are too fleeting
and occasional to constitute real prayer.

But be this as it may, it is in any case not the contemplative
prayer described by the holy Doctors who serve as our guides;
for the acquisition of this gift of prayer all human effort is,
according to them, unavailing. A special intervention from God
is required, an intervention which presupposes, it is true, a
certain preparedness in the soul, but one quite independent of
human volition and beyond the sphere of human effort.

This Divine operation does not usually, as we have shown,

manifest itself suddenly and unexpectedly; but it is none the less indispensable, and it constitutes, as must be noted, a novel and more perfect order of grace.

10. In the good but still imperfect heart this Divine grace has not full scope. There are too many obstacles in the way. In Christians who have not yet advanced beyond a simple piety much self-love remains. They dissipate the powers of the soul upon a hundred worldly objects; they suffer distractions through vanity, the love of ease, and concern for their own interests. In them, too, abound natural inclinations and human considerations. Also, the interior faculties, sensitiveness and imagination, largely influence their lives. Before they can have any facility in prayer, grace must oppose to these human motives others founded on faith; for the natural joys which delight the senses must be substituted the true consolations of piety. The advantages of virtue, the sweetness of the Divine yoke — these are the truths which God reveals to the pious soul, truths which sustain and guide it in the battle of life.

Later on, if it has followed faithfully the light which has come down to it by processes of reasonings deducted in accordance with the teachings of the faith; if it has applied itself whole-heartedly to virtue, breaking all fetters by a courageous self-mortification and a sincere humility, in spiritual dryness relinquishing all sensible consolations, then the Divine grace no longer finds the former obstacles to its workings or is confined to its earlier and limited operations; then the intelligence, which is no longer obscured as before; the will, which is no longer captive, have become fit to receive still higher favours. There is no further hindrance to the direct action of grace upon these master faculties, imparting fresh radiance to the intellect and predisposing the will insensibly, but most powerfully, to love.

11. In the first state the Divine grace adapted itself to the ordinary processes of human nature. It followed in its operations, as St. Thomas would say, human methods, having recourse to the deductions of reason, and setting the will slowly

to work. In the second state grace, to use St. Thomas's words again, adopts the superhuman course, following the direct promptings of the Holy Spirit. *Dona a virtutibus distinguuntur in hoc quod virtutes perficiunt ad actus* MODO HUMANO *sed dona* ULTRA HUMANUM MODUM (Sent, iii., dist. xxxiv., q. i, a. i).

While grace was content to direct the mind by causing it to follow the principles which faith teaches, and to excite the will to acts of love by means of arguments founded on faith, grace produced meritorious acts, indeed, but acts of slight value, while those produced by the ultra - human medium of free gifts — that is to say, by the operations of the Holy Spirit *illuminating the soul directly, and Himself pouring into it the Divine love* — will be of a higher perfection. *Et hoc est quod quidam dicunt quod dona perficiunt hominem ad altiores actus quam sint actus virtutum* (St. Thomas, i. 2. q. 68, a. 1). *Et haec opinio inter omnes vera videtur* (Sent, iii., dist. xxxiv., q. 1, a. 1).

In each case the soul, under the influence of this grace, grows in virtue and increases in merit. The results, however are very different. Under the action of the sap which circulates from root to branch the poplar-tree grows, it uplifts itself straight towards heaven; but it sends out no side branches, it affords to mankind neither the refreshment of cool shade nor the sweetness of palatable fruit. The oak, on the contrary, spreads itself abroad, and provides a shelter under its generous foliage. The apple, the pear, the cherry, the orange trees, yield pleasant fruit. The sap in these trees produces much more valuable results, whereby many profit. It is thus in those souls wherein grace works unrestrictedly. They attain to great sanctity, and their saintliness communicates itself to others, and many brethren are benefited.[1]

---

[1] We do not say that imperfect souls never act in response to these gifts, nor that in souls which have arrived at perfection there is never any cause of action other than the direct impulse of the Holy Spirit. Gifts and virtues occur together in both cases; but, as we shall presently explain, the exercise

§ 2. On Various Terms for Contemplation — Mystical Graces, Passive Prayer, Supernatural Prayer.

12. The word "contemplation" often alarms the faithful. They imagine that some extraordinary mode of prayer is signified, without the possibility of distraction and closely allied to ecstasy. They forget that there are various degrees of contemplation. When it is desired to define any operation, phenomenon, or any being whatever, you take this being, this operation, this phenomenon, in all its developments, and you describe it as it then appears to you, although not to the exclusion of cases where the phenomenon is less complete and perfect. The word contemplation, taken in its primary sense, signifies a secret phenomenon, an operation of the mind which, illumined by the vivid radiance shed upon some Divine truth, admires it, rivets its gaze upon it, and, oblivious of all else, tastes the joys of its vision. In order that the soul may remain thus, as it were, suspended in its admiration, graces more powerful than the ordinary must illuminate the mind. But these graces, which, as we have just explained, are the result of the direct operations of the Holy Spirit, are far from always producing this admiring suspension which is contemplation properly so called. It often happens that, as we shall presently show, the intelligence and the will only are affected, leaving the other powers — the memory and the imagination — to be the cause of painful distractions. And, further, the control even of the powers affected is not always complete. While the soul sees itself united to God by love that dwells in the superior part of the will, it may still have other thoughts and abandon itself to other occupations. The more the act of contemplation extends itself through the whole soul, the less capable is it of prolongation in all its full plenitude. Contemplative prayer

---

of these gifts is incomparably more frequent with the second than the first, and so much the more so, again, as they become more faithful.

admits, then, of distractions; it is not an extraordinary and almost miraculous condition.

13. Contemplation is sometimes described as passive prayer. If this were understood in the sense that the soul would be inert, contenting itself with receiving the Divine favours without any action on its own part, the term would be incorrect. If it is understood as signifying that the soul lies captive, incapable of any operations other than those which are communicated to it, this would only apply in rare cases, and not to contemplation in general; but it is correct in the sense that in contemplation the soul *receives* more than it performs. "*In donis Spiritus Sancti mens Humana non se habet ut movens sed* MAGIS UT MOTA" (St. Thomas, 2. 2. q. 52, a. 2, ad. 1).

14. Again, contemplation is sometimes called *mystical prayer*, also *mystical graces*, because those gifts of light and love proceed from the immediate action of the Holy Spirit upon the powers of the soul. The reason for the last-named appellation lies in the mysterious character of these graces, which often take sudden possession of the soul, illuminate it by unknown ways, and impel it towards God more forcibly than it could advance towards Him of itself. This name is also due, and perhaps even more largely, to the mysterious character of the truths which the soul embraces in this new state. It knows that the God of its love is an incomprehensible Being; of His perfections and virtues it forms a high, but at the same time confused and mysterious, idea.

15. This prayer is again referred to by certain authors as *supernatural prayer*. St. Teresa, for instance, prefaces her description of contemplative phenomena by saying: "I shall speak henceforth of supernatural things" *(Fourth Mansion,* chap. i.).

With regard to this, and in order that there may be no mistake as to the meaning of this word, it is well to state its significance precisely. In the language of mystical writers it is used in various senses. There are, in fact, three recognizable degrees of the supernatural.

First, the ordinary supernatural, which consists in the exercise of Christian virtues. Every act performed from a motive of faith for a spiritual end is supernatural. It presupposes the preventing and concomitant action of actual grace. In this sense ordinary meditation and vocal prayer are supernatural works. *Nemo potest dicere Dominus Jesus nisi in Spiritu Sancto* (x Cor. xii. 3).

Secondly, this supernatural is ever within our reach in the sense that God is always disposed to respond to our efforts, and to help us to perform these acts which He Himself inspires us to desire. But over and above this ordinary supernatural there are other and higher operations of grace which do not follow the common path of human action, but proceed rather by intuitions than by human reasoning. These presuppose a special act of God, and are consequently independent of our own efforts. Vainly we long to call them into being; our endeavours are futile; while we are equally powerless to retain them, should it please God to discontinue them.

"I term supernatural," said St. Teresa, "that which we are unable to acquire of our own selves, however great may be the care and diligence which we employ. All that we can do is to dispose ourselves for it, and this disposition is the great point."[2] It is in this second sense that acts of contemplation are called supernatural, nature aided by ordinary grace being unable to produce them.

Thirdly, the word "supernatural" is sometimes limited to extraordinary operations of grace, the resulting actions being contrary to the usual laws of nature, and consequently supernatural, not only in their essence, but also in their mode. Such are revelations, visions, ecstasies — in a word, all the phenomena of the miraculous.

16. This being settled, it can be said with Schram (§ 219)

---

[2] *La primera oration, que senti, a mi parecer sobre-natural (que-llamo yo lo que con industria ni diligencia no se puede adquerir, aunque mucho se procure, aunque disponerse para ello si, y debe de hacer tnucho el caso,* etc.) (*Letter to Father Roderique Alvarez*, February, 1576).

that ordinary contemplation is at the same time acquired and infused, active and passive, natural and supernatural.[3]

On the one side it is granted only to souls which by their previous efforts have removed all obstacles and are in the right dispositions, and in so far it appears to be the fruit of our own labours.[4]

On the other hand, it depends upon God's good pleasure. The "tasting" of Divine things (we use St. Teresa's expression) which is frequently experienced, and even an intimate union with God,[5] the general and loving knowledge of God on which it is founded, are all independent of the soul's own effort. In order to experience them, the action of God is required, and this action operates sooner or later according to the designs of Providence. We must not, therefore, endeavour to force our own way into this prayer, as we do with discursive prayer, and also, up to a certain point, with affective prayer.

This dual character of ordinary contemplation is recognized by Bossuet. "Meditation is excellent in its proper time, and most useful at the commencement of the spiritual life; but one must not be content to stop there, since *the soul, by fidelity in mortification and recollection, is commonly rewarded by a purer and more intimate way of prayer, consisting in a simple insight, vision, or loving regard directed towards some Divine object,*" etc. It is not the soul, therefore, which acquires this prayer for itself; it *receives* it, but receives it, *as a rule,* thanks

---

[3] It is doubtless because Schram "accepts the regular and ordinary progress from meditation to contemplation that Voos, the Latin translator of Scaramelli, reproaches him with confounding asceticism with mysticism. We should rather be tempted to make just the opposite reproach, alike to Voos and several others — namely, that of greatly exaggerating the line of demarcation between these two ways, and not being in agreement, in this respect, with the great mystics.

[4] *Cf.* St. John of the Cross, Ascent of Mount Carmel, i., ii., chap. xiv.

[5] God is the principal Agent here; it is He, indeed, who secretly and tranquilly sheds wisdom and light into the soul, which does not resort to many formulated and reiterated acts" (St. John of the Cross, *Living Flame,* strophe iii., § 6).

to its own fidelity, in mortification and recollection *(Opuscule sur l'Oraison de Simple Présence de Dieu,* chap. iii.).

CHAPTER III

THE UNION OF LOVE, WHICH IS THE FOUNDATION OF
CONTEMPLATIVE PRAYER

17. From the doctrine just expounded it follows that the
constitutive elements of contemplative prayer consist in actual
graces, and not graces *gratis datae*. These are conspicuous
graces of faith which illuminate the soul as to the greatness and
incomprehensible goodness of God, a loving attraction by
which God, calling the faithful soul, unites it to Himself by the
cords of a sweet and holy affection. The union with God is, m
fact, effected by knowledge and love, such being the teaching
of the theologians as well as the mystics,[1] and the more perfect
this knowledge and this love, so much the more perfect is the
union with God.

It will not be superfluous to show by passages from holy
writers that this is undoubtedly the way in which they
understand contemplative prayer.

---

[1] See, in the *État Mystique* (chap, viii., "L'Union Mystique") St. Thomas's
formulated doctrine on this point. Likewise St. John of the Cross:
"Contemplative prayer unites the soul to God by a sublime knowledge"
(*Ascent of Mount Carmel*, ii. 14). But this knowledge must be combined
with love, for "love alone has power to unite the creature and the Creator"
(*Obscure Night*, ii., 18 *et passim*).

"The soul delights to be alone," says St. John of the Cross, "waiting lovingly on God, without any particular considerations, in interior peace, quiet, and repose, when the acts and exercises of the understanding, memory, and will — at least, discursively, which is the going from one subject to another — have ceased, nothing remaining except that knowledge and attention, general and loving, of which I have spoken, without the particular perception of aught else" *(Ascent of Mount Carmel,* Book II., chap, xiii., p. 119).

St, John of the Cross returns incessantly in all his writings to "this confused, undefinable knowledge of God, to this loving attention, simple, and directed wholly upon one object, rather like unto a man opening his eyes to gaze lovingly" *(Living Flame,* strophe iii., § 6); and everywhere he specifies this disposition as the essential character of contemplation.[2]

18. St. Teresa, while employing a different phraseology, is in reality entirely in accord with the reformer of the Carmelite Friars. In this condition, according to her, the will[3] tastes of true delights, of perfect peace; without knowing how, it yields itself into captivity, it gives its consent simply to God, in order that He may make it prisoner; and God, in fact, holds it bound to Him by love. At times the understanding and the imagination share in this sweet and calm peace of the will; at others, they are, on the contrary, a prey to all kinds of involuntary distractions, without, however, diverting the heart from its application to God.

There is therefore a Divine operation, usually calm and gentle in its action, which takes possession of the will with such completeness that it has but to yield itself up to it, and it

---

[2] Some authors, endeavouring to explain the nature of the mystic states, have fallen back on certain passages of St. John of the Cross, which, as we shall presently see (No. 33), apply, not to the mystic state, properly so called, but to special and exceptional favours.

[3] Those to whom these words of St. Teresa seem obscure, not being accustomed to take the word "will" in the scholastic sense, have only to substitute the word "heart" to make the passage perfectly intelligible.

remains, without any further effort, united to God by love. Often this union exists in spite of digressions of the imagination and understanding, sometimes even apart from prayer, amidst the occupations and labours to which the soul is obliged to devote itself. When this sense of well-being, this inner happiness, communicated to the will, reacts upon the senses, and invades the sensitive appetite, then are experienced those true delights, secret and abundant, which the Saint speaks of as the Divine tastings.

It is therefore easy, when reading her works, to bear this in mind — that wherever St. Teresa speaks of ordinary contemplation she refers to the operation which the will undergoes when it finds itself, as she says, united to God by love without any act of its own. At the most it may have practised some recollection, have set the *noria*[4] in motion, but even this will often not have been necessary.

She thus describes only one of two elements recognized by St. John of the Cross — the feeling of love which is seated in the will. She does not speak of the general knowledge of God upon which her holy disciple particularly insists; but her words necessarily assume this. In fact, the affections of the will are always the product of an intellectual knowledge — *nihil volitum nisi praecognitum* —and one follows the other so closely that the act of the will participates in the form of the intellectual act from which it springs. This is just what takes place with contemplation. There is in the mind an indistinct general knowledge of God, and thence is borne into the will an affection equally confused and indistinct. It is precisely because of its general and vague character that the sentiment of love often persists, as St. Teresa affirms, amidst a thousand varied thoughts, and even amidst the divers occupations of life.

19. St. Francis of Sales, speaking of contemplation,

---

[4] The *noria* is a machine very common in Spain — a sort of waterwheel with buckets, which is put in motion by turning a long arm fitted to a revolving shaft. It allows of much water being drawn with very little exertion.

represents it as being a loving, simple, and enduring attention to Divine things, these not being considered in detail, as is the case in meditation, but simply and collectively, and consequently, according to St. John of the Cross, generally and indistinctly.

"All is seen generally, and nothing particularly," said St. Francis of Sales (*Love of God*, vi. 3-5).

To this perception of God and of Divine things is joined a sweet and gentle affection. "Earthly lovers are often satisfied with being near, or in sight of, the beloved one, without speaking to her, and without descanting apart either of her or her perfections, satisfied, it would seem, and content to enjoy the beloved presence, not because of any reflections that he makes with regard to her, but by a certain stillness and peace which the mind derives from her."

The holy Bishop, again, compares this soul, of which the will reposes thus in God, to a little child, who, lying in its mother's bosom and half asleep, draws gently and scarcely perceptibly the milk which nourishes it. "Thus," he says, "the soul reposing in the presence of God extracts almost insensibly the sweetness of this presence, without speech, without action, without any sort of activity on the part of any one of its faculties, unless it be by the sole point of the will."

It is thus always a confused, indistinct sentiment of love, from which the soul derives an inward satisfaction more or less sensible.

If it does not seem easy to understand how the soul should experience these confused and indefinable feelings of happiness, remember those vague sensations of joy, sadness, weariness, etc., which each one has felt for himself. At the tidings of some fortunate occurrence the heart dilates; at first we enjoy the full flavour of our happiness, then, other occupations having come to distract us, we cease to dwell on the cause of our joy; nevertheless, an inward satisfaction endures to tinge all the rest of our day. On the other hand, we have suffered some annoyance, some sorrow. The cause of our grief has passed; we are again wholly occupied with other matters, and yet we continue depressed and melancholy. At the bottom of our hearts a sadness, a vague vexation, confused, but deep and persistent, remains.

20. It is evident from all this that the foundation of contemplation is an intimate union of the heart with God — a loving union in no wise due to exact and reasoned considerations, but to a general and indistinct knowledge of God, which is a true gift from the Divine goodness. This union can persist amidst distractions of the imagination and digressions of the understanding; it brings a real happiness to the soul — a happiness which amounts at times to an overflowing delight, while at others it is merely an almost imperceptible, though none the less real, satisfaction. Later on we shall describe the accidental forms which, starting also from this common basis, constitute certain special kinds of contemplation; but we must first try to explain the nature of this contemplative union.

CHAPTER IV

HOW THE CONTEMPLATIVE UNION OPERATES

§1. *The Higher Operations of the Soul, according to St. Francis of Sales.*

21. THE nature of the contemplative union seems impossible of explanation without first dealing with certain points of doctrine, the *knowledge* of which "*is requisite for the proper understanding of any treatise on spiritual matters*" (*Love of God,* i. 12).

We cannot do better than borrow this doctrine from the holy Bishop, whose teachings, with all their accuracy and charm, will, we think, throw light on a subject in itself not a little obscure.

Having already (Vol. I., Nos. 154-156) explained the nature of the two appetites — the *sensuous,* or *appetite of desire* (to quote his words); and the *reasonable appetite or will* — the holy Doctor establishes a distinction of degree between the various motions or affections of the second-named appetite, that of the will. "Those affections," he says, "which we experience in our reasonable side are more or less noble and spiritual according as their object is a higher or lower one, and according as they belong to a higher part of the soul; for there are affections in us which are given birth to by discourse made in accordance with the experience of the senses; there are others based upon discourse deduced from human science; there are others, again, which proceed from discourse[1] made in accordance with faith; and, finally, *there are those which have their origin in the simple feeling and acquiescence which the soul exhibits towards the truth and the will of God.* The first of these are styled *natural affections*, for who is he who does not naturally desire health, the requisite provision of food and raiment, and sweet and pleasant companionship?

"The second affections are called *reasonable*, because they are all based upon the spiritual knowledge of the understanding, by which our will is impelled to seek after tranquillity of heart, the moral virtues, true honour, and *a philosophical contemplation of the things of eternity.*

"The affections of the third rank are called *Christian*, because they take their birth from discourse drawn from Our Blessed Lord's teaching, causing us to cherish voluntary poverty, perfect chastity, and the glories of Paradise. But the affections of the highest degree are described as *Divine* and *supernatural*, because *He Himself pours them into our mind*[2] and they relate and tend to God, *without the intermediary of any discourse or any* natural light, as will be readily understood by what we shall say later on, when considering the acts of acquiescence and the sentiments which operate in the sanctuary of the soul. And these supernatural affections are chiefly three — the love of the intellect for the beauties of the mysteries of faith, love for the utility of the blessings promised to us in the next life (hope), and love for the sovereign goodness of God (charity)" (*Love of God*, i. 5).

---

[1] In the speech of the sixteenth century we know that *discourse* was used where we now use *reasoning*, and they then said "discoursing" where we should say "reasoning."

[2] We see here an example of the word *supernatural* taken by St. Francis of Sales in the sense referred to above (No. 15), and the holy Doctor gives the same reason for this as does St. Teresa. "God Himself outpours them into the mind." They are not, therefore, at our own disposal.

Of such importance does this doctrine appear to St. Francis of Sales that he reverts to it a little further on. "In this mystical temple (the soul) there are three courts, which are three different degrees of reason. In the first we act according to the experience of the senses, in the second according to human science, in the third according to faith; and, finally, above and beyond all this, there is an eminence and a supreme point of the intellect and the Spiritual faculties which is not reached by the light of reason nor by argument, but by a simple vision of the understanding, and a simple act of the will, by which the mind acquiesces in and submits itself to the truth and to the will of God" (*Ibid.,* chap. xii.). Now, these last acts, which we style *direct,* are precisely the contemplative acts. Contemplation, as Bossuet and Fénelon lastly teach, is merely a series of acts of faith and love, so subtle, so delicate, that they consist of a simple consent of the will, no reasoning being required for their production.

22. The Venerable Libermann, treating of the difference between the contemplative acts and the inferior operations of the soul, employs, it is true, a less scholastic, and therefore less exact, language than the holy Bishop of Geneva whom we have just quoted; but it is fundamentally the same doctrine (*Écrits,* p. 212). "The soul," he says (and the expressions which we are about to quote fall constantly from his pen) — "the soul has two modes of operation: one which is insensible, when it acts solely by its own powers, and independently of any of the sensible faculties; and the other sensible, when it acts by the medium of the senses.[3] It follows, therefore, that the soul has

---

[3] Speaking with philosophic precision, this language must be taken with some reservation, for if the senses have a lesser part in the superior operations of the soul (direct acts), their assistance cannot be entirely dispensed with. There can be no thought without sensible species, no act of the will without a *thought*; only the part played by the senses is curtailed as much as possible — so much so that their action, so to speak, escapes notice. *In divina con- templatione, says* Blessed Albert the Great, *non fit abstractio ab usu potentiarum inferiarum, quia remanent secundum*

two ways by which it can unite itself to God, and consequently two ways of prayer, one insensible, the other sensible. God likewise operates in these two ways in our souls," sensibly through the affective impressions, and insensibly through the contemplative operations.

Under the name of "sensible operations" the Venerable writer classifies, as it seems to us, all those operations the existence and nature of which each soul can easily prove for its own self, or, at least, he restricts the term "insensible operations of grace" to those which St. Francis of Sales calls supernatural. Of these latter experiences, occurring as they do at the soul's summit, and consisting merely in swift realizations of the understanding and simple consents of the will, there is less conscious recognition.

§ 2. *Direct Acts.*

23. We have just referred to the direct acts. This term[4] is applied to acts which are not discursive, which are performed without reasoning and by simple attention, and which are at times so delicate that the soul is not aware of them. This is especially so when these acts, in the language of the theologians, take place within the heart, and are not *signified.* There are, in fact, acts of this kind which are not expressed *by any sign* whatever. The soul does not speak of them even to itself; in order to describe them it does not employ any sort of language or imagery. They are simple tendencies, aspirations of the heart, sentiments which are swift, but none the less real, and which can be very free and very spontaneous, and, consequently, very meritorious in God's sight.

These direct acts may be found in hearts which are full of worldly preoccupations, but then there is nothing supernatural

---

aliquem usum sed tantum ab actu secundum intensionem, quia anima non attendit operationem ipsarum, et actio debilitatur (In libro de myst. theol., cap. i. 6, circa 2).

[4] *Cf.* Bossuet, *Instruction sur les États d'Oraison,* q.v.

in their objects. Let us see, for example, what passes "in the heart of a mother, thinking of her beloved child. During the whole time that she entertains these loving thoughts, is she not exercising her natural affection? And how? First by direct acts which are nothing but simple interior movements, a mere tendency of the heart towards this well-loved child; secondly, by unpremeditated acts, because there is no premeditation in love; thirdly, by acts little or vaguely realized, because she is only aware of them by the confused sensation which she experiences, without any thought of analysing what is passing within her; fourthly, by acts in no wise signified, for she neither says with her lips nor even inwardly with her heart, 'I love that child.' She loves it, notwithstanding, by acts indisputably performed within her heart, and she loves, therefore, without expressing it otherwise than by loving. And if her child could, like God, penetrate into the heart of its mother, would it not perceive all her real tenderness for it? But yet these acts, without being premeditated, are always so deliberate, so consented to and desired, that if their object were criminal this mother would be sinning, and would be obliged afterwards to accuse herself in confession of having spent a considerable time in a disposition of heart and mind both voluntary and culpable" (Caussade, *Instructions Spirituelles,* 2ᵉ partie, *Dialogue Préliminaire*).

This simile of Father de Caussade exactly illustrates the swift and almost intuitive character of the direct acts. It helps us to understand how, when a soul is under the influence of any deep and ardent emotion, there must result a succession of quick, lively, instantaneous and unpremeditated movements of joy or grief, complacency or aversion, desire or fear. These movements are voluntary if the feeling itself, the disposition of the soul whence they spring, is accepted, consented to by the will; while the opposite is the case if the sentiment which produces them is repudiated by the soul, but persists notwithstanding. They are then velleities, undeliberate desires, *motus primoprimi*, which the soul rejects, and which are not imputable to it.

24. But if there is a similarity beween direct acts which are natural and those which are contemplative, there is also a notable difference. The direct acts, when profane, are always sensible; the senses, and particularly the imagination, play a great part therein; the sensitive appetite is always largely aroused. Thus, in the example just given, it is either by contemplating her child with her eyes, or in conjuring it up through the imagination, that the mother's heart feels all those stirrings of affection. It cannot be otherwise. That which is natural can but follow the ordinary laws of nature. Now, the composite nature of man requires that it shall arrive at knowledge and love by the way of the senses, and the object of this natural affection, having itself a sensible nature, is easily apprehended and loved through the senses.

On the other hand, God, being of His nature spiritual, is perceived and must be loved after a more spiritual manner by means of a knowledge and a love wherein the senses play a lesser part. It is true that at the outset, as we have already shown, the faculties of sense co-operate actively in the love of God, as the reason, directed by faith, presents motives for the exercise of this love to the soul; but as long as the Divine love rests on this basis it remains imperfect, and only a feeble and incomplete union with God can be realized thereby. In fact, representations, imaginings, and all the sensible operations of the human soul, have, as St, John of the Cross truly says *(Ascent,* ii, 12), no relation, no direct connexion with God; they do not furnish an immediate way by which we can unite ourselves with Him.

Much more are distinct intellectual conceptions powerless to enable us to apprehend the Divinity, to come into Contact with God. All that we can conceive of by the force of human reasonings fails to furnish us with any but a most imperfect idea of God. *Oculus non vidit, nec auris audivit nec in cor hominis ascendit* — The eye hath not seen, nor ear heard, neither hath it entered into the heart of man, etc. (1 Cor. ii. 9).

This, again, is the very true teaching of St. John of the Cross. According to this holy writer (*Ascent,* ii. 8), as the memory could never conjure up in the imagination any image which would represent God, so the understanding, with all its activity, could conceive of nothing which would be like unto Him, and the will could never taste the joys and rapture which approach to this supreme Good. Thus, the most sublime Speculations as to the Being of God, the deepest thoughts which may come to us or which we may formulate for ourselves with regard to His perfections, will be always very far removed from God, and can serve but imperfectly to unite us to Him.

In order that we may be united to Him *as completely as is possible in this life (segun que en esta vida se puede),* there must be a knowledge of God freed from the things of sense, and superior to that which is the fruit of the highest reason, even when illuminated by faith.[5]

25. Direct acts which are natural proceed, then, either from a sensible impression or some reasoned consideration, which, inspiring certain lively and powerful sentiments in the soul, dispose it to produce these swift acts. Direct acts, which are supernatural, are, on the contrary, due neither to sensible impressions nor arguments, however striking.

When the contemplative soul experiences the union of love, when it first finds itself bound to God by the sentiments of

---

[5] Long prior to St. John of the Cross, Blessed Albert the Great taught that in order to arrive at a real union with God, such as every fervent soul should aspire to, detachment from the things of sense must be practised. Here, amongst others, is a significant passage: "Cast out of your mind all the phantoms, species, images, and created forms whatever, that you may consider God in the inner recesses of your being with a naked heart and mind and will. This is the end of all spiritual excretes to go to God and rest in Him, interiorly, by a pure act of the intelligence and a very fervent emotion of the will, freed from all sensible images" (*De Adhaerendo Deo,* chap. iv.). We have shown elsewhere (*La Vie d'Union à Dieu*) that this is also the teaching of the greatest masters of mysticism (see analytical table, p. 608). "We dispose ourselves for contemplation by renouncing the things of sense, and casting ourselves upon God."

quietude, at once ardent and peaceful, intense and sweet, it perceives clearly, if it examines into its condition, that it is in no wise the appeal to the senses (as in the chant, or the beauty of religious services), nor the imaginative representations of sacred things, nor any exquisite and sublime thoughts, which are the cause of its love. If the senses are moved, as often happens, it is but secondarily and concomitantly, the more spiritual faculties being those most directly affected, and these it is which are taken possession of by the Divine love. In order to describe this condition, the mystical writers speak of these contemplative operations as taking place on the soul's summit, and this is the most exact and proper figure which could be employed.

But it must not be concluded that sensible means, pious considerations, or, again, imaginative representations — as, for example, of our Blessed Lady and of Our Lord — are valueless to a soul which has attained to the prayer of quiet. These methods may assist the contemplative operations, but they do not produce them (*dispositive agunt, non causaliter*); they remove the obstacles, they dispose the soul to a state of recollection where the union of love becomes more easy, but they only contribute indirectly thereto.

§ 3. *On the Part played in Contemplation by the Intelligence.*

36. Whence, then, proceed these direct acts of contemplation? It is evidently in the intelligence that the cause, the intellectual act, which always precedes the affective act, must be sought — *nihil volitum nisi praecognitum.* But the intelligence, as we have just proved, is put in motion, in the case in question, neither by sensible images nor by reasoned reflections. How, then, is it accomplished? By an obscure, vague contemplation, by a general and confused view of the Divine perfections.

When the contemplative soul finds itself before the Blessed Sacrament, it very commonly experiences an attraction, as it were, towards God. In this condition it neither thinks nor acts; it does not even pray: it adores. This union with its God is at times passionate, but more commonly sweet and peaceful, and usually full of rapture. But it is not through the faculties of sense, through the imagination, that it apprehends the presence of Jesus, its Beloved; it is by a more intimate and spiritual way. It is, in fact, by the summit of the soul, as the mystics say. If it has been able in the first beginnings of its contemplation (although this is not always indispensable) to call up the image of its Saviour, this is now no longer necessary. It attains more directly to the object of its love; it feels His presence, feels His goodness, feels His lovableness, rather than thinking any definite thoughts as to the perfections of its Beloved; it grasps, as it were generally and vaguely, the Divine beauties of Him whom it loves; and this apprehension, where the heart takes a larger share than the intellect, is far more perfect than any distinct contemplation could be.

27.   This superiority of a vague or negative contemplation over one which is distinct and affirmative is taught by all the masters. St. Alphonsus, who sums them all up, says: *Contemplatio negativa est longe superior quam affirmativa. Haec contemplatio negativa dicitur* CLARA CALIGO *quia ob nimiam lucis abundantiam intellectus obscuratur: quemadmodum qui intuetur solem, radiorum fulgore obcaecatus* NIHIL CERNIT, SED TANTUM INTELLEGIT SOLEM ESSE MAGNUM QUODDAM LUMEN; *sic Deus in ista caligine infundit animae lucem magnum, quae facit ut illa intelligat non jam veritatem aliquam particularem, sed acquirat generalem quandam et confusam notitiam ejus incomprehensibilis bonitatis, unde anima incipit efformare altissimam de Deo idiam, licet confusam* — Negative contemplation is greatly superior to the affirmative. It is spoken of as the *luminous obscurity*, because the intelligence is, as it were, blinded by an excess of light. He who gazes at the sun is dazzled by the effulgence of its rays, and discerns nothing; he only perceives that the sun is a powerful luminary. So God, in

this obscurity, sheds a great light upon the soul. It discovers no one particular truth thereby, but it derives a general and indistinct notion of the incomprehensible goodness of God, and thus formulates to itself an exalted though confused idea of Him (*Praxis*, No. 135).

Experience confirms this doctrine of the Saints, and shows that this general and indefinite perception of the qualities of Almighty God is more perfect than a distinct and reasoned knowledge of His perfections. As a matter of fact, we see every day simple, unlettered persons exhibiting great fervour and blessed with this gift, and having much juster ideas and an infinitely deeper and stronger conviction regarding the greatness of God than learned men possessing far greater knowledge.

28. "This obscure contemplation," says St. John of the Cross, "is called secret, because it is, as I have said before, the mystical theology which theologians call secret wisdom, and which, according to St. Thomas, is infused into the foul more especially by love. This happens in a secret, hidden way, in which the natural operations of the understanding and the other faculties have no share. And therefore, because the faculties of the soul cannot compass it, it being the Holy Ghost Who infuses it into the soul in a way it knoweth not, as the Bride said in the Canticle, we call it secret. And, in truth, it is not the soul only that knows it not, but every one else, even the devil, because the Master Who now teaches the soul dwells substantially within it. This is not the only reason why it is called secret, for it is secret also in its effects. It is not only secret beyond the powers of the soul to speak of it during the darkness and sharpness of the purgation, when the secret wisdom is purifying the soul, but afterwards also, during the illumination, when that wisdom is most clearly communicated, it is so secret that it cannot be discerned or described. Moreover, the soul has no wish to speak of it, and, besides, it can discover no way or proper similitude to describe it by, so as to make known a knowledge so high, a spiritual impression

so delicate and infused. Yea, and if it could have a wish to speak of it, and find terms to describe it, it would always remain secret still" (*Obscure Night*, chap, xvii., pp. 123, 124).

29. This obscure contemplation has many different degrees. To return to the simile of St. Alphonsus, without seeing anything distinctly in the solar disc, the rays may appear more or less dazzling. The sky may be quite dear, and the orb will then be exceedingly brilliant; or, on the contrary, a light haze may interpose and dim its splendour. So, too, this general and indistinct vision, obscure contemplation of the Divine perfections, may he very powerful and dazzling — such, for example, as the *clara caligo* of St. Aloysius, and the *great darkness* of St. Angela of Foligno; or it may, on the other hand, be almost imperceptible, and this is what takes place, so St. John of the Cross teaches, in the night of the senses, at the outset of the contemplative way, when the soul scarcely perceives it and understands nothing of its condition.

From the foregoing remarks a direct and intuitive vision of the Divine Being must not, however, necessarily be expected. Whatever the ontologists may say, the direct vision of God is reserved for our Native Land. God is known to us here below by His attributes, of which the soul forms to itself — *species intelligibilis* — a more or less thrilling idea. He is not attainable directly and in His essence.

§ 4. *On the Different Ways of attaining to the Knowledge of God.*

30. God may be known naturally in four ways: by reason illumined by faith, by the mystical rays of contemplation, by the purely spiritual and miraculous lights of the intellectual vision, and by the intuitive vision.

First, then, by the way of reason illumined by faith. The human intelligence can, by the sole force of reason, convince itself as to the Divine perfections, and say: "God is great, all powerful, infinitely good. God has created us; God loves us.

God is a Being above all beings; His nature is inscrutable." There are to be found rationalists, formal heretics, without faith, who accept these truths; but in their case it is the reason alone which recognizes the truth of them.

31.   When a Christian makes an act of faith with regard to these truths, he relies upon revelation. He starts from this principle, "God has said it, and I will believe it"; and his belief is thenceforth supernatural and meritorious. In this case the human intelligence acquires a power and a perception superior to its native strength; it now sees these truths standing out in a new and supernatural light, which is called the *lumen fidei.* In the growing but still imperfect soul this celestial light which irradiates the revealed truths is still faint; so, in order to arrive at these fundamental truths, and when it wishes to draw its conclusions, it has need of arguments. "God merits that I shall sacrifice everything for Him, and renounce my own entirely for Him." Further and more or less laboured arguments will still be required.

32. The contemplative soul perceives the same truths, as well as those other truths which proceed from them; but they appear clothed in great splendour, indistinct, perhaps, like the light of the sun, but like it dazzling, and like it taken in at a single glance. Above all, it perceives that God is an incomprehensible Being; that He surpasses any idea that we can form of Him. Convictions which faith supplied when following up the deductions of reason, the Holy Spirit confirms by another way. Acting directly upon the superior parts of the mind, He imprints the same truths upon it. He bestows a further certainty — a more perfect understanding than could have been arrived at by all the arguments fortified by faith which were available. The impression made upon the contemplative soul is so vivid that it is satisfied merely to see them, to contemplate them, and to delight in them.

The action of the Holy Spirit confines itself, then, to acting upon already acquired truths, making them more resplendent and the ideas which the soul has formed more luminous; or He combines and draws together, while He illuminates them, the divers gifts which the soul already possesses; or, again, He instils into the mind ideas which cause the soul to grasp these same truths more perfectly. The three methods are possible, and may even succeed each other with the same person. Often when the contemplative places himself in the presence of God it seems as if no new idea presented itself to the mind; but the thoughts which it recalls, and which have God for their object, assume a sweet and powerful radiance, making an impression which other thoughts fail to make, and arguing a special intervention of the Holy Spirit. Sometimes, also, a thought such as that of God's love for him, or, again, the incomprehensible greatness, the beauties, and inexplicable qualities of the Godhead, pierces him so suddenly, strikes him so forcibly, that he sees that it is God Himself who has given birth to this thought within him, and has thrilled him through with this idea. But these truths which seem so luminous are not, however, new to him. He knows that God has revealed them to him, and he accepts them lovingly through docility to the Divine teaching. But the favour which he has received does not cause him to forsake the way of faith, It is not a substitute for faith; it only strengthens, illuminates, and perfects it.

33. But at times God favours His friends with even more marvellous lights. In the preceding case the high, white, intuitive lights of contemplation do not lift the man out of the normal state. They axe supernatural, but in conformity with the nature of our intelligence as it exhibits itself here below. It is knowledge conveyed by means of intelligible species, more perfect, although of the same order as our intelligible human species. But it is a much higher mode of understanding which does not belong to our present state, although it is not repugnant to our nature; for it will be the manner of knowing which we shall also enjoy after death. It is the mode of cognizance of pure spirits by means of purely intellectual species, having no connexion with the words of human speech nor the phantasies of the imagination. It is often spoken of as

the intellectual vision; it opens out vast horizons to the soul. An angel in one single glance takes in truths, objects, facts, which we can only encompass one after another, and in long periods of time. Distant objects are recognized thereby, "all visible things of the heavens and the earth" as also "all simple or immaterial substances such as angels and souls" (*Ascent of Carmel*, ii. 24). Thanks to this truly miraculous[6] mode of perception, holy persons have been enabled to read the secrets of hearts, and to know and foretell the future.

These realizations do not unite the soul to God, because the soul unites itself to Him in knowing Him and loving Him. They are preternatural, not supernatural; they must be classed as graces *gratis data,* and not as actual graces. But by this method of angelic perception it is possible to obtain "sublime ideas regarding the Divine attributes, such as the all-powerfulness, the strength, the goodness, the graciousness of God. These high realizations, which are coupled with love," and which are not distinct and special, but "general, are granted only to souls which have attained to the Divine union." Further, "they themselves produce the Divine union." The soul, in fact, obtains them by a mysterious touch of the Divine — "a touch of realization and of love (*toque di noticia y sabor*) which penetrates into the inner recesses of the soul" (*Ascent of Mount Carmel,* ii. 26). They are of the order of the supernatural; they are actual graces of a new and highly exalted order. Not even the angels themselves can communicate them; only "Our Lord, dwelling substantially in the heart, gives them being." The highest degree of prayer to which a soul can rise is reached by this road, but the soul receives these communications of truly angelic light and love only after having passed through a complete purification by the denuding of the spirit and the absolute relinquishment of all that relates to the creature (*Obscure Night,* ii. 23). After this manner might the angels

---

[6] We take the word "miraculous" in the sense of departure from the laws of nature. This phenomenon is not a miracle properly so called, because it is not sensible.

pray during their time of trial, and thus, although without being able to increase their merits, pray the holy souls in Purgatory.

It is necessary to distinguish carefully between the mystic states, properly so called, and these phenomena of the angelic order. The saintly souls who receive these communications, and who are favoured with these mystical illuminations, do not always draw such a sharp line of demarcation between the two as does St. John of the Cross. Anyone, however, who should see only simple degrees of the same state in all the intimate occurrences related, or should seek to explain the mystical state by the description given of favours of another order, would be responsible for a very regrettable confusion.

34. These three ways of attaining to the knowledge of God which we have just set forth, do not reveal Him face to face. The simple believer, the contemplative soul, the disembodied soul, and even the angelic being before it entered into glory, know God only under intellectual species; of different kinds, indeed, but all alike intermediaries between God and the soul. In the intuitive vision, on the contrary, there are no more intellectual species; God Himself unites Himself to the intellect, and reveals Himself without any intermediary. By all other modes of cognizance, even by that which is purely spiritual, the soul sees God as in a mirror, an enigma; it knows Him but imperfectly. By the beatific vision it sees Him face to face; it knows Him directly as it is known of Him. *Videmus nunc per speculum in anigmate; tunc autem facie ad faciem. Nunc cognosco ex parte; tunc autem cognoscam sicut et cognitus sum* (1 Cor. xiii. 12).

§5. Of Bossuet's Teaching on this Subject.

35. We now deem it advisable to submit to the reader Bossuet's exposition of the nature of contemplation. We shall find a doctrine identical with our own, set forth here in beautiful language, and, as we think, more easy of understanding after the explanation given above. "Remember,"

he says, "that the soul, fallen from its original integrity and entirely devoted to the things of sense, arrives at the knowledge of itself with extreme difficulty; and (as St. Augustine says) wrapping itself in the image of the senses by which it is obscured, it becomes by this means all corporeal, and can no longer distinguish itself from the body. As a result of this condition, the things most completely ignored are the acts and motions of the intellect; the senses are paramount, and we become so absorbed in the corporeal objects which they convey, that, discerning nothing through this thick cloud, we come, after a fashion, to believe that the body alone *is,* and that all which is not the body or of the body is non-existent. Thence, also, it follows that the soul is so little affected by purely intellectual goods that its whole bent is towards the senses and the things of sense. It is only by strenuous effort and little by little, that the soul escapes out of this deplorable condition. I admit that it can recover itself by the aid of the reason, as some philosophers have done. Faith also effects a remedy even more promptly and efficaciously, but it is properly in contemplation that, having entered into itself, it begins, as it were, experimentally to disentangle itself from the body by which it feels itself weighed down, and to separate the operations of the intellect — its true actions — from those of the senses and of the imagination (which is nothing but a sense, more interior than the others, but at bottom equally gross, since, after all, that which enters it is never anything but the body).

"The soul, then, in this state of ignorance, swayed naturally by the habit of feeling, and believing, after a fashion, that nothing is real except what is felt, what is touched, what is handled, reducing itself little by little to pure intellection, eludes itself and thinks itself inactive, while it is really beginning to exercise its true and natural functions. The operations of the will are still more imperceptible than those of the intelligence, for while all thought is by nature so prompt and swift that the sublime poet wishing to express the celerity of a movement says 'Swift as thought,' yet the action of the will, if one ranks it with thought, will be found to be the swiftest of all human actions, because it is swift to such a degree that there is hardly time to feel it. The understanding ranges over divers propositions to form an argument or draw a conclusion, but the act of consent, so to speak, is given in an instant, and is only seen in its effects.

"The soul, then, in the state of contemplation finds itself so purged, or, as the spiritual writers say with Cassian, 'so slender and attenuated — *extenuata mens* — and its thoughts so subtle and so delicate, that the senses have no foothold. In this state of pure contemplation, the soul,' says Cassian again, 'becomes impoverished: it loses all the rich material of beautiful thoughts, beautiful imagery, beautiful language, with which its interior acts were accompanied. It is then reduced to speaking the pure language of the heart. Until this point is reached we converse always within ourselves in human speech, and we clothe our thoughts in the words which we should employ in order to make them known to another. But in the case of pure contemplation we arrive at speaking to God in a language which none but He Himself understands, and it is this which we have described as the language of the heart, especially in the act of love, which neither can nor will make itself known to God except through Him. Love expresses itself only by loving, and the heart then speaks to God alone. Whether it is possible, and, if so, in how great a degree, to reach the perfection of such an act during this life, and whether the point of dispensing completely with all imagery and words can be arrived at in the soul, I leave for decision to the perfectly spiritual. Here, where I desire to avoid all vexed questions, I content myself with saying that this purging proceeds so rapidly in sublime contemplation that at least a glimpse of perfect purity is obtained, and that if it is not attained absolutely there is something which closely resembles it. Thought, thus purged, as far as may be, from all that coarsens it, from images and expressions of human speech, from all those retrospective glances which our pride inspires, without reasonings, without discourse (because our object is to garner the fruit and the results of all preceding discourses), tastes the purest of all beings, which is God, not only by means of the purest of all the interior faculties, but also by the purest of all acts, and unites itself closely to the truth even more by the way of the will than by that of the understanding. The soul, then, enters truly into the school of the Holy Spirit, that inner school where it is wonderfully taught of God. 'How far removed is it,' says St. Augustine, 'from the sensations of the flesh, this school where peace and silence reign, this school where God makes Himself felt, where the councils of the heart are held, where resolutions are formed?' 'Once more,' says the same Saint, 'how far is it removed from the sensations of the flesh?' The astonished senses perceive nothing, and the soul which eludes their perception appears to be reduced to nothing: *ad nihilum redactus sum el nescivi.* 'I am reduced to nothingness,' said David, 'and even this nothingness which I find within myself in these depths into which God has brought me, is unsearchable' — *et nescivi;* which causes him to add: 'I am become as a beast before Thee' — *ut jumentum* — without reasoning, without discourse, and all that I can say in this condition 'is that I *am* always with Thee, and that I find nothing else in the darkness of faith into which Thou hast plunged me — *et ego semper tecum.* This is all that I can say, stammeringly, of the perfect practice and the imperceptible truth of the acts of the mind in sublime contemplation' " (*Instruction sur les états d'Oraisott,* I. v.).

§ 6. *How that Contemplation proceeds from the Gifts of the Holy Spirit.*

36. The doctrine which we have just expounded is in perfect accord with the masters' teachings as to the gifts of the Holy Spirit, which lead the soul, not as do virtues that are infused by reasoned motives and legitimately drawn

conclusions, but by illuminations and inspirations of grace, more intuitive than deductive.

And so, according to St. Thomas (1, 2, q. 68, a. 1), Suarez *(De gratia*, I., II., chap, xvii.), the gifts of the Holy Ghost are *habitus* distinct from supernatural virtues, and they dispose the soul to receive the light and obey the motions, not of reason illumined by faith (which is the function of the infused virtues), but of the Holy Spirit; lights and impulses which operate directly in the soul without the assistance of arguments. "Thanks to these gifts," says St. Francis of Sales, "the soul becomes pliable, tractable, and obedient to the Divine promptings and celestial inspirations of the Holy Spirit."

37. The majority of Christians, by their countless infidelities put many obstacles in the way of the operation of the gifts of the Holy Spirit. "One marvels," says Father Lallemant, "to see so many religious who, after living for forty or fifty years in a state of grace, saying Mass daily, practising all the holy exercises of the religious life, and having, consequently, the gifts of the Holy Spirit in a very high degree physically — one marvels, I say, to see nothing of the gifts of the Holy Spirit in their actions and conduct; how their lives are purely natural; how, when blamed or crossed, they show their resentment; how they display as much eagerness for praise, for the esteem and applause of the world, and take so much pleasure in it; and how they like and seek their own comfort and all that flatters their pride. There is no cause for astonishment, however. The venial sins which they continually commit hold the gifts of the Holy Spirit, as it were, bound, so that it is not strange if no results are to be seen in them" *(Doctrine spirituelle,* principe 4, chap, iii., article 3).

It is very dear that Christians who are but little advanced in mortification and self-denial are inapt for the frequent reception of the impulses of the Holy Spirit. How should they be under the habitual direction of the Holy Spirit, they whose lives are full of resistance to grace and hesitation to follow its guiding light; their wills entangled by a thousand natural affections, bound by sensual and selfish habits which they cling to and cherish? They are incapable of responding promptly to the Divine inspirations. In proportion as they free themselves from these imperfect attachments, they break the bonds which enchained the spirit of love in their hearts, and the gifts come into operation more and more.

38. By the verdict of the Doctors the gifts of intellect and of wisdom are, above all others, those by which contemplation is produced.

It is plain that the gift of understanding occupies a large place in contemplation; this it is that makes it possible to penetrate most deeply, to attain most directly to the things of God; this it is that enables the human reason to raise itself above its ordinary operations, weak and imperfect as they are, and communicates the power to perceive the Divine perceptions and greatness, dispensing as far as possible with the aid of the inferior faculties. It sometimes happens that a quite unlooked-for inspiration comes suddenly to mark out a line of conduct for the faithful soul, which, seeing that this inspiration is in harmony with the teachings of faith, accepts it freely, and follows it whole-heartedly. This is a result of the gift of counsel. The Holy Spirit Himself has put this sudden inspiration into the soul. So with the gifts of understanding: exalted ideas of the Divine greatness are poured into the soul, which, seeing that these thoughts are in conformity with Christian doctrine, cleave to them lovingly.

Let us give an example as an illustration of this theory. It is constantly the case with contemplative souls to find themselves suddenly pierced with the consciousness of the presence of God within them. The strength of the impression made upon them by the thought of this Divine presence show's that such a powerful feeling, such a penetrating realization, could not have been arrived at by the aid of reason, nor by the best considered arguments, but is, without doubt, a fruit of the gift of understanding.

39. With this illumination of the reason there is a

correspondingly strong impulse of love in the will. Then the contemplatives unite themselves closely with the Divine Guest of their souls. They rejoice in possessing Him, and all this takes place through acts of the heart, scarcely expressed, but intense and ardently affectionate.

According to many writers, these affective emotions, brought forth within the soul by a recognition of the Divine qualities, belong to the gift of wisdom which, according to them, should be a sweet savour of God and of Divine things. "Wisdom," says St. Francis, "is simply love which tastes and experiences the goodness and sweetness of God" (*Love of God*, Bk. xi., chap. xv.).

St. Thomas, however (2. 2, q. 45), remarks that this gift of wisdom does not consist exactly in the taste for Divine things, for it would then be of the will, which the holy Doctor pronounces inadmissible; it lies, rather, in the judgment which follows therefrom. According to him, this leaning towards supernatural things, this delight which we take in them, would be a product of charity.[7] And thus the attraction which Divine things have for us would not be the result but, on the contrary, the cause of wisdom. By this inner predilection which they excite in us we judge of the truth, the goodness, the fitness of Divine things, or, according to St. Thomas, it is this rectitude of judgment which constitutes wisdom.[8]

However this may be, it is certain that the soul, which is entirely united to God and in perfect submission to the action of the Holy Spirit, receives from Him a more lively understanding of Divine things, a more piercing vision by which to apprehend supernatural truths. It is equally sure that to this perception of the intellect there is a very intense corresponding affective tendency of the will, a sentiment of

---

[7] *Haec connaturalitas sive affinitas ad res divinas fit per charitatem qua quidem nos unit Deo secundum illud. "Qui adhaeret Deo, unus spiritus est."*

[8] *Sic sapientia causatn habet in voluntate scilicet charitatem, sed essentiam habet in intellectu, cujus est recte judicare* (2, 2, q. 45, art. 3).

love, full of sweetness. The heart finds its completion in this love; it discovers a great delight therein, whether it enjoys the rapture of its union with the Beloved, or yearns after a union more intimate still. It is also evident that the result is an experimental knowledge of Divine things which gives wisdom in an eminent degree — *Gustate ei videte quoniam suavis est Dominus.*[9]

The soul which has thus tasted God can appreciate Him, and possesses a sound judgment in all things.

40. We see here, therefore, the exercise of the gifts of understanding and wisdom. Under their influence a multitude of rapid acts, some clearly defined, some quite indistinct, succeed each other in the soul. It is also very often difficult to note them clearly, and to distinguish their characters. They consist in sentiments of complacency in the perfections of God and joy at the spectacle of His greatness—*Scitote quoniam Dominus ipse est Deus*—of praise, admiration, respect, absolute confidence, self- effacement, the offering of the entire being, the longing to love Him more and to see Him better known and loved—desires which are often fraught with anxieties, and which, not being satisfied, are the cause of actual torments to the soul. These sentiments, distinct or confused, as the case may be, vary according as the illuminating rays communicated by the Holy Spirit bear on such or such a truth, and cause the Divine things to be seen under such or such an aspect. Sometimes an impression of the goodness and benevolence of God tills the soul with consolation, as in the prayer of the Divine "tastings" of St. Teresa. At other times, on the contrary, a vague, but powerful sentiment of the Divine holiness and justice, enlightening the soul upon its nothingness and misery, leads it to realize the disproportion which exists between itself and the God of its love, and fills it with terror and desolation, as in the "night of the soul" of St. John of the Cross.

---

[9] Oh, taste and see how the Lord is gracious!

Such, as we believe, is the role of the gifts of understanding and wisdom in contemplation. The contemplative soul is simultaneously disposed to submit to the influence of the other gifts—that of piety—which instils sentiments of a filial nature towards God into the heart—*In quo clamamus Abba Pater*—of knowledge, when its attention is directed towards created things, and it judges of them according to the light which this gift communicates.

These gifts may, therefore, have their part also in contemplation. As to the other gifts — of counsel, of fortitude, of the fear of God — they serve in the ordinary conduct of life to bring forth acts full of prudence and generosity, but they can also intervene in prayer and cause it to take the most virtuous and, at times, the most heroic resolutions.

41. Given these outlines, it is easy to understand why contemplation, which is the effect of these gifts, is rightly styled supernatural in contrast to discursive prayer. It is natural to man to act by reason, and he can apply his intellect to the things relating to faith as well as to those which are profane; the necessary grace to ensure that it should be done in a Christian spirit will not be lacking, even as the Divine assistance will not fail him when he desires to treat of temporal matters. The action, then, of grace in this case is more within the reach of the Christian soul. But this is no longer so where the question is one of gifts. It does not, as a matter of fact, lie with us to suffer the workings of the Holy Spirit, to receive His light, to taste the sweetness of the love which these illuminating rays kindle in the will; above all, to feel the heart sensibly rejoiced. All this presupposes a special action of the Holy Spirit.

It is true that man can dispose himself towards these contemplative acts, but he cannot cause them. He disposes himself thereto indirectly by a perfect renunciation which clears away all obstacles to the action of the Holy Spirit; he prepares himself directly by the act of recollection which is favourable to the Divine operation; and as God is infinitely generous, and desires nothing more than to pour out His gifts, the soul, if very faithful, will come to be in a manner under the habitual influence of these gifts of the Holy Spirit. These are the souls of which St. John of the Cross speaks who, "from the moment of placing themselves in the presence of God enter into the possession of a confused knowledge, loving and full of peace and calm, whence they drink long draughts of the waters of wisdom and of love."[10]

This contemplation, however, remains supernatural, even though it may have become frequent and, as it were, habitual, because it derives more from God than from man; but it is supernatural, not miraculous: there is no derogation, properly so called, from the laws of nature.

43. We will conclude this chapter with the following proposition, given as a *résumé* of the doctrine just set forth. The contemplative operations are the operations of the soul which has "become more pliable and tractable to the Holy Spirit," and which, acting by means of the gifts, is no longer influenced by sensible emotions nor by the slow considerations of reason; but under the action of grace it produces direct acts in which the intellect has no part—acts of the intelligence which swiftly seize and embrace, as by a flash, the Divine perfections and acts of the will which inflame it with the love of its God. The soul thereby raises itself above the inferior faculties, as much as is possible in this life without the aid of miracle.

43. We crave the reader's pardon for detaining him so long over this chapter, and for not having treated it with greater clearness and in a more interesting way. In the prologue at the beginning of his book *(The Ascent of Mount Carmel)*, St. John of the Cross requests that his work may be read twice, as one reading would suffice to shed but a partial light on so difficult

---

[10] *De manera que luego en poniendose delante de Dios se pone en acto de noticia confusa, amorosa, pacifica y sosegada, en que esta el alma bebiando sabiduria, amor y sabor (Ascent of Carmel, 11-14).*

and obscure a subject.[11]

Having dealt with this same subject we are inclined to make the same request as does the Saint. If anyone has the courage to read us twice he will find this doctrine more easily digested, and, this point once clear, the rest will present no difficulties. We think we can give an undertaking that no one will regret the trouble which he has taken. However arid the study of these mystic phenomena may appear, they none the less open out many new vistas full of interest and edification. Without comprehending these superior operations of grace no correct idea of the interior life of perfect souls can be formed. With it, however, we understand the purity of their sentiments, the greatness of their merits, the liveliness of the love which they bear to God and God's tenderness towards them.

---

[11] St. John of the Cross, we may say in passing, is less obscure, however, than is commonly supposed. We hope that those who have read this present work will understand his writings without difficulty. The Abbé Calaber has furnished a good summary of his doctrine, and has put it within reach of every one in a pamphlet which we commend to the notice of all pious souls. It is styled *La terminologie de St. Jean de la Croix dans la "Montée du Carmel" et la "Nuit Obscure."* It is followed by an epitome of these two works.

CHAPTER V

ON THE VARIOUS KINDS OF ORDINARY CONTEMPLATION

Preliminary Remarks.

44. WE have just shown what the union of love is—how it is produced by a confused, general knowledge of God, which constitutes the common basis of ordinary contemplation. It now remains to describe, as we have notified above, those accidental forms which, coming to graft themselves upon this common stock, constitute the various kinds of ordinary contemplation.

"As," to borrow a simile from Father Surin, "a lute- player keeps his instrument in tune, however much freedom he may allow himself in his playing, provided that the principal chord which forms the foundation and basis of his melody continues in the same tone, so, provided that the union of the heart endures, one may touch every sort of string in prayer, if it is in accord with the principal and fundamental tone" (*Spiritual Catechism*, t.1., part ii., chap. ii.). Now as the same writer (*ibid.,* t.11, part ii., chap. i.), reverting to this simile, teaches elsewhere, "this is exactly what happens to souls who really seek only after God, and whose sole intention is to please Him;

those souls, namely, who are living the unitive and contemplative life. As soon as they engage in prayer they feel the vibration of the main chord—that is to say, they experience this union of love of which we have spoken—though the accompaniment remains the same, the modulations change, the powers of the soul being able to produce a great variety of thoughts and affections. The old writers begin by dividing contemplation into cherubic, or intellectual, contemplation, and that which is seraphic, or affective. Faith and charity both play their part, it is true, in contemplative prayer, but with some faith predominates, with others charity" (*Libermann).* "Sometimes it is the understanding, sometimes the will, which plays the principal part, according as God communicates more light or more love to the soul" (Father Lallemant).

§ 1. *Intellectual Contemplation.*

45. We will speak first of cherubic, or intellectual, contemplation.

The soul which is in this disposition of union with God may, under the influence of grace—*Spiritus ubi vult spirat*—have its attention directed upon the mysteries of the faith and the Divine perfections; then, instead of reasoning, as the meditative soul would do, instead of producing this great multitude of acts which are no longer fitted to its condition, it remains enthralled and absorbed in the object of its contemplation. Being, then, under the influence of the gifts of the Holy Spirit, and especially the gift of understanding, it penetrates much more deeply into such and such a mystery, such and such a truth, without the aid of reason; it becomes the recipient of illuminations still more brilliant and more vivid. "To meditate upon hell," said Father Lallemant, "is to see a painted representation of a lion; while by contemplation upon hell the living lion stands before you" (*Doctrine spirituelle,* principe 7, chap, iv., art. 5).

Such is cherubic contemplation, of which, as we believe,

St. Teresa speaks in chapter xvii. of her *Life,* when she describes the kind of prayer in which "God takes possession of the will and also of the understanding; which latter, discontinuing all discourse, remains absorbed in a ravishing contemplation of the Divine greatness. So many marvels are there revealed to it, that one effaces another, and it is unable to follow up any one in particular."

In this kind of contemplation the action of grace is felt not only upon the superior parts of the soul, in order that the union of love may be brought about there, but throughout the whole understanding for the communication of marvellous lights.

It is generally supposed that no other kind of contemplation exists.[1] But this is only one of the forms of contemplation, and not even the most common; it is far less frequently encountered than the various modes of affective contemplation.

§ 2. *On Affective Contemplation or Prayer of Quiet.*

46. Seraphic or affective contemplation is that wherein love is paramount. To this especially the name of prayer of quiet or quietude is applied, because of the repose which contemplative love brings to the soul. "Holy quietude," said St. Francis of Sales, "admits of different degrees"; and it is these various modes of affective contemplation which we are about to try to explain.

"*In quiete,*" said St. Alphonsus, "*amor communicatur immediate spiritui in ipso animae centro, deinde etiam ad sensus externos diffunditur, hoc autem non semper, unde*

---

[1] It is in consequence of this error that so many false notions as to contemplation exist, that it is thought to be so rare, and that it is considered useless to study its rules. We must, however, recognize that the nature and frequency of contemplation are better understood now than when these lines appeared for the first time, nine years ago ; the works by M. Lejeune, the Rev. Father I.udovic de Besse, and the Rev. Father Poulain, S.J., lately publisher!, have cleared up many misconceptions, and we earnestly hope that they will all now disappear. *(Note to the 3rd edition.)*

multoties accidit quod anima habeat orationem quietis sed sine ulla dulcedine sensibili."—"In quietude love is communicated directly to the mind, and this communication takes place at the soul's centre, then it is diffused among the senses; but this does not always take place, the result often being that the soul is possessed by the prayer of quiet without experiencing any sensible sweetness" *(Praxis,* 134).

In order to understand this doctrine better let us hear St. Francis of Sales. "Quietude sometimes extends to all the faculties of the soul united to the will, at others to the will alone ; in the will it is sometimes sensible, and then the soul derives an inexpressible satisfaction in the recognition of God's presence by means of certain sweet, interior sensations; at other times it is imperceptible, the soul being then possessed of an ardent bliss because it is in God's presence, although at the time that presence is imperceptible to it (*Love of God,* vi. II).

§ 3. *Perfect Quietude.*

47. Perfect quietude is that in which all the powers are affected.

This was the case with Blessed Margaret Mary: "My Sovereign Master presented Himself to me in the mystery which He desired me to consider, and He engrossed my spirit so completely, holding my soul and all my powers so enthralled in Himself that I suffered no distractions; but my heart felt consumed with the desire to love Him, and this filled me with an insatiable longing for Holy Communion and for suffering. His goodness held me so fast in the preoccupation of which I have just spoken, that it inspired me with a profound distaste for vocal prayer, so that I could no longer resort to it before the Blessed Sacrament, where I found myself so completely absorbed that I never knew weariness. . . . I could have passed days and nights there without food and without knowing what I was doing, like a burning taper, consuming itself in His presence in order to pay back love for love."

48. The impressions of grace, which the soul receives so abundantly while in this condition, and which overflow from its centre to all its powers, can either possess the soul in peace and repose, or, on the other hand, excite in it the liveliest transports.

"At other times," says St. John of the Cross, "also the Divine light strikes the soul with such force that the darkness is unfelt and the light unheeded; the soul seems unconscious of all it knows, and is therefore lost, as it were, in forgetfulness, knowing not where it is, nor what has happened to it, unaware of the lapse of time. It may, and does, occur that many hours pass while it is in this state of forgetfulness; all seem but a moment when it again returns to itself" *(Ascent of Mount Carmel*, Book II., chap. xiv.).

This is affective contemplation of the perfect but peaceful kind.

49. When the action of grace produces ardent transports in the soul, what the mystics call mystic inebriation takes place. "One pours oneself out then," says St. Teresa, "in praises to God, but without any method. The soul, lifted out of itself, convulsed by transports of the utmost sweetness, longs to break forth into songs and benedictions. Ah! what must the soul not experience in this rapturous inebriation? It desires to be all transformed into millions of tongues in order to praise its God. It gives vent to a thousand holy extravagances which travel straight to their goal, and delights Him who has prompted their utterance" (*Life,* chap. xvi.).

"The aspirations caused by this inebriation," says St. John of the Cross, "continue at times during its whole duration. At others the inebriation can exist in the soul without producing these burning aspirations, which are more or less intense, according as the inebriation of love is more or less pronounced" (*Cant, spir., str.,* xxv.).

The impression of the senses, the disturbances produced in the sensitive appetite, are, we think, a common cause of this livtly ardour. In fact, the memory and the understanding being

52

themselves turned towards God in this kind of prayer, not only is there nothing to hinder these impressions, but everything conspires to augment them.

Natural affection knows these transports. Who has not seen a mother cover her child with kisses and caresses, addressing it constantly in terms of the wildest affection and (to use St. Teresa's expression), indulging in a thousand extravagances? The explanation is that there are moments when the mother's entire faculties are absorbed in the love of her child. She thinks of nothing beyond it, and her heart, being free from all distractions, everything, on the contrary, warming and animating it, experiences the liveliest emotions, and she lavishes the most ardent signs of affection upon her beloved child.

50. The mystics, following St. John of the Cross *(Spiritual Canticle, strophe* xxv.), note two kinds of inebriation—the complete and the partial.

According to the description which the holy writer gives of the incomplete inebriation of beginners, it consists simply in these outbursts of ardour to which affective souls are subject—those burning feelings where desires are predominant, and the petitions always more or less personal and always definite; for the soul always knows what it desires and what it asks. On the other hand, in these contemplative outbursts which have their birth in the union of love already described, and which constitute complete inebriation, wishes and requests may still exist; but the dominant feeling is a lively sensation of love and joy and satisfaction in the perfections of Almighty God, of ardent conformity to His will, and a desire for His glory.

Further, these burning feelings are frequently confused and indistinct and without any clearly defined object; we perceive merely that it is love which has given them birth. Such words as "my God, my God!" for instance, may be uttered without anything else being found to say, or any further defining of the thoughts.

How, then, are the faculties of the soul occupied pending

the duration of this holy inebriation; what arguments is the understanding pursuing, what thoughts occupy it, what objects present themselves to the imagination? It seems as though these faculties were no longer active, for they do not appear to produce any results; although they are not, however, suspended, ravished, as would be the case in an ecstasy. It is this which causes St. Teresa to say: "This state is a slumber of the faculties, in which, without being entirely lost in God, they do not understand their own operations." Thus must be interpreted the language, at first sight so strange and inexplicable, of the Saint, who defines as a slumber of the faculties, a condition where the soul displays so much activity. Such, then, is perfect quietude.

Between this perfect, affective contemplation and intellectual contemplation there is this in common—that all the powers participate and are subject to the action of grace; only in the first-named it is the will which more especially has an impression made upon it, and love is the dominant factor. They both alike must be regarded as the highest forms of non-miraculous contemplation, and are rarer than those of which we are about to speak.

§ 4. *Sensible Quietude*.

51. We have quoted (No. 46) St. Alphonsus as saying that in quietude the love which is communicated directly to the soul in its inner recesses gushes out again upon the senses. St, Francis of Sales has also spoken of this quietude which is in *the will atone, to the exclusion of the understanding and the imagination;* but it exists in the will *sensibly,* the soul experiencing an incomparable satisfaction in feeling, by means of certain sweet, interior sensations, that God Himself is present. This is the form of quietude which we call sensible quietude, because in addition to the will the senses also are involved.

There is a close connexion between the intellectual

appetite, or the will, and the appetite of the senses; it is not surprising, therefore, that when one becomes subject to the impressions of grace, the other feels the effect more or less strongly. We have just said that when the other faculties—the memory and the understanding—are all under the same influence, the impressions of the sensitive appetite are generally very strong. In the quietude of which we are now speaking the understanding and the imagination are rather an obstacle than otherwise; the senses are less powerfully moved, and the sweetness which they experience is mild and peaceful.

It is also thus with human affection. When it has either moral qualities or such a reason as the relations of paternity, superiority, etc., as its cause, it has its seat evidently in the will; and yet the sensible side of our nature is nearly always more or less involved; the heart when under the influence of affection is usually touched, and it is very rare to find anyone who remains entirely cold while loving devotedly. If a father sees his child come back to him again after a long absence, he is made glad by its presence, and he feels this sweet emotion of affection satisfied, even while he lets his attention wander to different objects, as, for instance, while he attends to the occupations of his business. These necessary distractions, while occupying part of his attention, with the result that his satisfaction is less lively and expansive, do not entirely prevent him from enjoying the happiness of being with the object of his affections. It is the same with affections which are more intellectual than paternal love, and where the senses play a lesser part.

52. But if grace, communicated to the will in this form of prayer, reacts upon the sensitive appetite, it does not, as we have said, equally affect the understanding, which appears to be a stranger to the contemplative phenomena, although the fact that the understanding always takes some part in contemplation must not be lost sight of; for grace acts upon the superior faculties in order to communicate that vague, indistinct knowledge to which we have referred, and which

results in the union of love. The inferior part of the understanding remains, as it were, insulated from the contemplative operations and carried away by the imagination, or distracted by its legitimate occupations, produces all kinds of reasonings.

53. Let us now hear what the holy writers say of this kind of quietude. "The will," says St. Frances of Sales, "being once allured by the Divine presence, does not fail to taste its sweetness, even although the understanding or the memory should have broken away and deserted in order to follow after alien and unprofitable thoughts. It is true that the quietude of the soul is not so complete as when the understanding and the memory also co-operate with the will; but all the same, a spiritual tranquillity does not fail to make itself felt, because it reigns in the will, which is the mistress of all the other faculties. We have certainly seen a soul deeply attached to and united to God, in spite of the fact that the understanding and the memory were quite free from any interior occupation; hearing distinctly all that was said around it, and recollecting it all perfectly, although quite unable to respond or to detach itself from God, to whom it had united itself by the application of the will. I say it is so united that it could not withdraw itself from this sweet preoccupation without suffering a great anguish, which would find vent in lamentations even when in the full enjoyment of its consolations and quietude! We thus see infants moaning and uttering little plaints when, after ardently desiring the breast, they have begun to suck; or, like Jacob, who, when embracing the chaste and beautiful Rachel, uttered a cry, weeping because of the vehemence of the joy and tenderness which he experienced. So the soul of which I speak, having the will alone engaged, and the understanding, memory, hearing, and imagination free, resembles, as it seems to me, a little child who at its mother's breast, sees, hears, and even stirs in her arms without relinquishing the breast" *(Love of God*, vi. 10).

"But," St. Francis of Sales goes on, "the peace of the soul

would, however, be much greater and more sweet if no sounds were to be heard around it, and if there were nothing to disturb it either by the way of the heart or of the body; for it only longs to lose itself in the sweetness of the enjoyment of its happiness; and remark that when the will is held in quietude by the joy which it experiences in the Divine presence, it does not disturb itself in order to recall the other wandering faculties, since if it attempted to do so, it would lose its peace, withdrawing from the presence of its Beloved, and wasting its energies, hurrying hither and thither to collect its scattered powers, which, moreover, could never be so successfully recalled to their duty as by the will's perseverance in holy quietude; for little by little all the faculties are attracted, drawn by the pleasure which the will is deriving, slight touches of which, like perfumes, are passed on to them, inciting them to draw near in order to participate in the blessings in which it is rejoicing."

54. "It occasionally, or even frequently, happens," says St. Teresa, "that the will alone is united to God, and in a state of profound peace tastes the joys of its union, while the imagination and the memory preserve sufficient liberty to occupy themselves with their own affairs and to engage in works of charity."[2]

The Saint constantly insists upon this division of the faculties of the soul, and everywhere recommends that no notice should be taken of these side flights of the understanding and wanderings of the imagination. "These," she adds, "may go straying away even amongst the cruel and venomous beasts which dwell on the outskirts of the castle" (the Saint thereby intending to signify the gravest temptations), "while the soul remains united to God in the upper chambers—that is to say, in the most exalted form of contemplation" (*Fourth Mansion*, chap, i.).

"The will," she says elsewhere, "should remain in repose,

---

[2] *Life,* chap. xvii. ; *Way of Perfection,* chap, xxxii.

and not set the understanding to seek after all kinds of thoughts and considerations. Let it utter any words of love which present themselves, but let no sort of effort be made with the understanding, which is nothing but a noise-maker *(moledor, he who grinds noisily)*. If the will desires to make it (the understanding) participate in its own joy, it will not be successful; for, constantly, while the understanding is rotary, the will finds itself united to God and enveloped in a profound peace. It will, therefore, do better to abandon the understanding to its wanderings, while continuing to rejoice in the raptures which are granted to it" *(Life,* chap, xv.).

55. This sensible quietude which affects simultaneously both the will and the senses, comprises a large number of varieties, according to the divers operations of grace and the divers acts of the soul. "Sometimes," says St. Francis of Sales, "the soul is not only aware of the presence of God, but it hears Him speak by means of certain illuminations and interior convictions which take the place of speech; at times it feels Him speak and speaks to Him again, but so secretly, so gently, that its holy peace and quietude are not lost thereby. . . . At other times it is aware that its Divine Spouse is speaking, but knows not how to utter, because the joy of hearing, or the reverence which it bears Him, constrain it to keep silence. Or, again, it suffers from spiritual dryness, and such an extreme of langour of spirit, that it has only strength to hear, and is incapable of utterance" *(Love of God,* vi. 11). So, too, the union, which the will attains is exercised in many ways. St. Francis of Sales *(ibid.,* Book VII.) enumerates these different ways in which the union of the soul in prayer is accomplished. It may be by small and constant flights or by a continual insensible pressure and growth of the heart in Divine goodness; or, again, by a simple consent, "allowing ourselves without resistance, to become united to the Divine goodness."

The doctrine which the Saint expounds here applies, it is true, to various kinds of prayer, but several of the modes of union indicated are specially applicable to quietude.

§ 5. *Arid Quietude.*

56. This is the term by which we designate the quietude which affects the will alone, where it exists, to use St. Francis of Sales's words, imperceptibly. In quietude, as St. Alphonsus remarks, it often happens that the love which is communicated to the centre of the soul does not overflow again upon the senses, and the soul possesses the prayer of quiet without any conscious sweetness. Not only are the understanding and the imagination no longer under the influence of the contemplative operations, but the sensitive appetite itself is not affected, the union of love exists in the will alone.

To revert to Father Surin's simile, the lute-player has discontinued all his modulations; only the main string still vibrates.

Let us hear St. Francis of Sales upon this state of prayer. "The will is unaware of the happiness and contentment that it derives, and profits by them unconsciously. Nevertheless, the soul, which in this calm repose rejoices in this delicate sentiment of the Divine presence, though unaware of its happiness, always (when anyone attempts to take it away, or when anything turns it from it) shows how dear and precious this gift is to it. For then the poor soul laments, utters cries, and even sometimes sheds tears, as a little child, who is awakened before it has had sufficient sleep, shows by its grief at being awakened how dear its sleep was to it. When you attain to this pure and simple filial reliance in Our Blessed Lord, abide in it, my dear Theotimus, without so much as stirring even for the sake of making sensible acts either of the understanding or the will; for this simple, confiding affection, this loving slumber of the spirit in the Saviour's arms, comprises all that you could desire, or could go hither and thither to seek. It is better, then, to slumber on the Divine breast than to keep watch in any other place whatever" *(Love of God,* vi. 8).

Some pages further on (chap, xi.) the Saint comes back to

this mode of prayer, and again extols its value.

"At times the soul neither hears its well-Beloved nor speaks to Him again, neither does it feel any sign of His presence ; it is simply conscious that it stands in the presence of God who wills it to be there. . . . It continues in His presence, not merely hearing Him, *gazing* at Him, or addressing Him, but also waiting to see if it will please Him to look at us, to speak to us, or to make us speak to Him; or, again, doing none of these things, but abiding simply in the place where He wills that we should be."

And then follows the famous simile of the statue.

"My dear Theotimus, let us indulge in this fancy. If a statue which the sculptor had set up in a niche in some great prince's gallery were endowed with understanding and could reason and speak, and if someone came and asked it, 'Oh, beautiful statue, tell me why art thou in that niche?' 'Because,' it would reply, 'my master placed me here.' And if its interlocutor continued: 'But why dost thou remain here idle?' it would answer, 'Because my master has not set me here in order that I might do anything whatsoever, but only that I should stand thus motionless.' And if they continued to urge it, saying, 'But, poor statue, how does it profit thee to stand here after this fashion?' 'I am not here,' it would say, 'for my own advantage and service, but to obey and minister to the will of my master and sculptor, and this satisfies me.' 'Now tell me, statue, I implore thee, thou never seest thy master; how, then, canst thou be content with thus serving him?' 'No, certainly,' it would admit, 'I do not see him, for my eyes are not for seeing, as my feet are not for walking; but I am more than satisfied with knowing that my dear master sees me here and takes pleasure in beholding me.' But if they continued the argument with the statue and said : 'Dost thou not, then, wish to have the power of motion in order to draw nearer to the workman who has fashioned thee, and to offer him some worthier form of service?' it would certainly deny it, and protest that it desires no other thing but to do as its master required. 'Well, then,' they would conclude, 'thou hast no ambition to be aught but a statue, standing there motionless in this niche?' 'No, certainly,' the wise statue would say, 'I desire nought but to be a statue, and always in this niche as long as my sculptor desires it, satisfied to be here, and just as I am, because it is his pleasure whose I am and by whom I am what I am.'" St. Francis concludes with these words : "So this quietude, in which the will acts only through a simple acquiescence in the Divine good pleasure, desiring no other thing in prayer but to be in the presence of God and acceptable unto Him, is a quietude of sovereign excellence, inasmuch as it is free from all self-interest; the powers of the soul, and even the will, taking no pleasure in it, unless it be in its highest point, wherein it is content to know no other satisfaction but that of being without satisfaction for the love of the satisfaction and good pleasure of its God in whom it rests."

"This dry and arid recollection," says Father de Caussade on his side, "has a sweetness nearly allied to, and similar to, the foregoing (that of sensible quietude); for in it we are occupied with God, although without any conscious flavour; the heart lies quiet before God, but in a dry peace; this is usually a condition free from weariness, but also without sweetness."

57. The soul will make great progress if, instead of seeking after the spiritual sweetness of which it is deprived, it accepts the new condition and, in the words of the Psalmist, which the mystics like to quote in this connexion, consents to dwell as a dumb beast before God—*Ut jumentum factus sum apud te et ego semper tecum* (Ps. lxxii. 23). "At prayer," says Father Grou, speaking of souls which have attained to this condition, "assisting at Mass, or at Holy Communion, we must maintain ourselves in the simple disposition to accept whatever it pleases God to give us without repining if we have nothing, if we are dry, absent-minded, or even a prey to temptations." Elsewhere the same writer, speaking of Mary Magdalen, silently listening to the words of the Divine Master, adds: "It is not recorded that she spoke to Jesus Christ, or interrupted Him. She conducted herself before Him as a disciple before his

Master; she received His teachings and allowed them to penetrate gently into her heart. This is the model of perfect prayer, where the soul does not strive to give itself out in reflections and feelings, but listens to Him who instructs it without any sound of words. When God has given us the grace of calling us to this manner of prayer, we must never depart[3] there from under any pretence whatever, whether of distraction, dryness, or temptations, but persevere, overcoming any difficulties which present themselves, and persuading ourselves that we are accomplishing much, all that God requires of us, even when we feel that we are doing nothing and losing time. It is this prayer which more than anything else promotes our death unto ourselves and our life in God" (*Manuel,* Martha and Mary).

"Happy the soul," says M. Olier, "that is constrained to keep silence before God and is free to listen to Him, leaving its spouse to animate it by His spirit, to incite it to speak to Him and love Him by the operations of His light and of His love, and all this *as* it pleases Him and *when* it pleases Him" *(Letter 97).*

§ 6. *How Arid Quietude is not Sloth.*

58. It constantly happens that souls called to this kind of prayer and even their directors too, fancy that it is not "a quietude of sovereign excellence," as St. Francis of Sales used to say, but pure sloth. If, as in the case of the prayer which went before, the soul were consciously to taste and enjoy the happiness of being with God, it would realize that this was one way of loving Him. But it is not so any more. It is love,

---

[3] This is not to say that souls which have once been raised to contemplation should, under the pretext of listening to God, drive away all reflection and neglect all preparation for prayer. But the rules which we give later on will make our meaning clearer, and correct what might seem too uncompromising in these words of Father Grou, quoted above.

however, notwithstanding; for it makes an act of charity which thus keeps it in God's presence with no other aim than that of dwelling with Him and of doing His will. The acts of this love are delicate and imperceptible; grace, in a far greater degree than human effort, being responsible for their production; they are less conscious, but also more perfect.

"It is not by agitation, hurry and much action," says Father Grou, "that one attains to repose in God, but rather by the relinquishment of all these things in order to give place to the operations of God. God is ever performing and ever still. The soul which is united with God partakes alike of His activity and of His repose. It is always working, even when least aware of it, but it works in a profound peace. It does not anticipate the action of God, but waits for His summons. It moves itself under the Divine impress as the hand of a child learning to write moves itself under the impression of the master's hand. If the child's hand is not supple and tractable, if he insists upon forming the letters himself, he will write badly. No doubt the child is a factor in the production of this writing, but its action is directed by that of its master. The child's repose does not lie in not moving the hand, but in not moving it of itself and following the impulse given to it.

"It is so with the soul under the influence of God; it is not idle for a single instant, as is thought by those who have false ideas of what constitutes repose in God; God merely gives it the impulse and directs its actions. It is true that God's action as well as that of the soul is sometimes imperceptible, but it is always real, only it is then more direct, more secret, more spiritual. Even in the natural state how many interior acts there are which are unperceived by us, but which are nevertheless the causes of our exterior acts! I see, I speak, I walk, I look around, I am silent, I stand still, because I so will it, and as a rule, I pay no heed to this continual exercise of the will. Much more is this the case in the supernatural state. You pray without knowing that you are praying—the heart is united with God and is unconscious of the union."

How many imperceptible actions are thus performed? The heart turns towards God, takes its pleasure in Him, unites itself to Him.

"We must not, therefore, say that nothing is accomplished in the prayer of repose, and that it is merely time lost, but rather that we act after a very real but very secret fashion, where self-love finds nothing which nourishes it, engages it, encourages it, and in this lies the advantage of this prayer" (*Manuel*, p. 95),

59. Besides, if the soul is not praying in any way, it dreams. Now it is easy to distinguish a spiritual reverie from the prayer of quiet, however arid. In a reverie the soul perceives that it is not united to God; that it is not living in His presence; that it does not take hold of Him in any way. Its imagination alone works, and follows its own bent, making, perhaps, fine schemes of perfection—magnificent projects of apostleship, building, in a word, castles in the air, but without any loving turning towards God—without making a tranquil attempt to unite itself to Him. And this is so easily recognized, that when the soul in its prayer interrupts the union of love, however arid it may be, to fall into a reverie, it quickly becomes aware of it, reproaches itself, and endeavours to draw near to God. There is no conscious enjoyment in this union, but we are aware of its existence; we recognize it by knowing what it costs us to terminate or interrupt this prayer, no matter how great the dryness and distraction may have been. It is a pain to be separated from God—to leave His presence; we may have been unable to speak to Him, to find anything to say to Him, and yet it was happiness to stand before Him. Then all unconsciously we lived in and enjoyed the love of God; and who would dare argue that time is lost when it is employed in loving God?

60. Further, the authority of the saints and theologians confirms our teaching. Bossuet eulogistically describes the prayer of St, Jane Frances de Chantal, which St. Francis of Sales approved over and over again, even resorting to his authority to prevent the Saint from departing from it in the least

degree.

Now let us hear her own words:

"I no longer feel," she wrote to her saintly director, "that abandonment and sweet confidence, and I should be at a loss to make a single act; but all the same those virtues appear more solid and stable to me than ever. . . . My soul, at its extreme summit, remains in a simple state of unity; there is no union; for when it desires to make an act of union (which it too often wishes to attempt) it is conscious sometimes of the effort, and perceives clearly that it cannot unite itself; it can simply remain united. The soul only desires to continue there; it does not think about it, but in its inner self it forms a certain, almost imperceptible desire that God should do with it, and with all other creatures, in all things, all that it pleases Him to do. . . . Very often, according as the occasion arises, whether of necessity or affection, and all unsought, the soul glides into this unity." This was sensible quietude, and tasting in it the delights of her love, the Saint no longer feared to yield herself up to it; for she then adds: "With regard to this it is evident that it is all-satisfying. . . . But tell me, does this simple unity suffice during periods of spiritual dryness, when the soul neither sees nor feels, unless at its extreme summit?" (*sa fine pointe*). St. Francis of Sales had to reassure her on this point, and again reminds her that this entire abandonment into God's hands, even amidst spiritual dryness, is exceedingly salutary.

§ 7. *Affirmative and Negative Contemplation.*

61. This division of contemplation adopted by many writers seems in perfect accord with what we have said: *Contemplatio affirmativa est,* says St. Alphonsus Liguori, *quando anima beneficio lucis divinae, sine ulla sua opera cernit aliquam veritatem aut creatam ut esset infelicitas inferni aut increatam ut divinam misericordiam.* "If the soul, without any effort of its own, but thanks to the light which God communicates to it, sees clearly some truth, whether it be a

created truth, such as the pains of hell, or a Divine truth, such as God's infinite mercy, that is affirmative contemplation."

This is what we, in common with many writers, term cherubic or intellectual contemplation. *Negativa est quando dignoscit perfectiones divinas non in particulari, sed in genere cum confusa quadam noititia, sed quae ingerit conceptum longe majorem magnitudinis divinae.* "We describe contemplation as negative when the soul is not considering any one Divine perfection in particular, but the Divine perfections in general, and this only by means of a confused knowledge, which, however, conveys quite the most exalted idea of God's greatness." "In negative contemplation," as Father Meynard rightly affirms, "the will acts more than the understanding," and in this it does not, we think, differ greatly from affective contemplation.

62. We have already (No. 27) spoken of the superiority (as St. Alphonsus has just reminded us) of negative contemplation over that which is affirmative. We must not be surprised at this, because God, as the theologians say, knows and defines Himself less by affirmations than negations. "Let us affirm of God to the utmost extent all that creatures possess of being. Let us deny of God all imperfections and all limitations of being. Let us affirm, but, above all, let us deny—*negation is safer and worthier of the Divine Being.* In affirmation we always fall short of the inaccessible majesty of God; in negation we set it free from all that could diminish it, and we envelop it in a veil of mystery which exalts it in our estimation. This is why those who have sung the Divine perfections have always held that the human mind should proceed in the definition of these perfections by discreet affirmations, defined and corrected by reverential negations" (Father Monsabré, *Conferences de Notre Dame,* 7th Conference). The truth is that negative contemplation is contemplation, properly so called, out of which the union of love proceeds, and upon which affirmative contemplation comes at times to graft itself. It is, in fact, when the contemplative soul is united to God in a negative and vague

knowledge that it sometimes receives distinct illuminations which enable it to grasp certain truths, certain mysteries, or the meaning of some Divine utterance.

§ 8. *How the Various Kinds of Contemplation are often Mingled.*

63. In actual practice the various kinds of contemplation are not as sharply defined as might be supposed. What, for example, hinders intellectual contemplation and affective contemplation from succeeding each other in the course of the same prayer? In the same way, may not perfect quietude be merely transient? Often, as a matter of fact, in the middle of prayer that is very sweet and calm—often, even, amidst its daily work, the soul is subject to powerful and sudden emotions. The adorable Name of God or of Jesus, the most blessed name of Mary, or some holy, and sometimes quite vague, thought, will suffice to inflame the heart. This is what St. John of the Cross calls the contact of the fire.

"The contact of the fire," he says, "is that most delicate touch of the Beloved which the soul feels at times, even when least expecting it, and which sets the heart on fire with love, as if a spark of fire had fallen upon it and made it burn. Then the will, in an instant, like one roused from sleep, burns with the fire of love, longs for God, praises Him and gives Him thanks, worships and honours Him, and prays to Him in the sweetness of love. This is the flowing of the Divine balsam, which obeys the touch of the fire that issues forth from the consuming love of God which that fire kindled—the Divine balsam which comforts the soul and heals it with Its odour and its substance" *(Spiritual Canticle*, stanza xxv., p. 133).

And if the touch of which the Saint speaks is fugitive, the "celestial balm" which succeeds it remains in the soul and produces the most beneficial results. This is what St. Francis of Sales also teaches. "This recognition of the Divine goodness is expressed in St. Bruno's expression, 'O Divine goodness!' or that of St. Thomas, 'My Lord and my God!' or that of St. Francis, 'My God and my all!' This conviction, I say, lingering in the heart full of love, expands, spreads, sinks into the mind by an inward penetration, impregnating it all with its own savour, like some precious unguent or balm, which, falling upon cotton-wool, mingles with it and becomes ever more and more incorporated with it" *(Love of God,* vii., 1).

If it be not rash to seek to explain the nature of the Divine contact, it appears to us to happen after this manner, only transitorily, as we have also said with regard to contemplative "inebriation" (No. 49). Grace has taken entire and sudden possession of the soul and captured all its faculties; the understanding has received a sudden illumination in its highest point, an intuition, as it were, with regard to the goodness of God, a swift vision which suddenly strikes it, momentarily absorbing all its attention and affecting the will also. The sensible impression which resulted was at first very vivid, then it became fainter, and to the mystical inebriation of the moment the calm of quietude has succeeded.

64. So with arid quietude, there may be moments when the sensitive appetite is taken possession of and a gentle impress made upon it. "But if," says St. Francis of Sales, "to this simple abiding before God (without hearing Him speak or speaking to Him again) it pleases Him to add some such sentiments as that we are all His, and that He is all ours, O God, how desirable and precious is this grace to us!" (Book VI., chap. xi.). This is the sensible quietude which may momentarily succeed the arid quietude.

At other times it would be hard to say whether quietude is arid or sensible, sensible or perfect. In these moral questions the limits are not always very sharply defined. It is sometimes hard to determine whether the impressions made on the senses are sufficiently strong, or, on the contrary, too feeble to characterize such or such a way of prayer, but this is not of much importance in practice.

§ 9. *Contemplation and Vocal Prayer.*

65. If contemplation in its essentials (in the general knowledge and loving union with God, that is to say) can subsist in states of the soul as different as those which we have just reviewed, and even amidst the divers occupations of life, it will be evident that it is compatible with vocal prayer.

"I know a person," says St. Teresa, "who, never having been able to practise any but vocal prayer, possessed all the others also, and when she ceased reciting these her spirit went astray to such an extent that she could not bear it. . . . She recited *Paters,* reflecting upon the mysteries of our Blessed Lord's Blood-sheddings, and remained for hours thus praying. She came to me one day greatly afflicted, because, being unable to pray mentally or to apply herself to contemplation, she found herself reduced merely to a few vocal prayers. I asked her what she recited, and found that in saying the *Pater* she had risen to a state of pure contemplation, where Our Lord held her closely united to Him" *(Way of Perfection,* chap. xxx.; Dalton, p. 174-5). Thus, in the recitation of vocal prayers this pious soul was raised to the state of contemplation; it is possible, therefore, while praying vocally, to maintain oneself in the union of love, whether sensible or otherwise. And even with souls accustomed to this kind of devotion there is no better way of reciting their prayers, the canonical hours, the Rosary, etc,, and assisting at the Offices and ceremonies of the Church, than by continuing in a state of peaceful union with God, This is what Bossuet expressly advises: "The hours of prayer arrived, begin with great reverence by the simple remembrance of God, invoking His Spirit, and uniting yourself closely with Jesus Christ. Then go on in the same manner, including the *vocal prayers,*[4] *chanting of the Divine Office,*

---

[4] For those Orders of women where the chants and recitations of the Office are in Latin, it is very desirable that the religious should be able to practice this kind of prayer, for otherwise, not understanding the meanings of the

holy Mass, said or assisted at, and even the examination of conscience."

66. It is true that on those tolerably frequent occasions when contemplative grace makes its action powerfully felt, simple repose and the happiness of a silent abiding in the presence of God is preferred to vocal prayer. "The peace of the soul" (we have already quoted these words of St. Francis of Sales) "would be greater and more sweet if no sounds were to be heard round about it, and it were not disturbed either as to the heart or to the body." But when vocal prayer is a duty the soul must do violence to itself, and if it enjoys less abundant sweetness it will not on that account forfeit either the contemplative illuminations or the affections.

On the other hand, there are cases where the contemplative grace is weaker, and then the recitation of vocal prayers may be a help. Then the waters of contemplation have, in St. Teresa's words, risen to the point of overflowing; and the pious thoughts which are suggested by the sacred words cause them to rise, and the liveliest outbursts of love and sweet emotions are thus produced in the soul.

§ 10. *How the Soul may be Unconsciously Contemplative.*

67. St. Teresa has just given us a striking example of a soul which was contemplative without being aware of the fact. This will be easily understood from what we have said. We are not speaking of intellectual contemplation; the mind that is brilliantly illuminated by definite and distinct lights thrown upon this or that mystery cannot fail to be aware of it. But in the case of affective contemplation, where the heart plays a larger part, many are they who are thus favoured without their suspecting that this is contemplation, many who would never

---

words which they are using, they can derive no benefit from them. If while praying with the lips they are not in a way intimately united with God, they run the risk of praying badly.

recognize contemplation in the prayer of which we have been speaking, where the heart alone remains united with God, while the imagination and the understanding go free.

And this is even more the case in that other kind of quietude where the union of love is scarcely recognizable. Indeed, contemplation, as we have already said, is merely the exercise of the gifts of the Holy Spirit. Now, when the soul's principle of action lies in the infused virtues and obedience to reasoned conclusions (such as when pious reflections lead to an act of contrition made in the heart), this is readily recognizable. But if it operates by gifts, if it repents of its sins by an act of the gift of understanding and piety, there is no explicit reasoning, and the fact may pass unnoticed. It therefore often follows that souls possessing contrition to a high degree complain of being without it, because it is neither reasoned nor sensible.

CHAPTER VI

HOW CONTEMPLATION IS LESS RARE THAN IS COMMONLY SUPPOSED

§ 1. *The Testimony of the Mystic Writers.*

68. HAVE we not lowered the grace of contemplation in the eyes of many of our readers in the foregoing pages? It is true that, as Father de Caussade says, it is not usually represented thus,

"Are there not writers who, when treating of ordinary contemplation or ordinary passive prayer, manage to give such an exalted and magnificent idea of them that some souls are dazzled and others are discouraged from aspiring thereto?" (*Inst. Spir.,* dial. 4).

Those who form such an exaggerated notion of contemplation will, however, be greatly astonished when they read in the writings of the mystic authors statements absolutely incompatible with their point of view, but perfectly in agreement with our own.

"We are permitted," says Father Alvarez de Paz, "to desire the gift of contemplation; we may humbly beg God to grant it to us; it is even our duty to place ourselves in the proper dispositions by perfect self-denial and the diligent practice of all the virtues. And certainly," he adds, "we have only ourselves to blame if we never experience the ineffable sweetness of contemplation."[1] Father Lallemant, so justly renowned for his accurate and carefully considered writings expresses himself thus: "Without contemplation much progress in virtue would never be made, nor should we be fitted to help others to advance in it. We should never entirely rid ourselves of our weaknesses and imperfections, but remain always attacked to this world, never rising very far above the feelings of our human nature. We should never be able to render a perfect service to God. Unless we have received this most exalted gift it is dangerous to give ourselves up too unreservedly to minister to the necessities of our neighbour, etc."[2] The venerable writer would certainly not use this language if he regarded contemplation as a rare and exceptional phenomenon.

69. According to St. Teresa, contemplation is the crown, as it were, of the spiritual life; and she goes as far as to promise it

---

[1] *Nos certe in causa sumusquod nunquam contemplationis in effabilem suavitatem gustemus. De orai. ment.* (Book I., part iii., chap, xxvii.). All the masters admit that no one ought to desire to possess exceptional graces. And certain mystic theologians of the last two centuries having taught that contemplation is an exceptional favour are then much embarrassed in their attempt to reconcile this doctrine with the assertions of the earlier writers, who unhesitatingly affirm that it is permissible to aspire to these contemplative graces. "Scaramelli, after protesting that he would not contradict such learned men, first admits the thesis, and then demolishes it with corrections in the style of the rigorism of the eighteenth century" (Father Poulain, S.J., La Mystique de S. Jean de la Croix).

[2] This language of Father Lallemant's recalls the words of the *Imitation.* After showing the necessity for self-sacrifice, and pointing out that it is the only way which leads to contemplation, the author of this admirable work adds : *Nisi homo sit* in *spiritus elevatus, et ab omnibus creaturis liberatus, AC DEO TOTUS UNITUS, quidquid scit, quidquid etiam habet, non est magni ponderis* (*Imitation,* iii. 31).

to her daughters as the reward of their fidelity.[3] It is true that she begins by reminding them of facts which must not be overlooked: how that many souls that never attain to contemplation may still procure the glory of God and have great merit; and that not only can the soul be saved without contemplation, but that it is possible thus to go far towards perfection, farther even than others who are contemplative may do. But, nevertheless, without wishing to contradict these truths, she promises her daughters that God will, sooner or later, grant them the grace of contemplation if they remain faithful. "Consider that our Lord invites us all. He is the truth itself; we cannot doubt His words. If this banquet were not for all, He would not call us all thereto; and even if He called us, He would not say, 'I will give you to drink.' He might have said, 'Come ye all unto Me; ye shall lose nothing in serving Me; and as to these celestial waters (contemplation), I will give to drink of them to those whom I shall choose.' But since He puts no restrictions either in His invitation or in His promises, I hold it as certain that all those who do not halt on the way shall eventually drink of these living waters."[4]

In the Saint's opinion, the call to contemplation does not, therefore, come to all at the same time, God leading some less perfect souls earlier thereto; others, although farther advanced in sanctity, only arriving later; while some, notwithstanding their fidelity, may be withdrawn from this world without ever having attained to it. But, as a general rule, those who shall spend long years in perfect faithfulness will end by being admitted into the unitive and contemplative way.

In her book *The Interior Castle,* after describing the fourth mansion, where the prayer of the Divine joys, or sensible quietude, manifests itself, she concludes with these words: "I have treated of this fourth mansion at some length, because it is

---

[3] Way of Perfection, chaps, xviii., xx.p xxi.
[4] Chap, xix., p.116. Dalton, sub fine "Tengo for cierto, que todos los que no se quedaren en el camino no les fallara esta agua viva."

the one into which, as I believe, the majority of souls enter."[5] In her *Life* (chap, xv.), referring to this prayer which some writers persist in regarding in the light of a marvellous phenomenon, she had already, and with insistence, expressed her conviction that a large number of souls attain to it;[6] while in her book of *Foundations* (chap, iv.) she declares that in each one of their houses hardly a single religious could be found who had not advanced beyond meditation, all the others having attained to perfect contemplation.[7] She recognizes elsewhere that quietude, while communicating many saintly characteristics to the soul, leaves also many imperfections and weaknesses. The extraordinary begins, according to her, only with the prayer of union.[8]

In the *Fifth Mansion* (chap, iii.) she shows how souls may be brought by two different paths to this state of union — to that perfect conformity, that is to say, to the Divine will which is true holiness, and which ought to be the object of all our efforts and aspirations. Some attain thereto by an exalted and perfectly gratuitous prayer, in which God *suspends the ordinary operations of the senses*, and communicates marvellous dispositions to the soul; and she speaks of this prayer as the prayer of union.[9] Others attain to the same end

---

[5] "Me he alargado mucho en esta Morada, porque es en la que mas almas creo entran."

[6] *Hay muchas almas que llegan a este estado.*

[7] *En estas casas si hay una de las hermanas que la lleve el Señor por meditacion, todas las demas llegan a contemplacion perfecta.*

[8] What confirms us in this opinion is that the prayer of union, in St. Teresa's opinion, is merely a kind of inferior ecstasy. The senses play no part in it (*Life*, chap, xviii., and Letter to *Father Rodr. Alvarez*). Ecstasy, she says, differs from the union only in this: that it lasts longer and makes itself more perceptible to onlookers (*Letter to Father Rodr. Alvarez).* St. Francis of Sales adopts this theory (*Love of God*, vii. 3); see also *L'État Mystique*, chap, v., § 2). St. Teresa is consistent when on the one hand she approves and encourages the desire for contemplation, and on the other says and repeats that she has never desired the prayer of union. The first has to do with the ordinary, the second with the extraordinary, way.

[9] If the prayer of union, in St. Teresa's estimation, appears to be so much

and arrive equally at this fifth mansion by the death of the will—that is to say, by all kinds of trials patiently borne, and also, so we believe, by this arid quietude, which, according to St. Francis of Sales, owes its excellence to the fact that the will finds no lively satisfaction therein.

70. Let us now turn to St. John of the Cross. According to this holy writer, when the soul has already, to a certain extent, arrived at detachment from earthly things, "God begins to raise it to the state of contemplation, and this usually takes place very soon in the case of religious.[10] They have then merely to pass from meditation to contemplation." St. John of the Cross declares that there are exceptions to this rule. "God does not elevate to *perfect* contemplation everyone that is tried in the spiritual way" (*Obscure Night,* i.9, p.353). But, taking his writings as a whole, it is evident that he regards contemplation as the habitual crown of all generous effort made in the service of God. This is further proved by the distinction that he draws between a "general knowledge" of the Divine perfections, which is the basis of contemplation, and certain particular graces, "distinct perceptions, Divine contacts, feelings so hidden and so profound that they seem to have their being in the very substance of the soul itself " *(Ascent of Mount Carmel,* Book II., chap. 32). Of these latter favours he speaks quite differently, representing them as being much rarer, quite gratuitous, and impossible to foresee, "God," he says, "thus favours those whom He will, and for reasons known to Him alone." According to him, exceptional favours, visions, revelations, etc., are often dangerous (*Ibid.,* Book II., chap. ii.). The soul must "renounce them with constancy and generosity,

---

superior to quietude, much more will this be the case with the states of prayer which she describes later on—ecstasy, ravishment, etc.—which are certainly, in her eyes, of a different order altogether, and in the truest sense extraordinary.

[10] *Los comienza Dios a poner en este esta do de contemplacion; to cual suele ser may en breve, majormente en gente Religiosa (Living Flame,* strophe 3, g 5).

otherwise they will become rather harmful than useful in any real progress towards perfection" (chap. xvii.). Again, "Many souls who have not been enriched by such favours are undoubtedly infinitely more advanced than others who have received them in profusion" (chap. xxii.). Rather he constantly represents an obscure but supernatural contemplation, inspired by faith alone, as the true means of attaining to the Divine union, the way which leads to perfection.

71. If we read the various writings of Fathers Surin, Grou, de Caussade, etc., we shall come to the same conclusion—namely, that the contemplative way is the one to which souls who give themselves up without reserve to the service of God are ordinarily called.

"*I can affirm,*" says Father Surin, "*that amongst those persons who to my knowledge have given themselves wholly to God I have not remarked one who was not rewarded with this gift,* when they had habituated themselves for some length of time to the practice of meditating upon the mysteries and truths of the faith" (*Spir, Dial.,* Vol. I., Book IV., chap. ii.).

72. "I must say quite plainly," says St. Jane Frances de Chantal (*Reponses sur le Coutumier de la Visitation*) "that which for good reasons I had refrained from saying hitherto, but which the good of souls now constrains me to utter. It is this: that the longer I go on, the more clearly I perceive that our Lord conducts nearly *all* the daughters of the Visitation to this prayer of simple unity and unique simplicity of consciousness of the presence of God, by way of an entire surrender of themselves to His holy will, and to the protection of Divine providence."[11]

And in a letter to a Superior of her Order she says: "The

---

[11] Let us note in passing the following words of the Saint, which cannot fail to be instructive : "I know that this prayer gives rise to much questioning on the part of those whom God leads by the way of reasoning, and many of our Sisters have been troubled, accusing themselves of sloth and of wasting time. But, with all respect to those objectors, I assure you, my dear Sisters, that you should not be disturbed in your course by such words," etc.

almost universal attraction of the daughters of the Visitation is to a simple consciousness of the presence of God and a complete self-surrender. And I might dispense with the *almost,* for truly I have perceived that *all* those who from the outset have applied themselves properly to this prayer are attracted towards it immediately."

73.   We have shown (No. 5) St. Francis of Sales teaching how that by dint of meditation love grows and brings forth contemplation. But if this in his eyes is the natural outcome of devotion and fervour, it is far from being so with the ecstatic phenomena. "Many Saints are in heaven," he says, "who were never in an ecstasy, or even the rapture of contemplation" (Book VII., chap. vii.). In another passage, treating of *The Love of God* (Book X,, chap, iv.), he declares that quietude, or the repose of love, is vouchsafed by God from time to time "to souls which, in spite of their imperfections, yet love without measure." Let us recall Bossuet's words which we have already quoted: "*As a general rule,* the soul, by faithfulness in recollection and mortification, attains to this prayer of simplicity and repose in God." Scaramelli, who, however, makes the great mistake of ranking contemplation as a phenomenon of the extraordinary way,[12] declares that in the experience of his long life as a missionary he never found even one hamlet where there were not some souls at least who had attained to the contemplative way.

74.   The Ven. Father Libermann is no less explicit. "The prayer of affection," he says, "is not a permanent condition; it is only the path by which contemplation is reached if the soul is faithful." And this teaching flows constantly from his pen. Elsewhere, after showing how, when a soul has need of purification, God, after a first period of sensible consolation, causes it to pass through trials of dryness and aridity, "During the whole time," he adds, "that these privations of the senses endure, the faithful soul advances gradually into the

---

[12] See Vie d' Union, No. 419.

contemplative way, which leads it rapidly to the perfect union." In a letter to the Director of a Seminary he explained the method which he adopted for the direction of souls (*Letter* 196, written in 1839). He made it a point, first of all, to induce the novices or seminarists to strive zealously after perfection, endeavouring to make them overcome the chief obstacle to their sanctification. He then sought to establish them in stillness, tranquillity, and peace of heart. "This peace," he adds, "disposed them little by little to the inner life, and *led them always onwards to contemplation* and self-sacrifice." And a little farther on: "I was often astonished at the way in which they would tell me of their experiences, which were of the nature of pure contemplation, and this before I had said a word with the object of introducing them to this state." Later on: "When considerations had become distasteful to them, and I perceived that these had ceased to bear fruit, I led them to this simple looking upon God, and induced them to maintain themselves in His presence by faith."

75. But if contemplation involves no departure from the common way, it marks the highest point of the road, and is the last stage for those whom God does not intend to favour with miraculous gifts. It is, in a word, as the theologians say, the prayer which is proper to the unitive life.[13] It is easy to understand this. The contemplative operations, as we have said, take place in the superior portion of the soul. Before they could be produced with any frequency the inferior faculties (the imagination and the sensitive appetite), which are so powerful in sensual and even in pious souls, had to be enfeebled and, so to say, reduced by a valiantly fought combat and trials patiently endured. This is what St. John of the Cross means by saying

---

[13] *Dicendum est contemplationem qua spectat ad viam unitivem esse propriam perfectorum, quia talis contemplatio non quasi per occasionem et in transitu exercetur, sed per se et quasi ex habitu. Talis autem contemplatio requiret animum valde moderatum et compositum, diuque exercitatum et illuminatum; haec autem omnia non inveniuntur nisi in his qui gradum perfectionis attigerunt* (Suarez, *De Devotione,* cap. xi., No. 9).

that the soul must have had its active and passive night.

On the other hand, this prayer requires a perfect faith and an entire abandonment into God's hands; otherwise the soul, remaining too accessible to cares and preoccupations of every kind, will be confronted with insuperable obstacles to contemplation. For the same reason, purity of heart, as Father Lallemant calls it—that is to say, the true spirit of detachment—is necessary. Father de Caussade says with truth that "with a complete detachment of the heart there is accorded a correspondingly great facility for this kind of prayer, while with a lesser detachment there is a diminished facility."

Endowed with these dispositions, we may still, perhaps, be very far removed from holiness, but our feet will nevertheless be set in the unitive way. The free practice of the Christian virtues will have destroyed the contrary habits; temptations, without losing any of their strength, will have less hold on the soul; a swift repudiation, constantly repeated if they become urgent and tenacious, will suffice, as a rule,[14] to repel them. The soul which feels no farther need of arguments in order to decide it to choose the right will no longer rely upon them in its

---

[14] We say "as a rule," for there are cases in which, in repelling the temptation, it is helpful to call to mind some such thought as that of death, hell, the happiness of faithfulness, the glory thus rendered to God, the love thus manifested to Jesus, the superabundant glory which will recompense us in heaven for these painful conflicts. "The consideration of these truths," says St. Teresa (*Life*, chap. xv., 18,19,20), "particularly the nothingness of all earthly things and the greatness of the eternal reward, is very important for beginners. . . . These truths are necessary also for souls further advanced in this prayer, during certain seasons, when God desires to prove them and seems to be abandoning them. . . . There are days when even those who have made an entire sacrifice of their will to God, and who, rather than be guilty of the least imperfection, would go a thousand times to torture and death, need to resort to these first weapons of the armoury of prayer. Temptations, persecutions, assail them with incredible violence; also, in order to avoid the danger of offending God, they are obliged to build round about them a rampart composed of the truths of the faith, bearing steadfastly in mind the thought that everything has an end. and that there is a heaven and a hell" (*Cf. Love of God*, Book XI., chap. xvii.).

prayers, but will regard them only as a source of weariness.[15]

And God, whose paternal providence never fails those who are faithful to Him, leads them then into the way of contemplation, which will become easier in proportion as they advance in this life of renunciation of the world and of union with God.

§ 2. *Do many Perfect Souls exist without Contemplation?*

76. It would be puerile to inquire whether God can impart perfect or even heroic virtues to souls which are still at the stage of simple meditation. Upon thousands of martyrs who have never arrived at contemplation, eminent graces of illumination and strength have been poured out in their hour of trial, by the aid of which, and in the face of torture and death, they have given proof of real heroism. It is true that the gifts of the Holy Spirit which maintain the soul in contemplation are also the cause of perfect and heroic works, and for this reason contemplation and perfection are closely allied. But it is quite possible for the gifts of the Holy Spirit to manifest themselves in the conduct of life without taking effect at the hour of prayer. If the various writers are in agreement here,[16] they are none the less unanimous (according to Suarez) upon the point of the division of prayer into three classes which shall correspond with the three degrees of charity,[17] and also of

---

[15] *Cf. The Ascent of Mount Carmel*, Book II., chap. xiii.

[16] *Addendum vero est non esse contemplationem ita propriam perfectis, ut conveniat omnibus; non omnibus viris perfectis datur ut GRADU ILLO contemplationis fruantur quod interdum contingit ex*

divina dispositione pertinente ad ejus occulta judicia (Suarez, *De Oratione Mentali*, xi.. No. 9). Note, however, that the contemplation which Suarez speaks of as not being vouchsafed to all perfect souls, is that which operates without any effort, and habitually (see note to No. 75). It would, as a matter of fact, be difficult to prove that perfect souls are to be found who have never, even occasionally and transiently, enjoyed the contemplative graces.

[17] V. t. i.. No. 128. *Est haec partitio vulgaris inter scriptores praesertim mysticos et est in ratione fundata* (*ibid.*, xi., No. 5).

considering the prayer of contemplation as the attribute of perfect souls. We have adopted the course which the Saints and theologians have mostly followed, and which seems the most usual one.

This will be even more apparent if, instead of limiting the meaning of the word contemplation, as is too often done, to intellectual contemplation or perfect quietude only, it is taken in its more general sense, as we have done. Of contemplation, thus understood, we think that few saintly souls are deprived. They may not taste of the joys by which it is often accompanied, they may not experience that inward peace which is inseparable from even the most avid contemplation;[18] but when they betake themselves to prayer, those essential elements of contemplation, those secret operations of the Holy Spirit acting on the highest point of the intelligence by means of His gifts, are rarely denied them.

§ 3. *The Division of Souls into Three Classes, according* as *the Will, the Intelligence, or the Memory predominates.*

77. We shall understand still better that these contemplative phenomena are not always equally apparent if we observe the different results produced in souls by this grace of contemplation, as it adapts itself more or less to their various natures. It is with human souls as with celestial spirits. The

---

[18] The soul possesses this peace," says Father Grou (*Manuel*, p. " but does not perceive it, and even believes itself to be without it." "The will," says St. Francis of Sales, "'is unaware of the happiness and satisfaction which it enjoys, profiting by them only insensibly " (*Love of God*, vi. 8). In proof of the fact that the troubles and agonies of these perfect servants of God agitate the surface only of the soul, we find that they remain, nevertheless, masters of themselves, that their will is in no wise shaken by the trials which they have undergone, nor does their fidelity to God diminish; they are able, when necessary, to encourage others who arc Mao troubled, and to inspire them with that selfsame unalterable confidence, the absence of which they are lamenting in themselves.

Seraphim, the Cherubim, the other angels,[19] are full of admiration at the sight of the Divine perfections, and all alike are possessed with a burning love for their God. But with the Seraphim it is love which is the dominant characteristic, the distinctive feature, while in the case of the Cherubim it is light. It would seem that the Seraphim, all aflame with the love communicated to them by the Holy Spirit, are illumined by very reason of their love, because it leads them to contemplate the sublime beauties of God. The Cherubim, on the other hand, wonderfully illumined by the knowledge communicated to them by the Eternal Word, are at first only conscious of their rapture, and they turn with all the ardour of their love towards Him of whose perfections they have become aware. Flame emits both light and heat, but some flames are rather luminous than burning, while othets are more burning than luminous.

78. In human souls the same differences occur. With some, whom we will term the "seraphic souls" the faculty most directly affected by grace is the will; taken possession of by love, they apply themselves to virtue with ardour and perseverance. The seraphic souls feel themselves more especially impelled to make proof of their devotion to God; they seek for means to please Him. "What shall I do for God? What work shall I undertake for His glory?" Such is their first thought. It is only secondarily, and as a result of their love, that they set themselves to learn to know Him better. They will then, if they continue faithful, receive much light—above all, light of a practical kind; only that in their case it appears to be the *result* rather than the *cause* of their love.

---

[19] The different types which we are about to describe do not originate in differences of organism, as is the case with temperaments. They are distinctive traits of the souls themselves. In the first stage of the spiritual life, as we have already remarked, the faithful soul being still in a condition in which the senses are predominant, the temperament seems more noticeable. But after the purging of the senses has been bravely borne, the temperament loses much of its influence, and, the superior faculties waxing stronger, the spiritual physiognomy of each faithful soul is still more clearly manifested.

St. Peter, St. Gregory VII., St. Charles Borromeo, St. Vincent of Paul, St. Jane Frances de Chantal, the Ven. Mother Pelletier, seem to have been seraphic souls in whom the love that manifested itself in their remarkable labours more conspicuous than their illumination. So also Margaret Mary's attraction was rather to an active to a passive love; her longing to suffer and to labour for her God was greater than her desire for contemplation.

79. St. John the Evangelist, St. Augustine, St. Francis Of Sales, St. Teresa, St. John of the Cross, the Ven. Mary at &e Incarnation, on the other hand, rather resemble the In souls of this second order the dominant are those of illumination. When they are faithful God illumines them in a wonderful way, imparting to them Himself, of His perfections, the Divine mysteries, thoughts which fill them with admiration and rapture. They are ravished by the contemplation of Divine things, and then, as by a natural consequence, the love in their heart waxes stronger; for how is it possible not to love God when they perceive how beautiful, how great, how loving He is? When they are entirely faithful their love corresponds with their enlightenment, and for the God whom they so adore they will perform heroic acts of love. But they are less eager than the others to multiply works of charity. Called more especially to a state of passive devotion, they, more even than their seraphic companions, fed drawn to contemplation, with a lesser need for action. "My soul," says Ven. Mary of the Incarnation, "finding itself all-absorbed in the vast and infinite greatness of the majesty of God, cried out: 'O greatness! O length! O depth! O infinite height, vast, incomprehensible, adorable! Thou *art,* O Almighty God, and all else is not, except in so far as it exists in Thee and through Thee! O eternity, beauty, goodness, purity, love, my centre, my foundation, my end, my bliss, my all!' "

"Before this wonderful vision of the greatness of God she was so humbled that she longed to offer up her mortal life in homage to His immortality and all His perfections; but, being unable to gratify these longings, she martyred herself by penances more rigorous than any that she had hitherto practised. But these extreme mortifications only served still further to purify her spiritual vision, and to prepare the way for ever brighter light. This is why she goes on to say: 'After these penitential exercises my soul was filled with so much light that it was blinded and dazzled, if I may so speak, by the grandeur of the majestv of God' " (her *Life*, by Cl. Martin, i, 22, p. 102).

It is a superabundance of light, then, which incites these cherubic souls to penitence. The seraphic souls are brought to the practice of austerities by a more direct way; they find there a manner of exercising their affections and becoming one with the Well-Beloved. For in self-inflicted suffering we see an act of love which unites the soul to God; and as they are incessantly desirous of spending themselves in love by every possible means, they experience an urgent need for self-mortification.

Blessed Margaret Mary is a striking example of this disposition. "When I had poured out all my heart," she says, "and had stripped my whole soul bare, Our Lord kindled in it such an ardent desire *to love Him and to suffer* that He gave me no rest, pursuing after me so closely that I could think of naught, but how 1 could best love Him through the crucifying of my own self." (This was at the outset of her religious life.) "Then was shown me," she says elsewhere, shortly after her profession, "a great cross, of which I could not see the extremity, but it was all covered with flowers. 'Behold the couch of my chaste spouses! Little by little these flowers will fall away until nothing remains to thee but the thorns which, out of consideration for thy weakness, they now serve to conceal. And they will pierce thee so deeply that thou wilt require all the strength of My love to enable thee to endure the suffering.' These words rejoiced my heart, for I thought that never could I have enough of suffering, of humiliation, or contempt to slake my ardent thirst; nor could I ever know any suffering so great as that of not suffering enough. The greater my suffering, so much the nearer I came to appeasing this sacredness of love *which had kindled three desires in my heart,* and which urged me on incessantly—one to suffer, the other to love and go to Communion, and the third to die, in order to be one with Him."

St. Veronica's account of her own experience is equally striking, and shows no less clearly how, in the case of certain souls, grace acts rather on the will than on the intelligence.

"I was conscious at times of a longing after mortification: I denied myself everything that appealed to my inclinations; everything that my human nature craved for I refused to grant. And I did all this without knowing why. I do not ever remember acting with any conscious purpose" *(Diary,* vol. i., p. 44). "After dressing my little altars" (when she was still a child), "I used to throw myself on my knees, and remain so for long times together, but I do not know what I was doing. I was, as it were, outside of myself, so intensely happy as to be oblivious of all feelings of hunger or any other sensations; I was only aware of an ardent longing that God should be loved and honoured by aft His creatures" *(ibid.,* p. 48).

"From the age of fourteen I began to practise mental prayer, and found great consolation therein. I do not say that I received any illumination, for at the outset my only consolation consisted in abiding there for Our Lord's good pleasure. I began to desire suffering . . . and when my prayers were prolonged this longing after suffering became an actual craving" *(ibid.,* p. 52).

"When I returned home I withdrew to a place where I was unobserved, and performed some kind of penance. I did not know at all why 1 thus mortified myself; I was only conscious of a vivid wish for suffering. At one time 1 dragged myself about on my knees, or I made the sign of the cross with my tongue, or I held my arms extended. I did all this without any light from God, not really understanding what I was doing" *(ibid.,* p. 89).

80. The understanding, which in the case of cherubic souls is especially subjected to these impressions of Divine grade, is

a faculty which takes in the general outlines—attains to the perception, so to say, of a bird's-eye view, and finds an extreme delight in the contemplation of the beautiful. The memory, which in our present[20] conditions is closely connected with the imagination, and which acts particularly upon the objects of sense, finds the scene of its operations in special things or persons which it successively calls up. In cases where the memory and the faculties of observation in relation to objects and facts are highly developed, the most minute circumstances are observed; such persons devote themselves to details, are struck by a word, a gesture, some simple incident. Grace adapts itself to their natures, and if they are faithful it reveals to them in all their various occupations how duty is to be fulfilled, how God may be glorified; from a single word or a simple saying it unfolds some deep meaning, some salutary lesson, but it more seldom opens out vast horizons to their gaze. Their chief strength lies in scrupulous attention to the opportunities of perfection which are offered to them. We might liken these souls to the angels who are charged by the Lord with the care of the inferior creatures, and who watch over each one with a wonderful solicitude, rendering by their ministry great glory to God. *These angelic souls are in no way inferior to their seraphic or cherubic comrades, and can attain equally to the highest degree of sanctity.* THE WORTH OF A SOUL IS MEASURED BY ITS FIDELITY, AND NOT BY THE PREDOMINANCE OF THIS OR THAT FACULTY.

St. Alphonsus, who appears to have possessed this practical disposition rather than any great grasp or wide range of ideas, was an admirable Saint who received a mission, which he carried out with marvellous success, to combat Jansenism and unbelief. He who in the eighteenth century was the support and

---

[20] It is doubtless quite otherwise after death, as the imagination and the other senses no longer exist in the soul after its separation from the body. But if the memory is then capable of embracing a larger number of recollections simultaneously, it still deals with special facts and contingencies.

glory of the Church was not certainly lacking either in light or love; but in his case these gifts seem rather to have been the result than the cause of his great achievements. It was because he was so very faithful that God illumined and enkindled him. Each night, before going to sleep, this great Saint bound himself to formulate "ten acts of love, ten acts of confidence, ten acts of contrition, ten acts of conformity to the will of God, ten acts of love towards Jesus Christ, ten acts of love to the Blessed Virgin, ten acts of love to the Blessed Sacrament, ten acts of confidence in Mary, ten acts of resignation, ten acts of self-surrender to God, ten acts of self-surrender to Jesus Christ, ten acts of self-surrender to Mary, ten prayers that the will of God might be done by him"—in all a hundred and thirty different acts *(Life,* by Father Berthe, vi. 13). This simple trait, one amongst many, shows how, without being their inferior, he differed from a St. Francis of Sales, a St. John of the Cross, or a St. Teresa. If St. Alphonsus proved himself so careful to seek after ways of pleasing God, of progressing in sanctity, the practices which he imposed on himself—his terrible penances, for instance— prove the heroic nature of his faith and his love.

So St. John Berchmans resorted to a great multitude of devotional practices, and by these means attained to great enlightenment and an ardent love, arriving rapidly at a high state of sanctity.

81. We do not suggest that these angelic souls performing their various devotional practices with such care, and the seraphic souls multiplying these proofs of their love, have not already received illuminating gifts. In the case of all souls who have arrived at perfection eminent graces are to be found, conveying a high idea of God, and infusing sentiments of love towards Him. But we are referring to those operations of grace which in each several case are the first and most striking. Light, love, fidelity in the faithful discharge of every duty, go on increasing in proportion to the merits of each soul; only with some the light is more abundant; with others it is love which is the most active; while with others, again, faithfulness

is the distinguishing feature. Some are more led to adore, others to act, others, again, to attention or devotion to duty.

The mystic graces are very conspicuous in cherubic souls, less so with those that are seraphic, and less so, again, with souls of the third class.

So, also, a taste for spiritual writings—or, at any rate, mystic writings—shows itself in cherubic souls earlier than others—almost as soon, in fact, as they begin to emerge from the sensible way; they are quick to recognize their own condition and inner disposition, and take pleasure in the perusal of descriptions of them. This same inclination makes itself felt more tardily with the other souls, and its appearance argues a greater progress in love. They tend, in fact, more towards action than speculation, but they only recognize this mystic state in themselves when they have already made considerable progress therein.

The cherubic souls, in whom grace acts chiefly through the intellect, delight especially in the contemplation of Divine truths. They doubtless pass through periods of dryness, particularly when they require to be purified or are not faithful; but they are less subject to them than others, and are also less disposed to distractions.[21] Once purified, they tend more and more towards the unfathomable abyss of all beauty and all goodness which reveals itself to them; they aspire to unite themselves to it, to plunge into it, to lose themselves in its bliss.

With the seraphic soul arrived at a state of perfection, there is, indeed, this confused consciousness of the Divine greatness, which is an essential element of the mystic state, and which is to be found in those who are far advanced in perfections. Such

---

[21] "Thanks to the Divine goodness," said St. Francis of Sales, "I am entirely free from distractions whenever I am occupied in holy meditations. I do not know what I have done to our Lord; His mercy towards me is incomprehensible; for no sooner have I betaken myself to prayer than I become oblivious of everything except Him" (*Life*, by M. Hamon, I., VII., chap. ii.).

souls know Who is the object of their love; they recognize that their Well-Beloved is worthy of all their devotion; but, as a rule, there is not with them, as with cherubic souls, this abundance of light which floods the soul with happiness. But if the consolations of love are less sweet, they are in compensation more powerful; these souls are more subject than the others to periods of dryness; more, also, than those angelic souls who find great and visible consolation in the ordinary aids of piety, arousing thereby the envy of their seraphic comrades who are lamenting their coldness, while the others are thus filled with enthusiasm. It it possible to encounter seraphic souls who, even at the outset of the spiritual life, have enjoyed few consolations. Later on, having received graces of a very high order, they wish to love this God of whose grandeur they have caught a glimpse; they long to serve Him; they will it with a firm and energetic will; their whole prayer often consists simply in this act of the will, persisting amidst spiritual dryness. But they stand fast in these dispositions with less difficulty than do others, without any fresh illuminations being vouchsafed to them, and this even while the memory and intelligence are occupied with other things. Their prayer has often less of sensible sweetness without having less merit.[22]

When souls of the third class, by their proved fidelity in the service of God and complete detachment, have made great progress in virtue, they likewise receive those illuminating gifts from which an exalted conception of the Divine greatness and goodness proceeds, as well as that impulse of love which constitute the foundation of the mystic state. But these mystical graces which abide in the intelligence and the will are often combined here with a distinct illumination, bearing on some one special truth: a passage of Holy Scripture, or the grandeur and importance of their duties. It is this illumination of which

---

[22] St. Jane Frances de Chantal has given descriptions at various times of her devotions, which were much as we have just described. Blessed Margaret Mary enjoyed greater consolations, but in her case also she loved much rather than received special illuminations.

they are most conscious, and they are less aware of those other still more precious but hidden graces which are their real source of merit. They more rarely attain to the prayer of silence, and often achieve the mystic union in the recital of their vocal prayers.

82. The differences between these three classes of souls and the importance of distinguishing accurately between them will be better understood if we enumerate the various obstacles which must be surmounted, and the dangers to be avoided in the several cases.

Souls of the third, which we call the angelic class, in whom the memory predominates, possessing practical dispositions with a talent for detail, caring more for sensible objects, individual truths, ways and means by which they may draw nearer to God, these find it harder to enter into the way of pure faith. Instead of bringing their attention to bear directly upon God when He Himself calls them, causing the paths by which they have hitherto travelled to seem all barren to them, they continue searching after light and consolation in directions which have become profitless and even harmful. Certain methods, certain arguments, have long consoled and sustained them, and they wish always to recur to them.

They also attach themselves to practices which are excellent in themselves, but which lead only indirectly to God. Some, for instance, seek to find perfection by way of their austerities, others by their devotions. Some think of nothing but their occupations, their daily work; others of the reciting of interminable vocal prayers. This is the most dangerous reef for those in whom the memory and a talent for detail preponderates. It may prevent their arrival in the port of contemplation, and even after they have entered upon the contemplative way it may hold them back and make the Divine union more difficult of attainment.

83. Seraphic souls, it is true, strive after many ways of showing their love to God, but they are not attached to these methods in themselves; they consider the means much less than

the end, regarding them merely as the ladders which enable them to mount upwards to God. All means are therefore good to them; they do not attach themselves excessively to any one in particular. As on the one hand they ardently desire to act only for God, so on the other they have no special leaning towards this or that way of pleasing Him. They are specially fitted for the performance of great works; all that seems of a nature to rejoice the Heart of God excites their zeal also.

But their chief danger lies in the energy of the will, which may degenerate into stubbornness and obstinacy. If the angelic soul often lacks firmness in its good resolutions, the seraphic soul is frequently too much attached to its own opinions and is over tenacious in its desires, and so God's leadings in the case of these souls tend especially to render them supple, and to break their will.

Another danger for seraphic souls (less to be dreaded for them than for the angelic souls, but much more so, again, than for the cherubic souls) is that of refusing to relinquish the inferior way when the proper time has arrived. The ordeal of the transition from the meditative to the contemplative way is very painful to them and it is often considerably prolonged, because the mystical illuminations are less profuse and afford them less consolations. They find it hard to understand that they must now content themselves with so arid a prayer, and they sometimes yield to the temptation to give themselves up to active work at the expense of prayer.

84. The cherubic soul resorts to work less readily; it has not the ardent activity of its seraphic companion, nor (as in the case of the angelic soul) the fondness for detail, Which, on the contrary, it is rather inclined to neglect. It reflects more, stands silently in happy contemplation of the blessings which it enjoys—God's claim to its love, the Divine perfections, celestial joys. It is also more ready to pause in order to weigh the consequences of its actions, more quick to perceive all the advantages that will accrue from its works, as well as the difficulties and troubles which it will encounter.

The danger is lest they content themselves with the enjoyment of the light that they have received instead of conforming their conduct thereto; for while the mind is brilliantly illumined, the will is often lacking in energy. Before arriving at a state of heroic sanctity the cherubic soul groans over the slothfulness, the repugnance even, which the will displays in following the light shed by the intellect; it cries out for the graces of strength and energy.[23] A vigorous effort is needed before it can begin to act, and this effort costs it more, in point of virtue, than.in the case of the seraphic soul.

We say in point of virtue, for it is evident that a cherubic soul which has been very faithful and very generous will have acquired· a greater facility in self-sacrifice than a seraphic soul which has not corresponded fully to grace. So a faithful and courageous seraphic or angelic soul will be more illumined than a cherubic soul which has been faithless and cowardly.

85. To sum up. If a soul would attain to that degree of love to which God has called it, it must first correspond faithfully to such natural graces as are given to it and by which its dominant faculty is decided. It must then dispose its other powers for the reception of the holy influences of grace. This Divine grace penetrates successively into the triple sanctuary of the soul—into each of its faculties, that is to say—as soon as the door is thrown open for it. If the second door is not thrown open, it stops short at the outer sanctuary, and if the third stands closed it remains in the second. The more widely the door is opened, so much the more abundant is the inflow of grace. If we are not faithful to the first instalments of grace, we inevitably deprive ourselves of those which follow. If the angelic soul, called to

---

[23] The Saints themselves, when they are of the cherubic order, state that their minds are illumined before any strong impulse is received in the will. "If you knew," says St. Francis of Sales, "how God deals with my heart, you would bless His goodness, and implore Him to grant me the spirit of counsel and of strength to carry out these inspirations of wisdom and understanding which He communicates to me" (*Spirit of St. Francis of Sales*, part x.,§ xxxi.).

sanctify itself especially by the faithful discharge of the duties of its state of life, neglects them; if it does not allow the Holy Spirit free action in the memory and the inferior faculties so that He may incline them in the direction of the various works which it is called upon to perform it will not receive the high graces which, if it knows how to correspond to them, will perfect its intelligence and its will. If the seraphic soul does not obey the impulses which influence the will and prompt it to the sacrifice, neither shall it receive the light which, in accordance with the Divine intentions, would have been poured out upon its understanding. And when it has corresponded to this earlier grace, it must still dispose itself to receive the later. So the cherubic soul must first purge its mind, emptying it, so far as is possible, of all earthly things in order to fix its attention upon God, under pain of forfeiting the eminent graces of illumination which are reserved for it. It must afterwards co-operate with the Divine action, which will strengthen its will; and, finally, it must apply the memory and the inferior faculties to the works which Our Lord imposes upon it. And in showing itself thus faithful to the last, not only will the soul obtain the second and third instalment of grace, but the first will also be communicated anew and with even greater fullness.

In the case of a soul who has always been faithful, the dominant character of its grace never disappears, so that it will always be clear which was the faculty to receive the first touch of the Divine operations; but the other powers, although only secondarily affected, are so responsive to the Divine touch that they also bring forth their proper results with wonderful precision. We know that St. Teresa could have been an equally great Saint without her great works; but when God had chosen her to reform Mount Carmel and to found so many monasteries, she neglected no one necessary step, she quailed before no difficulties, she carried through all her enterprises successfully. In St. Jane Frances de Chantal and Blessed Margaret Mary we admire, above all, the strength of will and warmth of love which are their chief characteristics; but how vivid were the illuminations which these great souls received! how wonderfully they understood their duties! and how wise the counsels that they were able to give!

CHAPTER VII

THE MARKS OF CONTEMPLATION

86. IF it is possible to be in a state of contemplation unknown to oneself *(supra,* No. 67), it can also happen that it may occur to a soul without the knowledge of its director. What, then, are the signs by which he may recognize the presence of the contemplative graces in the soul which he is directing?

We must first remember that it is not at the outset of the spiritual life that the soul begins to experience this condition. Even in the case of advanced souls this prayer does not appear suddenly. But the vigilant director, warned by certain infallible signs, can foresee it. He perceives that a soul is giving itself up generously to the practice of mortification and self-sacrifice, that it accepts lovingly all those trials which Providence never fails to mete out to it—in a word, that it is giving proof of true and persevering fervour, that it is also abundantly favoured with sensible graces and that the affective feelings have become frequent and intense. Then the moment comes when, inflamed ever more and more with love, and moved by the sufferings of Jesus, it longs to suffer with Him and for Him. The imagination plays a large part, doubtless, in the outbursts of fervour. But if the soul is faithful, it frees itself gradually from the things of sense, "the operations of grace become more interior, and the Divine communications are made more and more directly to the spiritual faculties" (Libermann, *Écrits,* p. 186).

It is then that what St. Teresa calls supernatural recollection sometimes occurs; for days together, without any sort of effort, the soul remains recollected and filled with pious thoughts. If to this state of recollectedness the union of love in the will is not superadded, true contemplation is not yet present, but it is indicated, and will not long be delayed.

87. And then at last contemplation appears. More often than not, as we have shown in a former work (*Oraison de l'âme fervente*), its coming is fraught with pain. The soul is now going through that time of trial described as the night of the senses. The signs of this period, according to St. John of the Cross, are as follows: The soul can no longer employ its imagination and reason in prayer. It finds no more savour or consolation either in the things of God or in anything created. It is in a condition of acute distress, fearing that it has proved unfaithful to God, and that it no longer loves Him as hitherto (*Obscure Night*, i. 9).

But if the soul, says St. John of the Cross, can preserve its peace, if it enters into the way whither grace is calling it, giving itself up to the Lord, and listening to His voice in the recesses of its heart with a loving attention, little by little it begins to taste of a more hidden and a profounder satisfaction, not sensible now, but spiritual, which nourishes it as with a heavenly manna.

88. This is the true contemplation, the marks of which are given by the holy writer as follows, and note that the third mark alone differs from those which distinguish the night of the senses: to the former state of mournful distress a secret peace has now succeeded:

(1) A distaste for considerations, as no longer teaching anything to the soul, and a deep repugnance for discursive meditation. The books which it made use of formerly as helps to meditation no longer say anything to the heart.

(2) An habitual disposition of renouncement, so that the soul no longer attaches itself to anything apart from God; many human ties which formerly distracted the heart and formed a grave obstacle to prayer have now disappeared. The soul finds itself, as it were, weary of everything, and even although it may have to suffer from discursions of the imagination, it no longer takes any pleasure in fixing it upon the things of this world.[1]

(3) The third sign, *which is the most infallible,* says St. John of the Cross, *consists in the delight which the soul experiences in abiding alone with God,* giving Him all its loving attention, without concerning itself with any one special consideration, and *enjoying peace, quietude, and inner stillness (Mount Carmel,* ii. 13).

This spiritual peace, *the surest mark of mystical prayer,* is located in the will. It takes its birth naturally, as it were, from the love which the Holy Spirit Himself pours out upon this faculty. Rendered capable of exercising this love without any process of reasoning or any emotion in the region of the senses, the will tastes the sweetness of this love independently of the inferior faculties. This deep satisfaction that it experiences, this inner peace, must be carefully distinguished from any delight of the senses. This latter may coexist with the peace which the will enjoys, but the peace is often present without any sensible sweetness. "Do not suppose, Father," wrote Mother Teresa of St. Joseph, "that I am under the influence of any conscious fervour. No; I suffer much more than I enjoy, but my life of renouncement yields me an ineffable peace which sustains me in all my sorrows and difficulties" (*Life,* by Father Merrier; *Letter of November* 8, 1866). This peace, which no one who has not experienced it can comprehend, is very different from

---

[1] This inclination for renouncement, this distaste for everything, is noticeable more particularly in the superior parts of the soul; in the inferior parts certain violent inclinations may still persist, which, at the devil's instigation, will be the cause of grave temptations from time to time. Nevertheless, in this same inferior region numerous natural inclinations, which had formerly to be combated, no longer make themselves felt.

that which anyone may procure for himself by reasoning and saying that there is nothing to fear. It is communicated by God Himself, sometimes taking possession of the soul unexpectedly, and filling it with sweet, unshakeable tranquillity.

The happiness which it enjoys in thus fixing all its loving attention upon God makes the contemplative soul seek solitude and silence; while discharging all its social duties cheerfully, it is only happy when it is set free from them and can find itself once more alone with God.

"This soul," says St. Teresa, "sees within itself the birth of a love of God, pure of all thought of self, and it needs these times of solitude that it may the better possess its love" (*Life,* chap. xiii.). This last sign persists even in arid quietude, when the soul experiences a perpetual need for prayer, and seeks after solitude and silence, without, however, attaining to the enjoyment of God, all overrun as it is by every kind of preoccupation and distraction. The constant desire which it experiences to give itself up to prayer, this search, this thirst for God, shows that the will remains united to Him, and that this aridity is not a consequence of any want of fervour.

89. Such are the signs given by St. John of the Cross, and afterwards by all the other masters.

A contemporary writer suggests another sign. "It is necessary," he says, that a soul which experiences this contemplative state should have been purged by means of those passive ordeals of which we shall speak later on;" and by the way in which he subsequently explains these passive ordeals one would be inclined to suppose that only such souls as have previously undergone trials of a terrible severity and quite out of the common experience can attain to contemplation.[2] We must not, however, lose sight of the fact that the earlier trials, which are sent us with the object of detaching the soul from the

---

[2] This, at least, is the conclusion to which we have ourselves arrived after reading the book to which we refer, and we know of others who have also thus understood it.

pleasures of the senses and to prepare the way for contemplation, are much less severe than those which succeed them. Regarded from a point of view which excludes the essential part—namely, purification—the night of the senses consists precisely in this difficulty in meditation and this universal distaste to which we have referred. Later on, no doubt, the soul will undergo fresh purifications which are designed to complete the detachment and to facilitate contemplation. But these new trials are not the necessary prelude to all contemplative prayer.[3] On the other hand, all this purification is more or less severe, according to the degree of perfection to which God proposes to lead each particular soul (*Obscure Night,* Book II., chap. vii.). It would be a grave mistake, therefore, to take the ordeals through which we have seen the Saints pass, as an example of what usually occurs.

The signs enumerated by St. John of the Cross will therefore suffice us, and it is not necessary to supplement them. Neither can we agree with those who add to the signs enumerated above, that of the consciousness of the presence of God, even declaring this to be the main indication, calling it the prayer of simplicity, and refusing to recognize as mystic all prayer of simple vision only, where this consciousness of the presence of God is not indicated. As for ourselves, we are persuaded, especially if we consider the examples already referred to (St. Jane Frances de Chantal and the first Visitandines), that in this prayer of simplicity St. John of the Cross would have recognized a mystical prayer possessing the distinctive signs which we have just enumerated. In limiting himself to those three marks (the reasons for which he goes into at length), the great master of mysticism seems to us to propose a doctrine which is at the same time reasonable and in conformity with experience.[4]

---

[3] *Obscure Night*, Book II.. chap. i. et seq.

[4] We would refer any reader desiring to go more deeply into this subject to our other work, *L'État Mystique*. We are anxious to avoid all controversy here, and to confine ourselves to setting forth the generally accepted

90. The signs of contemplation become more striking and easily recognizable as the faithful soul advances in the mystical way, and its progress is in proportion to the generosity with which it devotes itself to the work of self-purification. In fact, the more it sweeps away all obstacles from its path, so much the more powerful and perceptible become the operations of grace. When, by dint of faithfully resisting all idle dreaming and profitless thoughts, it has succeeded in casting out of its mind all that does not relate to God and its own duties, the intellect becomes still more brightly illumined. When it has the further courage to detach itself from everything which is not God, it receives still stronger impulses of love by way of the will. The favours granted to the will are, as a rule, those of which it first becomes aware.

"The mystical inflowing," says St. John of the Cross, "streams directly into the understanding, and the will in some measure partakes of it, with a calmness and pureness so exquisite and so delicious to the soul as to be utterly indescribable; now God is felt to be present in one way, and again in another. Sometimes, too, it wounds the will at the same time, and enkindles love deeply, tenderly, and strongly; for, as I have said, *the more the understanding is purified, the more perfect and delicate, at times, is the union of the understanding and the will*, But, before the soul attains to this state, *it is more common for the touch of the fire of love to be felt in the will, than for the touch of the perfect intelligence to be felt in the understanding*" (*Obscure Night,* Book II,, chap, xiii,, p. 105).

"The soul," he says elsewhere, "resembles the window; the Divine light of the presence of God in the order of nature perpetually strikes upon it, or rather dwells within it. The soul, then, by resigning itself, in removing from itself every spot and stain of the creature, which is to keep the will perfectly united

---

teaching. This is why. in this third edition, we have curtailed the chapter showing how misleading certain writers are in their explanations of the terms *acquired* and *infused, active* and *passive* contemplation.

to the will of God—for to love Him is to labour to detach ourselves from, and to divest ourselves of, everything which is not God, for God's sake—becomes immediately enlightened by and transformed in God, because He communicates His own supernatural being in such a way that the soul seems to be God Himself, and to possess the things of God, Such a union is then wrought when God bestows on the soul that supreme grace which makes the things of God and the soul one by the transformation which renders the one a partaker of the other . . . . And as there cannot be any perfect transformation without perfect pureness, *so in proportion to that pureness will be the enlightenment, illumination, and union of the soul with God*, yet not wholly perfect if the soul be not wholly purified and clean" (*Ascent of Mount Carmel*, Book II., chap, v., pp. 80, 81).

91. To sum up, therefore, when there is any doubt as to the condition of a soul, the question as to whether it is or is not in the contemplative way may be decided by an examination of the following points:

Is the soul really advanced in abnegation, firmly established in the practice of virtue, and dead to itself? Does it experience a vague, unreasoned, but profound distaste for everything which is not God, or which does not bear some relation to Him? Does it perform all the secular functions of its daily life more from duty than inclination, seeking consolation in prayer only?[5] Does it feel repelled by all considerations, and discursive meditation? Does it at times experience a sudden, unexpected feeling of love for God, which takes possession of it, it knows not why; and this not as the result of any pondering upon or probing some religious truth, but merely at the thought of God and of Our Lord.[6] A Dove all, it experiences a feeling

---

[5] "For when we taste of the spirit the flesh becomes insipid" (St. John of the Cross, *Living Flame*, stanza Hi., § 7). It is the same with St. Gregory the Great: *Gustato spiritu, desipit omnis earo.*

[6] The further a soul advances, the more frequent become these impressions of the Holy Spirit; they make themselves felt amidst the works and occupations of the day. It often even happens with exceptionally faithful

of quiet happiness in being alone with Him, and without even having anything special to say to Him, like that pious peasant who used to pass long hours silently before Our Lord in the church at Ars, and who replied to the holy Curé's inquiry as to what he was doing during these long visits, "I look at Him, and He looks at me" *(Je l'avise, et il m'avise)*. And even when it is not conscious of any sensible consolation, does it not experience actual suffering when it is forced to interrupt its prayer and withdraw from its God? As a general rule, when a soul readily spends long hours in prayer, without effort, without weariness, often without even being able to say afterwards what has been the subject of its thoughts, this is contemplation.

souls to feel these touches of grace at the very time when they are least seeking for them. God may suffer them to continue in a state of spiritual dryness during their hours of prayer, and at other times they find themselves united to Him with a sweet and close union.

CHAPTER VIII

THE BENEFITS OF CONTEMPLATIVE PRAYER

92. THOSE who read these lines may perhaps be tempted to question the practical utility of this part of our work. To our way of thinking, however, it is very great, because this kind of prayer, less rare, as we have shown, than is too often supposed, is productive of much fruit; and if the soul which should practise it be ill-directed, it will fail to enter into this way to which God is calling it. Or even if it enters in, it may turn aside, and in either case will lose those most precious graces which in the Divine goodness had been destined for it.

Contemplative prayer is productive of much more fruit than discursive or affective prayer. "With contemplation," says Father Lallemant, "we may accomplish more in a month, both for ourselves and others, than in ten years without it." And these are the reasons that he gives: "It produces acts good in themselves and freed from the imperfections of human nature—sublime acts of the love of God, which are rarely accomplished without this gift; and, finally, it is a means of perfecting both faith and virtue and bringing them to their highest possible point" (*Doctrine Spirituelle*, 7th principe, chap, iv., article 4).

In contemplative prayer man's part is much less, that of God is greater. God gives, the soul has but to receive. "The soul," says the Ven. Father Libermann, "is but a receptive capacity; it possesses nothing of itself or in itself; it is with God that it should fill itself, and this by way of the prayer of union. Consequently, it has to receive, rather than to take. It therefore follows that the perfect state of prayer lies in the uniting of the powers of our souls to God by a contemplative silence, repose, and expectation. If this be so, *its* part is to co-operate by consenting to God's gifts and by accepting them. Also by disposing itself, by the grace of God, to unite itself to Him for the reception of His gifts" *(Écrits Spir.,* p.217).

"This prayer," says Bossuet, "in which we merely abide in a condition of simple attention to the presence of God, exposed to the Divine gaze, not hasting after anything, but accepting whatever may come to us—this is prayer with God alone; it is a union which comprises in an eminent degree all the other dispositions, and disposes the soul to passiveness." This is to say that God becomes the sole master of the inner life, and operates in it more particularly than is usually the case. "As *the creature labours less,* so *much the more powerfully does God perform.*" And since the operation of God is repose, the soul comes in a manner to resemble Him in this prayer, and with marvellous results. As the sun's rays cause the plants to grow, blossom, and bear fruit, so the soul which is attentive and lies basking peacefully in the rays of the Divine Sun of Justice, receives in greater profusion those Divine influences which enrich it with every virtue.

93. Spiritual writers combine as with one voice to proclaim the superiority of contemplation over the other forms of prayer, and there is not one of them who would not readily subscribe to what Father Surin says on this subject. This writer likens those who give themselves to this kind of prayer to three classes of men who travel, some on foot, some on horseback, the others in a carriage or by boat. (Had he lived in our days, he would have said by train, and this would be still more applicable.) "The first are those who practise discursive prayer; they go on foot, and advance by means of personal effort. The second are

those who practise affective prayer; they ride and have but little fatigue. The third are those who have arrived at contemplation; they travel much more expeditiously than the others, and without any sort of exertion" (*Catech. Spirit.*, t. i., 1 partie, chap. iii.).

It is also to the contemplative soul, above all others, that the words of St. Francis of Sales are applicable. "One single fervent soul renders more glory to God than a thousand negligent and lukewarm Christians can do," Blosius had already said: "Those who are united to God, and yield Him freedom to work what He wills in them at every instant, no matter when it shall please Him to move them, *are of greater service to the Church in one hour than others, whoever they may be, in many years*" *(Instit. Spirit* chap. i.).

The advantages of this way of prayer will stand out still more clearly in the picture which we are about to draw of the fifth degree of the spiritual life. We shall see there the results of contemplation which has become part of the life of the soul, when, instead of making itself felt only from time to time, it has become the habitual manner of prayer.

PART II.—DISPOSITION OF SOULS OF THE FIFTH DEGREE, OR PERFECT SOULS

CHAPTER I

HOW SOULS ATTAIN TO THE UNITIVE LIFE

§ 1. *Preliminary Remarks.*

94. WE have shown the faithful soul's progress in the fourth mansion; how from a sensible fervour it advances to one which is rather spiritual. Profoundly desirous of loving God and attaining to self-detachment, it seizes upon innumerable occasions for self-sacrifice, renunciation and submission to the Divine will, without needing to resort to long arguments in order to convince itself of the rectitude of its actions. At the outset this result is only achieved through the influence of the sensible graces; then, as the soul, amidst spiritual dryness and trials, becomes more and more confirmed in generosity of intention, it ends by accomplishing the most difficult actions, and this even in emptiness and aridity, and without feeling any satisfaction therein.

But many failings, as we have seen, still remain to it. For years together, it may be, life will be a blend of deep fervour, unhesitating and generous sacrifices and small attachments and immortifications, which it regrets, but is unable to overcome. It has visions of great perfection, it aims at complete abnegation, but it is still weak, and not sufficiently detached from self. How, then, is it to arrive at an entire self-denudation? This is what we are about to explain; for this true renunciation, this habitual conformity of the human to the Divine will, constitutes that state of perfection which is the first degree of the unitive life.

§ 2. *The Abridged Way and the Ordinary Way.*

95. St. Teresa teaches that certain exceptionally favoured persons are to be found, to whom God, at this stage of the spiritual life,[1] vouchsafes the gift of a much higher kind of prayer than any which has hitherto been communicated to them. She speaks of it as the prayer of union, and, as we have already said, she considers it as one of the beginnings of ecstasy.[2]

The majority of souls attain to the unitive life rather by means of the second way, which St. Teresa[3] also points out, and which consists in a very exact practice of renunciation and of all the Christian virtues. "I recognize," says the Saint, "that this other way exacts a greater amount of suffering, but the reward will be so much the greater if we obtain the victory. . . . In the first case (in the semi-ecstatic union) the happiness which the soul experiences in seeing that it is living such a new

---

[1] St. Alphonsus puts the prayer of union later, *after* the purification of the spirit. But there is no absolute rule; God gives it when it so pleases Him.

[2] Many writers understand the prayer of union, as they call it, differently, but for them there is no distinction between this and the state which we have called perfect contemplation. Indeed, in perfect contemplation the soul is already closely united to God. St. Teresa recognizes this. She also speaks of union, of faculties united, referring to ordinary contemplative prayer. Conformity to the Divine will she also refers to as union, but, as a rule, by the expression "prayer of union" she means the first degree in ecstasy. In mysticism it is very important to inquire carefully into the meaning of various terms as employed by the different writers, for these often vary considerably between one author and another.

[3] *Fifth Mansion*, chap. iii.

life affords it great support, while in the other case (the union of conformity) the soul, without departing from its usual mode of life, has to give itself up unto death."

In the case of Christians who are over-soft and self-indulgent, we have known[4] this trial of being deprived of all sensible graces to miss its appointed aim, and to leave them rooted, as it were, in a lamentable state of mediocrity. Others, endowed with greater fervour, have passed successfully through this ordeal, but because their detachment was not complete or their confidence not sufficiently strong, they have not entered fully into the way which God opened out for them, but have remained in an intermediate condition, half-way between the illuminative and the unitive ways.[5] Those who attain to the unitive life are the generous, sanguine hearts who yield themselves up to God's guidance, and respond to His every sign. And they arrive at it the more rapidly inasmuch as they forget themselves and care only to give glory to God. Those who, although solidly pious, return too much upon themselves, *anxiously* scrutinizing their least actions, or are greedy for consolations, longing to be upheld, tardy in self-sacrifice, slow to make any acts of trust and surrender, waiting for encouragement—these take much longer to reach perfection. Those, on the other hand, who go forward simply and straightforwardly, in forgetfulness of self, always mindful of the greatness and goodness of God and of His love for them, aiming only at pleasing their Divine Master—these advance with giant strides towards perfect love.

96. But even for such souls as these the time of trial is sometimes prolonged. During whole years, perhaps, they may have to struggle after self-detachment, and to resign themselves to conflicts and sacrifices without number.[6] During this painful

---

[4] Vol. I., No. 175.

[5] Vol. I., No. 330 *et seq.*

[6] Have these trials reference to the purging of the senses only? We think that for the attainment of perfection the soul must also undergo a certain purification of the spiritual faculties; but, then, the two sides of human

probation it is in prayer that the soul must seek the necessary strength. As it becomes increasingly enlightened by the contemplative gifts vouchsafed to it, it will arrive at a much higher and truer idea of the greatness of God and the mysteries of our holy religion—in a word, of all the truths of the faith— and the heart will be enkindled with the fire of pure love. At other times, on the contrary, the consolations of prayer will be denied to it, but its fervent desires, its unshakeable confidence, will touch the Heart of God, and it will obtain those efficacious graces which will deliver it from all its miseries. It will come through these trials emancipated; from the dominion of the faculties of sense; the imagination will no longer exercise its tyrannical empire over the soul, the human desires will have calmed down, and the natural inclinations have been weakened. It will henceforth belong to that order of souls which "no longer either desire superfluities or desire anything superfluously, loving only what God wills, and as He wills it."[7] Then all that was in opposition to the Divine will having been expelled from the soul, it remains transformed in God by love; the two wills, the soul's will and God's will, have become uniform; there is nothing in the one which is displeasing to the other.[8]

---

nature are so closely interwoven that it would be difficult to define the exact line where the purging of the senses would stop and the purification of the spirit would begin. St. John of the Cross, after describing the distressing tribulations of the night of the spirit, and declaring that this must necessarily be undergone before the Divine touches of knowledge and love which produce a veritable blaze in the soul can be felt, adds: "For other degrees of this union, lower than this, which are of ordinary occurrence, so intense a purgation is not required" (*Obscure Night*, Book II., chap. xii.). There is, therefore, for many souls, according to this holy writer, an attenuated purification of the spirit, far less terrible than that which we shall describe later on (Book VI., chap, ii., § 4).

[7] *Love of God*, Book X.. chap. v.

[8] *Ascent of Mount Carmel*, Book II., chap. v. Let the reader compare these words with another passage already quoted, where the same author clearly explains this state of union (*Direction of Fervent Souls*, Vol. I., No. 346).

97. It will then have arrived at perfection, for the dispositions that we have just enumerated are precisely those which St. Thomas attributes to the perfect[9] as opposed to *beginners (débutants)* and *proficients (profitants). Perfectio potest in hac vita haberi dupliciter: uno modo in quantum ab affectu hominis excluditur omne illud quod contrariatur charitati, sicut est peccatum mortale, et sine tali perfectione charitas esse non potest . . ., alio modo* IN QUANTUM AB AFFECTU HOMINIS EXCLUDITUR, *non solum illtud quod est charitati contrarium, sed etiam* OMNE ILLUD QUOD IMPEDIT NE AFFECTUS MENTIS TOTALITER DIRIGATUR AD DEUM; *sine qua perfectione charitas esse potest, puta in incipientibus et proficientibus.*" "Perfection can be had in this life in two ways: in the one by the exclusion of all that is contrary to charity—that is, of mortal sin—and without this kind of perfection charity cannot exist . . . ; in the other by the exclusion from a man's affection not only of what is contrary to charity, but also of all that prevents the affection of the mind being wholly directed to God, and without this perfection charity can exist—that is to say, in beginners and proficients" (2, 2, q. 184, a. 2).

§ 3. *The Signs of the Unitive Life.*

98. It is not always easy to decide whether the soul has really broken all its ties and arrived at a state of perfection, or whether it is still in the condition which we term fervour, where the ties, being considerably weakened, are often hidden

---

[9] The reader will note the sense in which we use this word. When this term is applied to Christian souls, theologians in no way pretend that they are altogether perfect. They subscribe wholeheartedly to St. Bernard's saying: "There is no perfect soul which does not desire to perfect itself further; it is even a sign of perfection to aspire to a higher perfection" (*Nemo perfectus est, qui perfectior esse non appetit, et in eo quisque perfectiorem se probat quod ad majorem tendit perfectionem* (*Epist. ad Drogonem* ; cf. Bonar, *Via compendit. ad Deum*, chap, xiii.).

from the soul itself. It is specially easy to be deceived when the abundance of the sensible graces prevents the revolt of the passions, so that the soul forgets its own evil tendencies; or, again, when it is out of the way of temptation, and is temporarily preserved from the occasions which might prove fatal to it.

99. A first mark of the perfect life is that contemplation has become habitual.

So long as the soul "still loved superfluously"—that is to say, with a too natural affection—it was favoured from time to time with "unions, states of recollection, and the repose of love . . . but it attained to these Divine unions with the Bridegroom but seldom, being preoccupied and diverted by loving, apart from Him and without Him, things which it ought to love only in Him and for Him" (*Love of God*, x. 4).

When this kind of prayer becomes usual it is a sign that detachment is complete and the soul's union with God habitual.

Hitherto it has travelled in an intermediate way, sometimes blessed with the gift of contemplation, but more frequently obliged to resort to the lower forms of prayer. But henceforward when it begins to pray it finds itself invariably taken possession of by a sweet and peaceful attention to God, without being capable of reasoning, or even of desiring to do so. It has then acquired the habit, perfect in its way, of contemplation.[10] Or, again, it often happens that this

---

[10] *Ascent of Mount Carmel*, Book I., chap. xiv. We have already quoted Suarez's words: Contemplatio petfeciorum non quasi per occasionem et in transitu exercetur sed per se ft quasi ex kabitu {supra, chap. vi.). We must, however, bear in mind that habitual does not mean constant. The perfect soul is not always in a state of contemplation, nor is it able to experience the delights of sensible quietude at will. " The soul, like a man escaped out of a narrow prison, emerges from the trials of the night of the senses, and with a heart more dilated and more joyous advances along the path of perfection. . . . The imagination and the faculties are no longer engaged in reasonings ; the spirit rests with great ease in sweet and loving contemplation. . . . Not that this state precludes the occurrence of darknesses, aridity, and anguish— for these may be even more extreme than in the earlier time of trial—but the

contemplative union, whether sensible or otherwise, persists in the midst of divers occupations without any great effort being required to sustain it, and this even at times without any exertion at all.

100. But the mystic union is far from being always readily identified. We have said that even if easily recognizable in cases where grace acts more directly upon the intelligence, it is much less apparent when it is the will which is principally affected by grace, and it is less so again where the memory and a talent for detail predominate.

And then some souls have the appearance of contemplation without the reality, and this either because the devil knows their condition to be unsatisfactory and leaves them in peace during the hour of prayer, in order to keep up this dangerous illusion in them, or because their quiet dispositions and gentle dreaming spirits facilitate their continuing in a peace which has nothing mystic about it. But the surest way of ascertaining whether a soul has attained to the unitive life is to observe whether it possesses the usual characteristics of perfect souls, which characteristics we shall now describe.

§ 4. *Different Degrees of Union with God,*

101. But first we must make an important statement.

From the moment when perfect purity, entire submission— that is to say, to the will of God—and a complete self-denudation in His sight, are present, the soul loving habitually and by its own consent only what God wills and as He wills it, the state of union or the unitive life is present. But "this union of love admits of several degrees, varying according to the soul's capacity, and the measure of grace which the Lord accords to each. The same differences exist amongst the blessed in heaven. Some enjoy God more perfectly than do

---

duration is shorter, and after some days of storm and tempest the sky of the soul recovers its wonted serenity " (Obscure Night, ii. i).

others, but all behold Him, all are happy and content, because their capacity corresponds to the measure of their merits. So at times in this life's pilgrimage we meet with different souls enjoying an equal peace and tranquillity in their state of perfection, but one may have attained to a higher degree of union than the other, and yet each is equally satisfied according to its disposition and its knowledge of God." So speaks St. John of the Cross (*Ascent of Mount Carmel*, Book II., chap, v.), and several times in his works he declares that the more completely a soul has been proved by trials and temptations, so much the more perfect will be the union to which it is called.

CHAPTER II

ON THE INTENSITY OF CHARITY IN PERFECT SOULS

102. EVEN in its lowest degree this state of union is a very exalted one. Those who have attained to it have one single wish only, to be united to God, to possess God, to rejoice in God. *Tertium stadium est ut homo ad hoc principaliter intendat ut Deo inhareat eo fruatur, et hoc Pertinet ad perfectos qui "cupiunt dissolvi et esse cum Christo"* (St. Thomas, 2, 2, q. 24, a. 9, c.). This is an act of love of God, intense and very pure. Fénelon appears to fail to recognize a cry of pure love in these words of the Apostle. He seems to see in them some alloy of natural love which detracts from its pure disinterestedness. But in his opinion the longing to possess God, to enjoy Him, is not perfect unless it rests solely on the motive of giving Him glory, so that those alone are disinterested who desire to enjoy God for His greater glory only.

But this yearning for the Divine union, this longing to possess God, often has its birth in the soul, as we must remember, spontaneously, from the moment when the thought first comes to it of this God, so good and so beloved. We do not pause to inquire why we desire to be united to Him, we go out after Him freely and to our great merit, without any definite reasons, but only because we love Him, and by virtue of this love we tend instinctively to unite ourselves with Him. *Amor est virtus unitiva*, says St. Dionysius the Areopagite, as quoted by St. Thomas (1, 2, q. 28, a. 1; cf. 2, 2, q. 28, a. 9, et 2).

Underlying this act there is without doubt an indeliberate, instinctive, and inevitable seeking after its own interest, but this does not in any way detract from its merit or perfection. *The soul truly sees nothing but God: it is oblivious of itself;* it is God, as the essential good, who is thus perceived by the intelligence and sought after by the will; it is His infinite perfection which ravishes the heart and is productive of this strong attraction which is nothing but an act of love free from any reference to self. *Cum homo Deus possidet sui obliviscitur et eum totis virtbus diliget.[1] Si in mea beatitudine, says Lehmkuhl, non tarn considero quod mihi bene sit, sed potius earn concipio quatenus prcesens intueri possim Deum omnibus bonis summe affluentem, atque ita in hac ipsa cognitions perfeda seu visions meum gaudium collocoi in se et per se actum perfectissimae caritatis exerceo.*

103. "If, on the other hand, the soul looks into itself, if it seriously reflects that God is not only the supreme good, but its own personal good also, it will then desire to possess Him as such; and it desires God, it longs after Him as the author of its joy, *quatenus beatificantem.* This love, then, which we call hope, is a love of concupiscence, but of a holy, regulated concupiscence by which we neither draw God down to us nor for our profit but join ourselves to Him as to our ultimate joy. In this love we love ourselves at the same time that we love God, but without preferring ourselves or making ourselves equal with Him in this love. The love for ourselves is mingled with our love for God, but that for God is paramount; our self-love enters into it, indeed, as a simple motive only, and not as a chief end. Our own advantage has some part in it, but God holds the principal place" (*Love of God*, xi. 17).

The second love is supernatural; grace has illumined the soul, it has revealed God to it as its true good and decided it to turn to Him, to long to possess Him. A wise and right way of

---

[1] St. Bernard, quoted by St. Alphonsus, Theolog. Moral., *De praecepto charitatis.*

contemplating God is to consider Him as our chief good, because this is what He actually is, and it is laudable to seek after Him as such. Besides, there is not only, as in the preceding case, an instinctive, spontaneous movement towards something that attracts us—*Fecisti nos ad te Deus, et inquietum est cor nostrum donec requiescat in te*[2]—there is also the deliberate consideration of our own profit. The mind, perceiving our advantage, our good, to lie in God Himself, and that He offers Himself to us for our happiness, proposes it as such to the will. It is this deliberate turning back upon oneself which prevents the love either of hope or of concupiscence from attaining to the perfection of true charity.

104. Side by side with this supernatural act of hope there may and does exist at times a natural act of self-love, or (which comes to the same thing) love of one's own happiness.[3] The soul, having considered God as its sovereign good, and having desired Him supernaturally, may take into consideration the bliss which the possession of God would afford it and desire this natural satisfaction deliberately. The heart, in fact, distinguishes all that the mind distinguishes; to each separate perception of the mind there may correspond (and this instinctively) a different movement of desire in the will. Now, it is certain that the intellect is able to see God's hand even in the natural happiness which He allows us to enjoy; the will may therefore be brought to bear more on one than on the other, or on the one and not on the other; or, again, it may bear simultaneously upon both, and in this case there would be two acts—one supernatural, the other natural. In this way it is possible to wish to give alms partly because it is a good action, and partly because of the credit which it brings. It is therefore a dual act, one part good, the other part bad.[4] So eternal beatitude

---

[2] "Thou hast made us for Thee, O Lord, and our hearts can find no rest but in Thee" (St. Augustine, Confessions, i.).

[3] *Sic,* says Billuart, *peccator impoenitens qui per lumen fidei cognoscit paradisum, ilium amai arnore naturali* (*De charitate*, Diss. i.. article 3, §2).

[4] In this case, if each of the motives has acted upon the will with sufficient

may be desired because we shall possess God thereby—and this is a supernatural act—and also because our human nature will find advantage and satisfaction therein, and this is a good but purely natural act.

It is this natural self-love which causes us, for instance, to say: "Oh that I were in heaven, in the enjoyment of perfect peace, set free from all the worries of this earthly life!"

105. These first principles laid down, let us apply them to perfect souls. They are animated by the three affections of which we have just spoken—pure love, the supernatural love of hope, and the natural love of happiness, the first-named acts having already become frequent. The Divine greatness and goodness are, in fact, the objects of those direct acts of perception and of love which form the basis of contemplation. For in its outbursts of love the contemplative soul loses itself, as a rule, and becomes blind to everything but God. Uttering such simple words as "My God," or often without any speech whatever, it formulates an act of complaisance in the perfections of God and experiences a vivid desire to unite itself with Him. These constitute, as we say, the direct acts, but, as we have already explained (No. 23), they are none the less very spontaneous and very meritorious, and are more frequently repeated than are the reasoned acts.

So a contemplative soul, embracing its crucifix, may in a few minutes make a greater number of acts of love, and these acts more intense and, from the point of view of motive, more perfect, than a pious soul would do during prolonged prayer. Further, in the case of the souls of whom we are now speaking, contemplation has become so frequent that even amidst the occupations of life, and for long hours together, they may continue without losing this feeling of the presence of God,

---

strength to produce the determination, an act which appears simple is in reality a complex one. But if, on the contrary, the two motives were simultaneously obeyed, neither being completely responsible, but both alike partially so, then the act is a simple one, and in the case in question it would be partly good and partly bad.

which carries with it a multitude of loving impulses. But even when the perfect soul is not under this influence, and during its days of spiritual dryness, a latent movement towards God still persists. The least cause, such, for example, as a glance at a picture of Jesus, or a simple thought, is often sufficient to give rise to secret but ardent feelings of love.

And these are acts of a deep, sincere love, because they amount to perfect detachment. With imperfect souls the affective outbursts are more often velleities than acts of the will; they mark the tendency of a heart desirous of loving God rather than one in which the love is fully formed, because the full determination to sacrifice everything for Him is lacking. The feelings of love in perfect souls are much more real and of much greater worth from the fact that they presuppose an entire self-abnegation.

It follows that a single day in the life of these perfect souls is replete with meritorious actions, and we understand SS. Francis of Sales and Louis of Blois (*supra*, No. 93) when they say that such souls stand infinitely higher than good but imperfect Christians.

CHAPTER III

THE FRUITS OF THIS ARDENT CHARITY

§ 1. *Love of Solitude.*

106. THE dispositions which we have described as constituting the signs of contemplation are all to be seen together as part of the habitual condition of souls of the fifth degree. There is nothing strange in this. As contemplation has become very frequent, so too have its fruits. We then showed with St. John of the Cross how the effects of contemplation are seen in a lively distaste for the world and all things earthly, a great happiness in finding ourselves in God's presence, enjoying Him in a sweet peace, and consequently a lively desire for solitude (St. Teresa, *Fifth Mansion*, chap. ii.).

"It is a strange characteristic of persons in love that they take a much greater pleasure in their loneliness than in the company of others. For if they meet together in the presence of others with whom they need have no intercourse, and from whom they have nothing to conceal, and if those others neither address them nor interfere with them, yet the very fact of their presence is sufficient to rob the lovers of all pleasure in their meeting" (*Spiritual Canticle*, stanza xxxv., p. 373).

So is it with the contemplative souls. They long to be always with God, to taste the sweetness of intercourse with Him. Even during its periods of dryness, when the sensible faculties are, as it were, void and barren, the soul still feels the

Divine attractions. It is happy when it escapes from human society to abide wholly alone with God. It is happy likewise when taking part in some religious ceremonial; it then, as a rule, needs no great efforts in order to be recollected, the heart takes flight swiftly towards God. So, too, the various means which it formerly adopted as aids to meditation, its acts of thanksgiving, etc,, now appear superfluous and fatiguing. "This mystic butterfly takes no further count of anything that it formerly did. It no longer slowly weaves its cocoon thread by thread—its wings have grown, and it can fly; could it be content to crawl along"? (*Fifth Mansion*, chap, ii., p. 106).

§ 2. *The Spirit of Detachment.*

107. Detachment in the contemplative soul has now become more complete. Things which it held to strongly in previous years, even when it had already given itself sincerely and fervently to God, it now regards almost with indifference. Its treasure is elsewhere, its treasure is God only, and where its treasure is there is its heart also. It is thus freed from any excessive attachment either to relatives, friends, or earthly possessions. "Formerly it feared penance, now it is strong; it wanted courage to forsake relations, friends, or possessions; neither its actions, its resolutions, nor separation from those it loved could detach the soul, but rather seemed to increase its fondness. Now it finds even their rightful claims a burden; it fears contact with them, lest it should offend God. It wearies of everything, realizing that no true rest can be found in creatures" (*Ibid.*).

It is no longer violently perturbed by those natural inclinations, anxieties, and human preoccupations from which even fervent souls have so much to suffer. The few cares with which it may, and necessarily must, be encumbered—no one here below being exempt—merely, as a rule, succeed in touching the surface of the heart without penetrating at all deeply. It is really alive only to the things of God.

108. But it must not be supposed that perfect souls are less distracted by natural inclinations and preoccupations because they are no longer a subject of temptation to them. When St. Paul made such lamentation with regard to the buffets of Satan he was in a much higher state of perfection than the souls of which we are now speaking. If there are many temptations which no longer assail these perfect souls, others still persist. Devils, even more malignant and powerful than those which assail the common run of Christians, at times succeed in arousing their slumbering passions. Our Lord, who permits these conflicts to His faithful servants for their ultimate glory, knowing them to be capable of resisting and overcoming, allows these accursed angels the fuller liberty. We see sinners in whom vices are unable to develop because of others which counteract them. So imperfect souls retain many natural attachments which occupy their thoughts, hold their hearts captive, and protect them against certain temptations. Perfect souls are more indifferent regarding the things of the world, and their only weapons with which to combat wrong desires are acts of love. But their conflicts, if harder, are also possessed of much greater merit.

109. This complete detachment, this holy indifference, which are the characteristics of the pious soul, are, however, as we should hasten to affirm, as far removed from the cold and contemptuous apathy of the Stoics as from the indolence of the man without a heart.

The perfect soul does not ignore the distinction between good and evil, pleasure and pain. If God sends temporal blessings, health, talent, or wealth, it offers Him its gratitude, and these good gifts of God become for it the occasions for rendering Him a more perfect service. If at times it desires them, it is in order to use them for the Master's glory,[1] and its

---

[1] *Temporalia*, says St. Thomas, *licet desiderate non quidem principaliter ut in eis finem constituamus, sed sicut quaedam adminicula quibus adjuvamur ad tendendum in beatitudinem, in quantum scilicet per ea vita corporalis sustentatur, et in quantum nobis organice deserviunt ad actus virtutum* (2,

entire reliance upon Providence causes this desire, when it occurs, to be always moderate and quiet. The ardours of the love which it feels for God greatly weaken, no doubt, yet do not avail wholly to stifle, all lower attractions. It will feel an inclination for certain occupations which suit it—study, work, the duties of its state of life, but these natural attractions, which it makes use of at the bidding of duty, are kept in check, are directed, and above all sacrificed when this is necessary.

With regard to relations and friends, St. Teresa, as we have just seen, says that the contemplative soul is saved from excessive attachments. Will it, then, feel only coldness and apathy towards them? Quite on the contrary; the affection which has now become supernatural will be only deeper and truer. We have heard what accents of tenderness fell from St. Paul's lips (vol. i., No. 78). Those Saints who have preached detachment and perfect indifference most fully (St. Teresa and St. Francis of Sales) have known all the refinements of a saintly affection.[2] The holy Spirit of God which inspires the faithful soul to a complete self-abnegation, inclines it at the same time towards its neighbour. From the very fact that it thinks itself nothing, it devotes itself to others with the greater facility; the harder it is to itself, the more alive it becomes to the joys and the sorrows of its brethren. No, it is not the union of our will with the Divine will, but rather selfishness and vice, which stifle all tenderness in the human heart and prevent devotion to others.

§ 3. *Longing for Heaven—the Anxieties of Love.*

110. "Weary of the world, the soul ardently longs to

2, q. 83, a. 6 c).

[2] The Ven. M. Marie de Sainte Euphraisie Pelletier, foundress of the Congregation of the Good Shepherd, who was so wholly detached from self and so closely united to God, had the tenderest feelings of a maternal affection for all those under her care, and her spiritual daughters in particular.

depart thence" (*Fifth Mansion*, chap. ii.). On the one hand it no longer feels at home on this earth, its amusements and pleasures possess no further charm. Besides, it is exposed to great trials. It experiences the full strength of the attraction of God's love, and it feels pain in recognizing how weak it is, in feeling the temptations which are leading it away from Him, and making it abhorrent in His eyes. *Infelix ego homo, quis me liberabit a corpore mortis hujus?* How depict the anguish of a heart which finds itself incapable of loving God.

"Sometimes," says St. John of the Cross, "a certain longing after God begins to be felt; and the more it grows, the more the soul feels itself touched and inflamed with the love of God, without knowing or understanding how or whence that love comes, except that at times this burning so inflames it that it longs earnestly after God. . . . The soul feels it to be a living thirst. So was it with David when he said, 'My soul hath thirsted after God, the strong, living.' It is as if he had said: The thirst of my soul is a living thirst. We may say of this thirst that, being a living thirst, it kills. Though this thirst is not continuously, but only occasionally, violent, nevertheless it is always felt in some degree. I commenced by observing that this love, in general, is not felt at first, but only the dryness and emptiness of which I am speaking; and then, instead of love, which is afterwards enkindled, what the soul feels in the dryness and the emptiness of its faculties is a general painful anxiety about God, and a certain painful misgiving that it is not serving Him. But a soul anxious and afflicted for His sake is a sacrifice not a little pleasing unto God" (*Obscure Night*, Book I., chap, xi., pp. 40, 41).

"O my Theotimus," says St. Francis of Sales on his side, "how the heart, urged on by its affections to give praise to God, experiences a poignantly sweet pain and a poignantly painful sweetness, when, after a thousand attempts to extol Him, it realizes how far short it has fallen! Alas, poor nightingale, ever striving to make its songs rise higher and to perfect its sweet melodies, the better to sing the perfections of the Well-beloved! Praising, it delights in its own praise, and in the very ecstasy of its praise it grieves at the shortcomings of its praise" (*Love of God*, v. 8).

111. And God takes a delight in these yearnings of the faithful soul. He provokes them by means of the graces which He grants, by the secret light which He communicates. "Drawing continually, so to say, fresh darts from the quiver of His infinite perfections, He wounds the souls of these lovers, showing them clearly that they love Him not half as dearly as He deserves to be loved. Although He sees a soul to be already wholly His, He draws and lets fly from time to time a myriad shafts of love, revealing to it by ever new ways how wonderful are His perfections, and how inadequate the outpourings of all human affection. And the soul, whose power of loving falls so far short of its desires, seeing the wretchedness of its efforts, when compared with its aspirations and yearning desires to love Him whom no human heart can sufficiently adore, suffers, alas! almost indescribable agony, for the higher it attempts to soar on the wings of love, so much the greater are the resulting pangs.

"The loving heart, longing to love God without measure, perceives that it can never love Him nor desire Him sufficiently. And this insatiable craving is as a barbed arrow to the generous soul, even although the very pain is sweet, because he who longs to love desires also to long, and would deem himself the most miserable man in the world did he not continually desire to love that which is of the most sovereign excellence. Longing to love, he suffers, but in this loving to long there is joy" (*Love of God*, vi. 13).

112. We have dwelt at some length upon this state of the soul, which we have called the anxiety of love, because if it constantly recurs it is a very favourable sign, and much fruit will result. "It is God Himself," says St. Francis of Sales, "who thus wounds the souls whom He desires to bring to a high perfection" (*ibid.*).

St. John of the Cross places this anxiety of love at the close of the night of the senses. St. Francis of Sales shows it to us in the most advanced souls, and St. John of the Cross describes it again in heroic souls. These vehement desires, this anguish, so purifying and so full of merit, make themselves felt at various stages of the spiritual life. They are often already indicated and foreshadowed in the affective life of the Christian soul when, under the influence of the sensible graces, it is conscious of an ardent desire for sanctification, a desire wherein the imagination doubtless plays a great part, and where perhaps a love of its own excellence has as large a share as the love of God, but which serves none the less as a vigorous impetus. At this point these desires become more disinterested and worthy of the name of anxieties of love. Dissociated from the imagination, they are so much the more ardent and perfect. They gain, too, in vigour and perfection in proportion to the soul's progress; the greater its detachment, so much the more powerfully will it be drawn towards God.

"The caverns are the powers of the soul, memory, understanding, and will, and their depth is commensurate with their capacity for great good, because nothing less than the infinite can fill them. What they suffer when they are empty shows in some measure the greatness of their delight when they are full of God, for contraries are known by contraries. In the first place, it is to be remembered that these caverns are not conscious of their extreme emptiness when they are not purified and cleansed from all affection for created things. . . . But when they are empty and cleansed, the hunger, the thirst, and the anxiety of the spiritual sense becomes intolerable; for as the appetite of these caverns is large, so their suffering is great, because the food which they need is great—namely, God" (*Living Flame*, stanza iii., pp. 458, 459).

The yearning for heaven which these souls experience is thereby accentuated. In heaven alone can they love God freely; there nothing will hinder the full flow of their love, their thirst will be quenched, their every aspiration satisfied. They can praise Him, exalt Him, unite themselves to Him, and rejoice in Him to their heart's content. *Ad hoc intendunt*, says St. Thomas, speaking of perfect souls, *"ut Deo inhaereant et eo fruantur, et ideo cupiunt dissolvi et esse cum Christo."[3]*

§ 4. *Disinterested Zeal—Love of the Cross.*

113. From out of this love, so pure and so brilliant, a burning zeal naturally proceeds. The soul "would have all men know God; meanwhile it is bitterly grieved at seeing them offend Him. . . . How intensely must it not suffer, then, at the thought of those multitudes of souls destined to be lost amongst heretics and infidels, while the loss of Christian souls causes it even deeper sorrow. It knows, of course, that God's mercies are very great, and that in spite of all the irregularities of their lives these Christians may yet repent and be saved; but, nevertheless, it fears that many amongst them will be lost" (*Fifth Mansion*, chap, ii.).

We have shown how with imperfect souls their desire for God's glory and the good of souls contains a considerable admixture of personal considerations. This is much less the case with fervent souls, but perfect souls hold their own interests cheaply; their happiness lies in sacrificing themselves to God. Whether it be through others or themselves, whether to their own advantage or to their detriment, provided Christ be preached, they are happy, and this with a lively happiness. *Dum omni modo. . . . Christus annuntietur, et in hoc gaudeo, sed et gaudebo* (*Phil.* i. 18).

114. Realizing that in accordance with the example of Jesus Christ it cannot promote the glory of God without suffering, the perfect soul feels a sincere desire to "bear heavy crosses for His sake" (St. Teresa, *Fifth Mansion* chap. ii.). This feeling lacks, perhaps, the vehemence of the early days of its fervour, when it longed for it knew not what. It now

---

[3] *Cf, Love of God*, Book V., chap. x.

contemplates suffering more calmly, more reposedly, but with a volume of love which is greater and more intense. Further, "all that it achieves for God seems nothing in comparison with what it desires to do" (ibid.). This it is that keeps it humble, and enables it to face without difficulty the trials which God will vouchsafe to it for the proving of its love.

§ 5. *Yearning after Holy Communion.*

115. Athirst for God, sighing for Him more vehemently than the hart after fountains of living water, perfect souls are conscious of an ardent desire for Holy Communion. Should they be deprived of it even temporarily, they suffer, although, perfectly submissive as they are to God's good pleasure, they find an alleviation of their suffering in conforming to His holy will. But if this deprivation be repeated and prolonged, how great is the torment to these loving hearts!

In Christians who have passed beyond the period of sensible fervour, who have emerged from their spiritual infancy, and attained to the calm maturity of the perfect, this longing after Communion is decidedly not the product of a heated imagination or a deluded mind. It is the fruit of grace and the work of the Holy Spirit. And we consider those directors to be extremely rash who interpose themselves as a barrier between these souls and their Lord, not fearing to prevent this daily Eucharistic union as ardently desired (if we may so say) on the one side as on the other.[4]

And very futile do the reasons alleged under such circumstances appear. They say, for instance, "They already communicate three or four times a week—that is about two hundred Communions in the year, and they are not satisfied." To this we might reply: "And so you would take on yourself to

---

[4] This passage is obviously in harmony with the directions of the Apostolic decree on Daily Communion issued December 30, 1905. [Note of the Translator.]

keep them from their Lord a hundred or a hundred and fifty times a year?"

"But then others would take offence, their susceptibilities would be wounded. Hence feelings of jealousy, perhaps internal dissensions, might arise."

"Such fears," we would reply, "are greatly exaggerated, and even in the event of their realization what great harm would accrue? If those to whom a daily Communion is permitted have arrived at the degree of perfection which we have assumed, they will be oblivious of the murmurs of which they may be the object, or these will serve only as an opportunity for the exercise of patience and the perfecting of their virtue. And as to the malcontents, would it not be better to chasten their self-love rather than to encourage it by an act of culpable weakness? And so for the sake of sparing certain jealous and over-susceptible people a foolish grievance, those whom Jesus invites to the great benefit of the Eucharist are to be deprived thereof." What an inversion of the proper order of things! And let no one say, "God will make it up to them in other ways." God can, doubtless, in His wisdom bring good out of evil. To save an obedient and submissive soul from being deprived of graces which you hold back from it, He may restore them by another channel; but have you the right to hinder God from employing His ordinary chosen means for the outpouring of His gifts? Is it allowable, save for a good reason, to deprive the soul of the sacramental graces which it asks for? Oh, if these directors themselves had experienced this thirst for the Eucharist from which God's true friends suffer they would not be so pitiless!

CHAPTER IV

CHARACTERISTICS OF CHARITY IN PERFECT SOULS

§ 1. *Their Calm and Tranquil Energy.*

116. THE intensity of the will is too often confounded with violence. But the two are very different. Listen to the Ven. Father Libermann on the subject: "In the natural order of things, a young man who desires any given thing desires it passionately; a man of mature age at least as strongly, but after a calmer fashion. The older man's will is usually stronger than that of the younger; the advantage being only apparently on the side of the young man because in his case it is more passionately expressed, the exhibition making the will appear more energetic, while all the time it is merely more active. Grace, operating upon the senses, is in its youthful stage (this is the affective state); later on comes the mature age, where the expression of feeling is less passionate, but where the inner action of the soul may be, and commonly is—at least, when we are faithful—more energetic, and consequently more intense (the contemplative state).

"The lives of the Saints furnish us with a host of examples. When our Lord Jesus Christ said to His Apostles that all would forsake Him during His night of agony, St, Peter, tenderly and vividly affected by the presence of the Divine Master (the sight of whom in the flesh filled the Apostles with feelings of devotion incomprehensible to those who have not

130

thus seen Him), penetrated with this sensible devotion, answered: *Et si omnes scandalizati fuerint in te, ego nunquam scandalizabor* (Although all should be scandalized because of Thee, yet will not I be scandalized). And a moment later: *Etiamsi oportuerit me mori tecum, non te negabo* (Though I should die with Thee, yet will I not deny Thee). In these bold words we plainly see the sensible ardour of love proceeding from an intense impression. This love had its defects, as was clearly shown in the rashness of the words, which defects are usually to be found in this sensible devotion where it is violently exhibited. But in the main it was a real love, and these sincere words of St. Peter show its violence. Later on, when St. Peter was in prison awaiting his crucifixion, his love was much calmer, and yet the intensity of his affection in the accomplishment of this act was much greater than during the night of the Passion" (*Écrits*, p. 402).

117. This tranquillity and quiet strength which perfect souls enjoy, is largely due to the fact that they no longer feel the assaults of the passions or the opposition of the world as vividly as before.

Love is by nature gentle, gracious, peaceful, and tranquil. If at times it seeks to take the citadel by storm and creates a tumult in the mind, it is because it finds some obstacles to its workings. But when the avenues to the soul are thrown open to love, and there is no opposition or contradiction, its progress is peaceful and of unparalleled suavity.

As we see a mighty river boiling and dashing itself noisily in rugged places where rocks form opposing obstacles to the free (low of its waters, but gliding on smoothly and without any effort in the plain; so the Divine love, meeting hindrances and resistances (such as exist in all men, though in different degrees), uses violence, combating evil tendencies, touching the heart, compelling the will by divers agitations and efforts, so as to remove all obstacles, or at least to pass them by"[1] (*Love of God*, vii, 14).

"When it pleases our Lord to bring us to the perfection of real love, to indifference and a sovereign disdain for the world and all that concerns it, of our own selves and all that touches our self-love and our own interests, the soul no longer experiences that extreme repugnance and violent opposition to all earthly things ; it thinks of them no more; to such an extent has it despised them, forgotten them, put them on one side, that all the attractions of vanity and earthly affections have ceased to affect it. It no longer perceives them, because in everything it sees God, acts for God and in God, and its heart loves Him alone" (Ven. Libermann, *Letter of May 6*, 1839).

118. It follows from all this, that contemplative souls no longer act from natural enthusiasm; they are to a great extent emancipated from the dominion of that imagination which in the majority of men is responsible for so many hasty intentions and more or less wise projects, and which is the source of so many illusions. Their actions are not so much their own as the impulses of the Holy Spirit.

Self-love, too, which so often and so readily spoils our feeble virtues, has less hold over the unitive soul. It has less purchase upon it, so to speak; the soul, grown calmer and more passive, is not so much tempted to a vain complacency. At first, in order to incite itself to do right, it sought and found arguments, it formed resolutions. In the affective life it gave itself up to many and vehement protestations. Now all, as a rule, is changed, and its mode of action is more secret. This is one reason why the contemplative soul, although more perfect, has a lesser opinion of itself than the affective soul. In all its undertakings, in the works to which its zeal inspires it, we see neither this restless activity nor the juvenile enthusiasm which is noticeable in beginners; but this does not prevent its acting

---

[1] Referring to himself, the Saint says: "Although the cares of life have calmed down the early ebullitions of my heart, my resolutions, by the Divine grace, have endured" (*Letter to a Lady*).

with equal generosity, and, above all, much greater constancy and firmness. No checks cast it down, no humiliations discourage it. It does its best, and leaves the result in God's hands, counting largely (and this distinguishes it markedly from the imperfect soul) upon the Divine grace, and very little upon human aid.

119. The will of God is, in fact, the perfect soul's one care—that God's will should be done on earth as it is in heaven, that it should be accomplished in the person of its neighbour and in itself through the execution of the designs of Providence. This is its most ardent wish. It cares little what God may decide to do with it. "Having yielded itself entirely into God's hands, the great love which it bears Him has made it so submissive to His will that it desires nothing but that He should do with it as He sees fit" (*Fifth Mansion*, chap. ii.).

The Venerable Father Libermann quotes a charming phrase of the Venerable Father Eudes which exactly illustrates this submission, or rather this complete union with God's will. "I thought when I last wrote to you that I wished to come to you, but I see now that I was mistaken, and that I did not wish to come for another two months, because the Divine will detains me here for two months more" (Venerable Libermann, *Letter of December 14*, 1834).

$ 2. *The Humility of Perfect Souls.*

120. We have just referred to one of the causes which preserve from pride the soul that has reached the fifth degree. We must now give the chief cause. Its humility is principally due to the light poured into it by the Holy Spirit, illuminating it not only with regard to the Divine splendours but as to its own nothingness and weakness also. Why is humility regarded by common consent as the touchstone of true virtue? Only because the Holy Spirit, who accords the gift of fortitude to generous souls and enables them to accomplish the most difficult acts, grants to them at the same time the gift of

understanding, revealing to them both the holiness of God and man's wretchedness.

Some directors dread nothing so much for the advanced souls under their care as the temptation to a vain self-complacency. Admiring their high excellence and their generous fidelity to grace, they fancy that these souls must be carried away by self-admiration and contempt for others who may be less faithful. This danger is always a real possibility, since Lucifer and his angels, with all their marvellous privileges, did not escape it. Experience, however, teaches that of all temptations pride is the one which has the least hold over perfect souls. Those who dread it so much on their account forget, or are not aware that these souls stand absolutely face to face with the nothingness of the creature, understanding better than their directors the greatness of Our Lord's part in their virtues, and experiencing the liveliest horror of their own imperfections; in proportion as they see more clearly the greatness of God, they see their own littleness, and God enlightens them in the measure of their faithfulness. They are also much less tempted to self-satisfaction than imperfect souls.

§ 3. *Singleness of View and Simplicity of Intention in Perfect Souls.*

121. Endowed with a calm, tranquil strength, freed from all feverish agitations of the imagination and the sensible faculties, attaching itself always, under all circumstances, to the will of God alone, the perfect soul leads a life of extreme uprightness and great simplicity. God, the infinitely simple Being, has communicated something of His sublime simplicity to this perfect soul. As Father Grou truly says, "All the operations that God works in the soul for its sanctification may be reduced to one—its simplification." This holy writer shall himself explain this transforming—or rather this simplifying—process in the soul as it progresses.

CHARACTERISTICS OF CHARITY IN PERFECT SOULS

"When the soul has given itself wholly to God that He may do with it as it pleases Him in time and in eternity, He first simplifies it in its essence, instilling into it a principle of infused and supernatural love which becomes the simple and only motive of its actions. It begins to love God without any other motive than that of loving Him. It loves Him for Himself, and not for itself. It reduces everything to this affection, without even thinking about it especially, or being conscious of it. Love is this soul's simple and only thought; it is always outside itself, as it were, at least it tends more and more to rid itself of self in order to be transformed into the beloved object.

"God simplifies it in its intellect. The multitude of thoughts which formerly troubled it now fall away; it can no longer reason or deliberate. A simple but indistinct light illuminates it; it walks by this light without distinguishing any special objects thereby. Its prayer, burdened formerly with considerations, affections, and resolutions, becomes simple. The soul is at the same time absorbed and unoccupied; it feels and enjoys without knowing what it experiences. There is no definite line of thought; it is a vague and general sensation which it cannot explain. Do not question it as to the subject of its prayers; it does not know. Either no definite idea has presented itself to the mind, or it has not followed up those which have offered themselves. It only knows that it has betaken itself to prayer, and that all has been with it there according to God's good pleasure—now dry, now full of consolation, now sensibly recollected, now involuntarily distracted, but always at peace and united to God in its essence. Hours pass thus without weariness or distaste, although the soul is apparently devoid of all thoughts and affections, because its thoughts and its affections are simple and their immediate end is God, the infinitely simple Being. The soul is very much in the same state even when it is not at prayer; whether reading or talking or occupied in its domestic duties, it feels itself all the time less engrossed in whatever it is doing than in God, who is the object of all its actions; God, indeed, is the inner preoccupation of its mind, so that in this respect prayer and the concentration of the mind on God are continual, and no external things can distract it from Him. This simplicity of the soul's aim perfects itself from day to day, and the soul's great desire is to brush aside everything that might bring it back to a multiplication of interests.

"God simplifies the will by reducing it to one single end, one only object, one desire, which is the accomplishment of the Divine will. The soul is no longer exhausted, as in former days, by a thousand wishes, hopes; and fears. The affections are concentrated on One alone; it loves all that it ought to love — parents, husband, wife, children, friends—but in God only. It no longer knows whether it desires anything or no, because its will is blended with God's will, and He, moment by moment, wills for it that which is best for it. Thus it is that the simplified will finds its rest and its centre in the will of God.

"God simplifies it by detaching it, little by little, from self and from all thoughts of its own interest—of all heed, even of the actual situation before it. Everything that it formerly cared for—amusements, conversation, reading, inquiry—all has become insipid. All human intercourse inspires it with disgust, and it lends itself thereto from a sense of duty and of what is becoming only. God calls it ceaselessly to interior things and separates it from all external objects. He takes from it by degrees all thought of self and of what befalls it, because were its vision thus divided and directed, now upon God and now upon self, it would no longer be simple. So that it comes at last not to know its own condition nor to think about it any more; not to concern itself with its state, but to dismiss all personal considerations, so that God may be its sole thought. And for the same reason God deprives it of any quickness to note where its own interest lies, because its eye and its Intention could not be single if to God's interests were added a desire to seek after its own things as distinguished from His. It no longer, therefore, looks upon its own virtues, its own perfections, its own good works, as things which concern itself, in which it has a personal interest; but it sees all in relation to God, as things which proceed from Him and belong to Him, and of which He can dispose according to His good pleasure.

"God simplifies the soul in all its external conduct. No double dealings, no shams, no dissimulations, no intrigues, no prejudices, no affectations, no human respect; it goes forward simply as God moves it. It speaks, it acts in accordance with its duty as it sees it, without considering what anyone may say or think. Its speech is simple, true, natural; it prepares nothing; it utters what the Holy Spirit of God may suggest to it to say, without troubling about the consequences. Even if its honour, its possessions, its life, were at stake, it would neither speak nor move of itself; it leaves all in God's hands, and sees Him only in all that may befall it through the medium of any of His creatures" (*Manual of Interior Souls—On Simplicity*).

122. Father Grou is not the only writer who notices the transformation which the soul undergoes as it advances towards perfection and arrives at this exquisite simplicity. We have already quoted a very apposite saying of St. Francis of Sales upon the subject.[2] Father Surin teaches the same doctrine. "When a man has devoted himself for a considerable length of time and with great diligence to the exact practice of the virtues and the amendment of his faults, God, as a rule, ends by uplifting his mind and giving him a taste for Divine things. And because the man has already acquired the habit of virtue, God draws him to the one thought of uniting himself to Him by love, and of following the attractions of grace, without turning aside to attend to the minutiae of definite acts. Then the soul ceases to take any exact thought as to its actions in detail. So, for example, the beginner in music applies himself to the scales in order to learn to sound the notes one after the other, and he who learns to play the lute reflects where he shall place his fingers, or which string he shall touch, that one may correspond with such a tone, and the other with the other. But when he has

---

[2] See above, vol, i., No. 229.

acquired the habit of playing, without considering where he shall place his fingers or taking any thought, when he sings, of the note which he shall take, he plays and sings, thinking all the while of other things without taking any heed of rules" (*Love of God*, i. 9).

§ 4. *The Serenity of Perfect Souls.*

123. These souls enjoy a deep peace. It is not yet, it is true, a peace as profound as that which is enjoyed by the holy soul which has passed through the ordeal of the night of the senses, and to which the words of Isaias may be fitly applied: *Declinabo super eam quasi fluvium pacis*—I will pour out upon her rivers of peace, which shall overflow and penetrate into every part of her (Isa. lxvi. 12). But without being so wonderful as the other, the perfect soul's peace is very great and much to be desired. *Pax multa diligentibus legem tuam* (Ps. cxviii. 165). "It will in no wise lose its cheerful serenity, because no privations can sadden one whose heart is free from any attachments" (*Letter from St. Francis of Sales to St. Jane Frances de Chantal*, October 14, 1604).

"No earthly events can trouble it, unless it should see itself in danger of losing God, or should witness any offence offered Him. Neither sickness, poverty, nor the loss of anyone by death, affect it, except it be that of persons useful to the Church of God, for this soul realizes thoroughly that God's disposal is wiser than its own desires" (*Fifth Mansion*, chap. iii., p. 114).

The trials which the soul undergoes—for it cannot be wholly exempt—do not rob it of its peace, and St. Teresa explains the reason of this. It is because they affect merely the surface of the soul; "they do not penetrate to the depths, they affect the senses and faculties only" (*Fifth Mansion*, chap. iii.).

The great maxims of the Gospel are but partially understood by imperfect Christians, even when pious: *Qaerite primum regnum Dei el justitiam ejus. . . . Vestri capilli capitis omnes numerati sunt. . . . Beati qui lugent. . . . Beati qui persecutionem patiuntur,* etc. (Seek ye therefore first the kingdom of God and His justice. . . . All the hairs of your head are numbered. . . . Blessed are they that mourn. . . . Blessed are they that suffer persecution.) These faithful souls, on the other hand, enlightened by the Holy Spirit, apprehend all their truth and all their import, and are thus freed from many anxieties.

CHAPTER V

THE EXTERIOR CONDUCT OF PERFECT SOULS

§ 1. *How all their Works are influenced by Love.*

124. THE works of perfect souls are precious in God's sight, and their great value lies in the fact that their inspiring motive is love. Possessed by a constant desire to love God and to glorify Him, this holy intention is always present with them; no great efforts are required for its renewal, because the inclination of their hearts is always in this direction. Even their most insignificant works tend towards this end, and they realize the counsel of the Apostle: *Sive manducatis sive bibitis, omnia in gloriam Dei facite.*

In this a source of merit lies, invisible to men's eyes, but none the less fruitful. Acts of virtue performed by perfect souls have a value above those of other Christians, because in them the love of God has a much greater part. When they apply themselves to self-mortification, for instance, they are impelled thereto by the fear of not loving God with sufficient purity of intention and by a desire to love Him with all the devotion that He merits; their sacrifices, therefore, will be acts of a love that is very pure and really disinterested. And so with their patience, their charity towards their neighbour, their faithfulness in their religious exercises, etc.

125. But to take an example which will make this clearer.

THE EXTERIOR CONDUCT OF PERFECT SOULS

We know the act of self-sacrifice which consists in applying to the Holy Souls in Purgatory all the satisfactory value of our own good works, without making any reservations for the purpose of expiating our own personal sins. This action, which receives the encouragement of the Church, and which is assuredly worthy of all praise, is termed The Heroic Act of Charity towards the Souls in Purgatory.[1] Many pious persons perform this act without, for all that, exhibiting any very great heroism. Some, touched with compassion for the suffering souls, do not realize that, in relinquishing to them all the benefits of their own expiatory acts, they are depriving themselves, and exposing themselves to grievous sufferings when their own day of reckoning comes. Or, again, they are counting upon God's mercy, and trusting to be released from the debts which they have thus contracted, without even having deserved it. This certainly is an act of charity, but it lacks the disinterestedness which would make it so meritorious.

Others, and with a greater show of reason, have every expectation that God will accept their bargain, and they therefore anticipate that they will have to suffer a long time for their sins of this life. This prospect is not without terror for them; but they know that this voluntary transfer, made to the souls of their brethren in this painful act of expiation, is highly meritorious, and that a superabundance of happiness will result to them in heaven. They therefore make this very sensible calculation: "Better to endure great sufferings, which are only temporary, and win a happiness which shall be eternal." This disposition is a more meritorious one than the foregoing, and is often seen in fervent souls.

---

[1] We should remark, in passing, that this act is not to be indiscriminately recommended for every one. It is obviously something above the ordinary way, and the inspirations of Divine grace must be apparent before it is permissible. Where would be the wisdom of suggesting such a serious action to souls who would perform it out of pure sentimentality, and without understanding its import?

But some persons make this act of charity with dispositions more perfect still. "After all," they say, "I shall have richly deserved it; and since by my cowardice in this world I have too frequently dispensed myself from undergoing the punishment which my sins have merited, I shall then no longer be able to evade it, and I shall be constrained to pay my debt fully to the Divine Justice." The Holy Spirit, who directs these souls habitually by His gifts, inspires them with His own thoughts, and particularly with a great horror of sin and a lively desire to repair their wrongdoing and satisfy the Divine Justice, as well as with a great love of all that God disposes and orders. These, as the Saints teach us, are the sentiments of the Holy Souls in Purgatory, causing them to accept their heavy load of expiation[2] with love and joy. This excellent disposition is also to be found, but in a lesser degree, it is true, in fervent souls; but it is much more habitual in the case of the perfect souls.

126. The perfect souls, enamoured of God with an insatiable devotion, have yet another way of looking at this act. In these sufferings to which they resign themselves, they see a way by which their love for God will be augmented for all eternity. When St. John of the Cross came to die, at the age of forty-nine, his one regret was that he would no longer be able, by prolonging his sufferings, to increase that love of God with which he was henceforth to be consumed for ever. While depriving themselves of the benefits of their satisfactory acts, these perfect souls believe that they will be recompensed for the resultant suffering by a redoubling of their love. And this hope of loving God more, and being more perfectly one with Him in heaven, leads them most joyfully to make this act of self-sacrifice.

We see, therefore, that this one act may be the fruit of very different dispositions; and this is why the works of the more advanced souls, without differing externally from those

---

[2] See St. Catharine of Genoa, *Traité du Purgatoire.*

of other Christians, weigh much more heavily in the scales of the infallible Judge.

127. We have shown how the action of grace operates with far greater ease in the case of perfect souls. If it still employs human methods, which consist in following the deductions of reason, often also (and that more frequently as the soul becomes more detached and more docile), grace acts directly upon the intellect and the will, shedding precious light into the mind, and impregnating the will with strong impulses towards the Supreme Good. Thus illumined and attracted to God, the perfect soul, as we have said, no longer follows the processes of meditation in prayer, but becomes contemplative. Marvellously aided, at the same time, by the eminent grace which it receives, it continues in the practice of the Christian virtues with a perfection hitherto unknown to it. St. Teresa, who applies the term supernatural to prayer which has been attained by the ultrahuman way of gifts, uses this same word for virtues which have been similarly acquired (*cf. État Mystique*, No. 35).

Quicumque Spiritu Dei aguntur ii sunt filii Dei (Rom. viii. 14)—For whosoever are led by the Spirit of God, they are the sons of God. They are not merely servants, working to gain their wages; they are children, loving their Heavenly Father with a truly filial love (*ibid.,*viii. 15), and in return they participate in His most precious treasures.

The servants, aided by ordinary grace, apply themselves to the fulfilment of their duties; they study to conform their actions to the teachings of faith and comport themselves as wise and sensible Christians. The children are under the direct influence of the Holy Spirit, who Himself illuminates them and impels them forcibly towards the practice of virtue. He communicates a marvellous strength to them, and is the cause of their accomplishing perfect actions.

§ 2. *Natural Qualities: are they developed by the Practice of Virtue, or do they merely serve to heighten this Virtue and make it more Meritorious?*

128. What we have said of fervent souls is even more true of perfect souls. Exempt from ensnaring passions, less susceptible to the illusions of the imagination which has lost much of its influence, they possess, in comparison with imperfect souls of equal intelligence, a great superiority of judgment. We even meet with simple, uncultured persons of ordinary intelligence who are excellent judges of character, and whose decisions in everyday life and worldly affairs show a rare good sense. But it is especially in religious matters, in the conduct of the soul, that the superiority of their judgment appears; it is here that the effects of the gifts of the Holy Spirit are most clearly manifested, communicating its precious light to the mind.

But, it may be argued, this rectitude of judgment which you take for a result of perfection, is it not rather the cause of it—at any rate, in part? Is it not just because these individuals are well endowed with intelligence that they have gone so far in the path of virtue?

129. This leads us to a careful consideration of the delicate question of the influence of natural gifts in spiritual advancement.

It is common enough to find the progress or falling away of souls attributed to an excess or deficiency of energy in the character, to a more or less happy temperament, or to the higher or lower degree of intelligence with which they are endowed. And yet St. Francis of Sales, in his work on *The Love of God*, devotes one whole chapter (Book XII., chap. i.) to show how "the progress of holy love does not depend upon the natural disposition."

It is positively certain that the happiest natural gifts, the most receptive intelligence, the most energetic disposition, cannot lead the soul to holiness, for this is a supernatural work.

The mistake is frequently made of attributing to these purely human qualities merits which have their cause elsewhere. The unerring judgment of the Saints, their splendid steadfastness, are far more the result of grace than of nature. It is the infused strength of the Holy Spirit which causes their heroism; His light is their wisdom. And so it is with less advanced souls. It is true that in their case the influence of the Divine gifts is at first sight less evident. The natural virtues, not being eclipsed and, as it were, absorbed in the supernatural qualities, are more noticeable; but the soul's progress to perfection must be attributed to grace and not to temperament.

130. But although we decline to admit any positive influence of the natural virtues in the work of sanctification, we realize that natural defects may have a negative influence, producing an adverse effect, and hindering any progress in holiness. God does not, as a rule, call those who live in an atmosphere of indifference, surrounded by persons without any religion, to an equal state of perfection with priests and religious; nor does He call to a high state of perfection those whose minds never develop and who are able to grasp the main facts of Catholic doctrine only.[3] There are natural obstacles which would hinder any great progress in sanctity. So, as it seems to us, foolishness or lack of judgment, excessive

---

[3] We refer here to those persons of limited intellect and semi-imbeciles who seem condemned to a perpetual infancy. Those who, however simple and ignorant they may be, are in the enjoyment of all their faculties, can attain to a very high state of perfection. Brother Giles, one of the earliest of the companions of St. Francis, said one day to St. Bonaventura; "Oh, how happy are ye, ye learned men, far ye know a thousand things by which ye can glorify God, while as far us, all ignorant that we be, what can we do?" And St. Bonaventura replied; "The grace of being able to love God sufficeth." "But. Father," Brother Giles answered, "can an ignorant man love God as much as one that hath learning?" "He can," said St. Bonaventura ; "and I say that a poor simple woman can love God as much as a doctor of theology." Then Brother Giles in a fervour cried out: "O poor and simple woman! love your Saviour, and you can be even as Brother Bonaventura is!" And so he continued three hours as one enraptured (St Francis of Sales, *Love of God*, Book VI., chap. iv.).

softness or extreme rigidity of character, or an uncontrolled nervous temperament, may be obstacles to sanctification, and hinder' the Christian soul from making any great strides towards perfection.

In the case of perfect souls this adverse influence of the temperament is greatly diminished.

They act habitually by way of the soul's summit—that "point which is above all its other parts, and which is independent of all natural dispositions" (*Love of God*, Book II., chap. i.). "The character," says Father Libermann, "has a great influence at the outset, when we are still in the sensible state; but later on, when we have acquired the mastery over the senses and are no longer subject to them, when the soul is in a condition where its operations are more intellectual, this colour given by the natural qualities is less apparent. Its influence is then only of the slightest; it is under the dominion of grace, and appears, as it really is, a mere mould" (*Letter of August 9, 1842*).

The temperament, therefore, can alter the expression, so to say, of the holiness, give it such or such a form, but can neither increase nor diminish it. Thus, the difference of sex, worldly position, etc., give a different physiognomy to the various servants of God. The saintship of a man differs from that of a woman; solitaries like St. Paul the Hermit do not resemble soldiers such as St. George; nor do missionaries like St. Francis Xavier resemble doctors like St. Thomas; nor are kings like St. Louis similar to mendicants such as St. Benedict Joseph Labre. But these differences which are due to their several natures do not touch the real cause of their holiness, or make one more perfect than the other.

§ 3. *The Mystical Union and External Works.*

131. Beyond these dissimilarities which are due to nature, there is also a variety in the gifts that the Saints receive from God. *Divisiones ministrationum sunt, idem autem Dominus, et*

divisiones operationum sunt, idem vero Deus qui operatur omnia in omnibus (1 Cor. xii. 5, 6). When we see some Christian heroes devoured with activity and having a strong power of initiative, we are sometimes tempted to fancy that this spirit of enterprise proceeds wholly from their characters, and to attribute to them a class of piety substantially different to that of Saints whose lives have been lived in the cloister. In many eyes the contemplative gifts presuppose a soul which is wholly passive, and they are regarded as being quite unadapted to the life of a warrior like St. Louis, or fighters like St. Gregory VII or St. John Capistran.

The truth is that in the case of these great servants of God grace plays a much larger part than nature—*Haec omnia operatur unus atque idem Spiritus, dividens singulis prout vult* (1 Cor. xii. 11)—and the graces which they receive are of the kind which God bestows upon perfect souls, and not upon beginners. The gifts of the Holy Spirit are enlightening and directing them, supporting them through all their most arduous labours.

132. Amidst the clamour of their many avocations, they remain in close union with God, and this intimate union is not the result of long reasonings or imaginative representations, as in the case of imperfect souls; rather is it by means of a simple and swift insight, that direct act of understanding and of love which constitutes the true contemplative union. Recall the passage already quoted above (No. 54), where St. Teresa shows how the prayer of quiet often persists in the midst of secular occupations. We gave as the reason for this persistence the explanation that, as contemplation occurs in the soul's summit, so the inferior operations may well be unable to affect or disturb it.[4] This is exactly what occurs with the perfect souls.

---

[4] Nor is it essential to contemplation, as some appear to believe, that it should produce a sensible effect upon the body, interfere with its operations, and more or less fetter the faculties of the soul. It is true that in perfect contemplation, where the soul is wholly absorbed in God, it experiences an extreme difficulty in speaking or in reciting vocal prayers. Drawn

Their exterior life will be very active— very busy; but their interior life will be one of close union with God and of constant submission to the Holy Spirit.

And the more they progress, the more this sort of dual life will be accentuated. Imperfect Christians are, as it were, necessarily absorbed by their occupations, and cares of a lower kind. Not being favoured with those special graces which act on the higher parts of the mind and will, they devote all their powers to the business in hand, and when they wish to unite themselves with God they are obliged to divert their attention momentarily from the objects which engross them, and turn it towards Him. Perfect souls, on the contrary, continue to dwell in union with God while attending to their affairs; and in proportion as they oppose fewer obstacles to the mystical operations and as these become more powerful and more constant, this coexistence of the mystic life and the active life becomes also more habitual and more apparent.

133. The Ven. Mary of the Incarnation wrote to her son: "When God wills you not to lose sight of Him in spite of your outward occupations, He will accomplish it Himself; and this more especially when His Spirit shall have mastered yours and He shall have taken possession of your innermost centre, in order to hold you in a close actual state of union with His Divine Majesty by the gaze of love. Then all your occupation will be powerless to distract you from the Divine intercourse. I say your centre, because in this world it is impossible to deal with temporal matters without devoting a reasonable amount of thought and attention to them. In this state of union and intercourse with God in the superior regions of the soul, His holy presence is never lost. When we are actually occupied outwardly the union consists in a simple looking towards the

---

irresistibly towards God, its one desire is to love Him; every other occupation wearies it and repels it. This is often the case in sensible quietude; but in barren contemplation and that which St. Teresa and Ven. Mary of the Incarnation refer to here, and which is allied to the active life, this interference with the faculties, this fettering, does not occur.

Divine Object, and we speak to Him at intervals only, when He permits it and calls us thereto" (*Letter 99 of October* 18, 1663).

CHAPTER VI

THE MERITS OF THIS STATE OF PERFECTION: HOW IT DIFFERS FROM THE STATE OF SANCTITY

§ 1. *On the Value of Perfect Souls.*

134. WE have done our best to portray the perfect souls. Great is their merit; this familiarity with God, this inward peace, this profound tranquillity, this liberty of spirit, this vigour in action, this wisdom in all their works, are blessings greatly to be desired.

"The *Sixth Mansion*" says St. Teresa, "only differs from the *Fifth* in the magnitude of its results; *but this difference is a very great one*" (*Fifth Mansion,* chap. ii.). The pools of our valleys are masses of water like the ocean; the hills of our Anjou are eminences like the mountains of the Alps and the Himalayas; and see the difference between the one and the other!

But however immeasurably short of the lives of the Saints the lives of perfect souls may fall, they are none the less extremely beautiful. God it is who leads them; God who works in them, who lives in them. And in this lies the merit of their actions; for as there is less of the human, there is more of the Divine. Under this beneficent influence the human will inclines towards virtue with a calm and peaceful, but at the same time strong and powerful, affection; and this simple, tranquil, but intense act is already most meritorious. How numerous must be the direct and therefore unperceived acts which are produced by these souls, "so supple and tractable to the Holy Spirit!" (St. Francis of Sales). How constantly in their prayers and in the course of their labours do they not (and often unconsciously) make acts of love, of faith, of contrition, of submission to the Divine will, etc! What treasures of merit do they not thus continually accumulate! This verily is the triumph of grace.

And beyond this, as they know but one desire—to do the will of God—He in response will do their will also. It is this which makes the perfect souls so powerful when they devote themselves to the salvation or spiritual advancement of others.

"A just soul," as Our Lord Himself said to Blessed Margaret Mary, "can obtain pardon for thousands of sinners."[1]

135. "It is to this happy lot of the unitive life that, according to Father Surin, all religious and persons with a special vocation for the devout life are called. And if they do not attain to the enjoyment of this happiness, if they secure no share in these celestial blessings, the fault is purely their own, since the Holy Spirit of God disposes and incites them thereto continually" (*Letter to Father Tillac of August* 25, 1661).

Let us pray that Our Lord will deign to multiply the number of perfect souls in His Church; that He will grant to us, and to all who are dear to us, to be raised to this happy state and to continue therein.

§ 2. *Imperfections which are to be met with in the Fifth Degree.*

136. "O Christian souls, whom the Saviour leads to this state," says St. Teresa to the inhabitants of the fifth mansion, "I implore you by the love of Him, cease not to be on your guard: avoid occasions of sin, for even in this condition the soul is not so strong that it can expose itself without peril." "It is still," says Blessed Suzo (*Fifth Rock*), "very far from the attainment of perfect union with God."

---

[1] Revelation made at the jubilee of 1682.

According to St. John of the Cross, until those most severe ordeals which he terms the night of the senses have accomplished the purification of the soul, many imperfections will still remain. "It still retains the remnant of that heaviness of the spirit which is the natural consequence of sin. Hence a certain languor of action,[2] a certain softness, noticeable, for example, in the fight against temptation or in the achievement of sacrifices. It is still subject to distraction of mind, outpourings of the heart upon external things, which form an obstacle to the Divine union" *(Obscure Night,* ii, 2).

The soul's yearning desire for heaven is, in part, the result of a pure and burning charity; in part, a love of repose, and a scarcely supernatural wish to be delivered from the burden of this life's conflicts. It is resigned, it is true, and "finds a consolation in the thought that it is detained here below by the will of God, but this is not sufficient," and does not quite do away with the acute sufferings caused by this bitterness of exile. In fact, "notwithstanding all the qualities which we have attributed to it, the soul has not yet attained to that perfect union with the Divine will which we shall see in the higher degrees. . . . It can go no further, because it has not yet received additional strength" *(Fifth Mansion,* chap. ii.).

137. Let us add that many souls mount up to this degree, and then lack the perseverance which should keep them there.

---

[2] In his life of Father Surin, M. Boudon relates how this holy man succeeded in making Mother Jane of the Angels victorious over the demons who tormented her, by ridding her of all her faults and imperfections. And the last of these faults, the extirpation of which resulted in the victory, is just that one to which St. John of the Cross refers—" a heaviness in which the soul longs for rest, and continues in a state of sloth, vainly occupied with its thoughts, and in a state of dull grief when things go wrong with it. This fault was recognized somewhat tardily in Mother Jane's case, and then all the demons set to work to defend it as their last outwork in her sensible faculties. The Mother herself had not perceived it, for, as a rule, no one detects it in themselves, for it does not lead directly to any evil, only to a certain lukewarmness which hinders good" (part lit., chap. viii., abridged edition, by Father Bouix, chap, xxxviii.).

"These inhabitants of the fifth rock," asks Blessed Suzo, "do they not give themselves wholly to God?" "Yes," Our Lord Jesus Christ makes answer, "but intermittently, with the result that many do not persevere, and go back to the fourth rock, following their own will, and living on without a complete self-renunciation. Then they repent and give themselves again to God, and thus return to the fifth rock."

Brother Suzo: "But whence does this inconstancy arise?"

Jesus Christ: "Their own will is not wholly dead. Nevertheless, God loves them well, and they are more perfect than any that you have yet seen. They stripped themselves of their own will at the outset, in order to give themselves to God; and although they do not always persevere in this renunciation, their lives are almost entirely lived upon the fifth rock, and after death the stain of their inconstancy must be effaced by Purgatory. Yet they will enjoy great glory in Paradise."

§ 3. *Two Subdivisions of the Fifth Degree.*

138. It is for this reason that the author of *The Dialogue of the Nine Rocks,* who comes forward as the interpreter of Blessed Suzo, reckons, as we suppose, two degrees, the fifth and sixth rocks, where St. Teresa only counts one, the fifth mansion. In each alike we find true renunciation, a sincere and complete union of the human with the Divine will. But this renunciation, which is already frequent and even habitual at the fifth rock, does not preclude the possibility of repeated falls. We see, in fact, at the outset of the unitive life, that it is in hours of weariness and suffering especially that the soul, more and more detached, presses ever closer to its God; whereas at other times it is exposed to the risk of some relaxation of energy. At times, for instance, when it is no longer under the stress of trials, it meets with things which give it pleasure, creatures whom it can and ought to love, and whose qualities delight it; or some work, some necessary occupation, which appeals to its inclination. And if it does not take heed it will

love all these things, in St Francis of Sales's phrase, "with some superfluity." At the point of perfection at which it has arrived these attachments will no doubt be but slight, and it will have only passing weaknesses with which to reproach itself; and these will have been perpetually retracted by sincere and entire acts of renunciation and by promises to love nothing but God only. And then its prayers, so full of love and of self-abandonment to God, will alone suffice to efface these few stains and to maintain it in its habitual disposition of real self-abnegation. And yet it will again forget itself, and in the pursuit of these creatures that attract it, it will obey the instincts of nature rather than the inspirations of grace, and follow love rather than duty.

Later on, if it has continued to advance, its renunciation will have become more constant, and will operate in prosperity as in tribulation. This will be the sixth rock. Here are to be found those friends of God who are all on fire with His grace, and who, for the sake of being pleasing unto Him alone, have sincerely detached themselves from self, even unto death" *(Dialogue of the Nine Rocks—Sixth Rock).*

And yet even in these souls something still is lacking. Their faults of frailty are more rare, their virtue is more established, their self-abnegation more constant, but their humility is not yet perfected. "They compare themselves with others, and desire to receive the same favours and consolations which other friends of God enjoy" *(ibid.).* However high the degree of perfection to which they may have attained, they do not yet possess the profound humility of the Saints, nor their heroic detachment.

PART III — ON THE DIRECTION OF PERFECT SOULS — RULES OF THE CONTEMPLATIVE LIFE

CHAPTER I

ON THE IMPORTANCE OF A KNOWLEDGE OF THE RULES OF THE CONTEMPLATIVE LIFE ON THE PART OF DIRECTORS

139. HITHERTO, as the reader has doubtless remarked, we have used the terms contemplative life, unitive life, and state of perfection,[1] indifferently; for contemplation is so marvellously adapted to the establishment and maintenance of the soul in that constant state of union with God which constitutes perfection, that the habitually contemplative soul is by this very fact a perfect soul.

But if the benefits of contemplation are so great, it is of the first importance for a director to know its rules, for he could not otherwise guide these perfect souls wisely in their appointed way. If formerly, at the outset of the spiritual life,

---

[1] Thus also the theologians. *Cf.* Suarez, *De Devotione*, chap. xi. 5. *Vie d' Union*, No. 366: "*Purgativa et illummativa via activae vitae, unitiva contemplativae apta consensione respondent.*" John of Jesus-Marie, *Théol. Myst.*, Vol. II., chap, ii., p. 13. Cardinal Bona likewise: *Cum vita spiritualis duplex sit activa et contemplativa.* Elsewhere (chap, xi.) he says: *Activa et passiva — ad activam duo priores status (incipientium et proficientium) pertinent, tertius (perfectorum) ad contemplativam (Via comp. ad Deum,* cap, viii., n. 6). We showed in the *Vie d' Union (passim)* that this, in fact, is the traditional doctrine.

they needed encouragement and support in the practice of meditation, it is now no less necessary that they should be led and directed in this new and unknown path by which God is calling them, and into which they are afraid to enter.

140. St Teresa severely censures those directors who fail to adapt their direction to the condition of contemplative souls, and she returns more than once to the charge.

"I have met with souls," she says, "cramped and tormented because he who directed them had no experience; that made me sorry for them. . . . Directors who do not understand the spirit of their penitents afflict them soul and body, and hinder their progress" (*Life,* translated by D. Lewis, 1904, chap, xiii., p. 99).

Father Balthazar Alvarez says that it sometimes happens that Our Lord Himself has brought religious to this way of prayer, and he continues: "Now, no one has any right to interrupt this progress. *Directors cannot, with a safe conscience*, recall to an active state those whom God calls to repose; they would endanger by it both their souls and bodies" (*Life of Father Balthazar Alvarez*, chap. xiii.; English trans., vol. i,, p. 152).

In such cases they will try to reassure themselves by saying that God has no need of persons when He wills to bring a soul to perfection. But although God may have need of no man, it is none the less true that He often makes His grace depend upon the co-operation of those whom He has chosen as His auxiliaries, *adjuiores Dei sumus.* How many heathen, who might be saved, will not actually accomplish their salvation unless they meet with some zealous missionary priest! Similarly, how many of the faithful who are called to perfection will fail to attain to it for lack of an enlightened spiritual guide!

It is a common thing to comfort souls by telling them that they have nothing to fear at the Day of Judgment so long as they are obedient. It is true that, since they have acted under obedience to His own representatives, the Sovereign Judge will not lay on them the blame for having turned aside from the path which would have been most advantageous to them; but because they were not responsible for the error, it only follows that they will not be punished for it, but this is not to say that they will still attain to that degree of glory which might otherwise have been theirs.

Now hear St. Jane Frances de Chantal: "This attraction [to the prayer of a simple consciousness of the presence of God] is so natural to us that the souls which are forced away from it seem dragged away from their centre; they lose their freedom of mind, and sink into a condition of constraint and perplexity which hinders them greatly in their way. *I have only too much experience of this truth." (Letter to a Superior of her Order,* quoted above.)

141. St. John of the Cross is perhaps still more categorical. He deplores with even greater bitterness the mistake described by St. Teresa and St. Jane Frances de Chantal. We quote a passage—one of many—taken from the *Living Flame of Love* (English trans., stanza iii., §§ 42-43):

"The interior goods which silent contemplation impresses on the soul, without the soul's consciousness of them, are of inestimable value, for they are the most secret and delicious unctions of the Holy Ghost, whereby He secretly fills the soul with the riches of His gifts and graces; for, being God, He doeth the work of God as God. These goods, then, these riches, these sublime and delicate unctions, this knowledge of the Holy Ghost, which, on account of their exquisite and subtle pureness, neither the soul itself, nor he who directs it, can comprehend, but only He who infuses them in order to render it more pleasing to Himself, are most easily, even by the slightest application of sense or desire to any particular knowledge or sweetness, disturbed and hindered. This is a serious evil, grievous and lamentable. O how sad and how wonderful! The evil done is not perceived, and the barrier raised between God and the soul is almost nothing, and yet it is more grievous, an object of deeper sorrow, and inflicts a greater stain, than any other, though seemingly more important, in common souls which have not attained to such a high state of pureness. It is as if a beautiful painting were roughly handled, besmeared with coarse and vile colours; for the injury done is greater, more observable, and more deplorable, than it would be if a multitude of common paintings were thus bedaubed. Though this evil be so great that it cannot be exaggerated, it is still so common that there is scarcely one spiritual director who does not indict it upon souls whom God has begun to lead by this way to contemplation."

And here the Saint inveighs vigorously against those directors who, seeing only pure sloth in this silent contemplation, oblige the poor souls to meditate and formulate acts (p. 472):

"Such a director as this does not understand the degrees of prayer, nor the ways of the Spirit, neither does he consider that what he recommends the soul to do is already done, since it has passed beyond meditation and is detached from the things of sense ; for when the goal is reached, and the journey ended, all further travelling must be away from the goal. Such a director, therefore, is one who understands not that the soul has already attained to the life of the Spirit, wherein there is no reflection, and where the senses cease from their work; where God is Himself the agent in a special way, and is speaking in secret to the solitary soul. Directors of this kind bedaub the soul with the coarse ointments of particular knowledge and sensible sweetness, to which they bring it back; they rob it of its loneliness and recollection, and consequently disfigure the exquisite work which God was doing within it."

Further on (§ 56, p. 478) the Saint gives vent to complaints more bitter still, not fearing to apply to such directors a well-known text of St. Paul's.

"These spiritual directors, not understanding souls who have already entered into the state of quiet and solitary contemplation, because they know it not, and perhaps have never advanced beyond the ordinary state of reflection and meditation themselves, look upon the penitents of whom I am speaking, as idle—'for the sensual man,' the man who still dwells with the feelings of the sensual part of the soul, 'perceiveth not these things that are of the Spirit of God'— disturb the peace of that calm and tranquil contemplation given them by God, and force them back to their former meditations."

"But it may be said that these directors err, perhaps, with good intentions, because their knowledge is scanty. Be it so: but they are not therefore justified in giving the rash counsels they do, without previously ascertaining the way and spirit of their penitent, And if they do not understand the matter, it is not for them to interfere in what they do not comprehend, but rather to leave their penitent to others who understand him better than they. It is not a light fault to cause by a wrong direction the low of inestimable blessings, and to endanger a soul. Thus, he who rashly errs, being under an obligation to give good advice—for so is every one in the office he assumes—shall not go unpunished for the evil he has done. The affairs of God are to be handled with great caution and watchful circumspection, and especially this which is so delicate and so high, and where the gain is infinite if the direction given be right, and the loss also infinite if it be wrong" (p. 479).

Such is the language of St, John of the Cross upon this point. It would be superfluous to add anything further.

CHAPTER II

RULES TO BE FOLLOWED IN THE DIRECTION OF CONTEMPLATIVE SOULS

§ 1. *Necessity for entire Self-Sacrifice.*

142. ALL rules for the direction of contemplative souls may be summed up thus briefly: As there is but one way of bringing souls to contemplation—that of renunciation—so there are no other means by which they may be sustained therein and helped onwards than by renunciation.

This virtue of renunciation is already practised by the perfect soul, but we would say with Blessed Suzo: "It is not sufficient to die unto oneself; this dying must be repeated again and again unto our life's end." And then: "We never die so completely unto ourselves and unto the world that something does not remain to be further renounced and made a subject for self-mortification."[1]

The further we progress, in fact, *in the way of love, the more completely we understand the full significance of those great words: Abneget semetipsum.* The Holy Spirit by illuminating the soul more and more in proportion to its

---

[1] Discours III., *De la Mort Spirituelle*, edition Cartier.

fidelity[2] and the height to which He proposes to lead it, reveals to it all its secret attachments, its seekings of self, of its own ease, its own will. These, it is true, are but passing imperfections, fleeting acts which do not prevent the faithful soul from dwelling in a continual state of unity with the Divine will and receiving the precious graces of contemplation; but they may none the less prove an obstacle to a yet closer union and still greater blessings.

Let the perfect soul listen with docility to the secret promptings of the Holy Spirit; let it ask for them; let it pray to God for the light which shall reveal to it its own imperfections and for the strength by which it may combat them. It will then be enabled more completely to cast out all that is human, all that is not God, and it will realize more fully that great motto of the Saints: "God alone!"

143. The disposition to which it should aspire (we again quote Blessed Suzo) "is a moral extinction of thought and of affection, a kind of infinite renunciation in God, by which the soul commits and abandons itself so wholly unto Him that it no longer possesses any understanding or will; but everywhere and always it obeys the power of God, which guides it, all unperceived, in accordance with His good pleasure.

"This renouncement cannot be continuous in this life, neither can it be so perfect and complete that the man should not go back upon himself at times and flag in so doing. He may give himself up sincerely to God, with the firm resolve never again to claim what is no longer his own, since he has abandoned it, yielded it, annihilated it in God and in His good pleasure; yet, for all this, the frailty of human nature is such that the soul reverts from time to time to its own desires, to the possession of its own will, and it commits faults by reason of this same return unto itself" *(Traité de l'Union de l'Âme avec Dieu,* § 1, traduction Cartier).

---

[2] "These hidden truths are not arrived at," says Blessed Suzo. "by study and research. We attain to them by renouncing ourselves humbly in God" (*Livre de la Sagesse éternelle, sub fine,* traduction Cartier).

As soon as the soul perceives its fault it should acknowledge its wretchedness, humble itself profoundly in God's sight and detach itself afresh, renewing its resolutions still more strongly. Thus will it die unto itself, that it may live only with the life of its God: *Vivo, jam non ego, vivit vero in me Christus.*

144. This renunciation must be universal. It must bear, therefore, upon everything to which the heart of man naturally clings—to earthly possessions, the world's esteem and that of self, the joys of human affections, prosperity, and the free exercise of the intellectual faculties. The progress which has already been made in the practice of poverty, humility, and mortification should not make the contemplative soul forget its weakness, for the natural tendencies, even when they seem to be repressed and destroyed, are sometimes very prompt to spring to life again.

145. But detachment from this world's goods, which is indispensable for those who would be perfect, must become yet more complete if a further growth in perfection is desired. Even those who are not called upon to bind themselves by vow to the practice of poverty must have its spirit, using their possessions only in conformity with the Divine will, never employing them in order to procure for themselves superfluous gratifications, ever ready to give their wealth for the glory of God and the good of their brethren. They will aim at simplicity in their houses, their dress, their food; all that they could dispense with without running counter to any duty, they should be ready to forego. Far from shrinking from privations, they will say with St. Francis of Sales: "I am never better off than when I lack everything."

146. The perfect soul should detach itself from all human supports, and be ever ready to make a sacrifice even of its most lawful affections to its Lord. God makes use of man in order to do good to men. "We are God's auxiliaries," says the Apostle. All those who share in the Divine authority—parents, superiors, directors—play their part in His beneficent action.

They have a right to the gratitude and affection, as well as to the obedience, of those who are subject to them. No less lawful is that feeling of supernatural affection which prompts men to devote themselves to the service of their brethren: superiors to stoop to their inferiors, to lavish their solicitude and their advice upon them. The more they give themselves, so much the more their hearts are softened and the greater waxes their love. Finally, all affection between souls who are united only in order that they may the better help each other to love their Lord, is lawful and blessed by God.

But these affections, pure and useful as they may be, can become an obstacle to a higher state of perfection, for our human nature all unconsciously seeks a too human satisfaction therein. It is sweet to be upheld, comforted, encouraged; it is sweet to see souls respond to the devotion lavished upon them; it is sweet to find friendly hearts understanding and sharing in our tastes, our desires, our hopes, our joys, our sorrows. But he who delights in these natural joys is starting aside from perfect renunciation. In order to follow the example of Jesus, numberless sacrifices must be imposed upon the heart; we must turn away many and many times from pleasant companionship, and, where circumstances require it, must accept separation cheerfully.

147. There is not a single hour of life wherein the soul is unable to make some act of self-sacrifice. Are there not those natural predilections which will often decide its choice of occupation unless the soul keeps watch over itself? It must renounce its tastes, overcome its repugnance, and throughout all its actions seek nothing but the greater glory of God. It must also fight against all love of its own ease, even in the smallest degree, all seekings after bodily satisfaction; for he who would be Jesus Christ's must crucify his flesh. *Qui Christi sunt, carnem suam crucifixerunt.*[3]

---

[3] We have explained and developed these thoughts in a little pamphlet intended for truly fervent and generous souls (*L'Abnégation Parfaite et le Parfait Amour*, Anger. Grassin et G. Grassin; Paris, Amat, ; 15 c. each, 1 fr.

But, above all others, the mortification of the spiritual faculties must be most carefully attended to. Let us follow St. John of the Cross in applying the doctrine of perfect renunciation to the various faculties of the soul.

§ *2. Renunciation of the Understanding, the Memory, and the Imagination.*

148. With regard to the understanding, we were in accord with his teaching in saying that when the soul perceives God to be calling it by the consciousness of the union of love which it experiences, or when it finds itself unable to meditate, it should discard all arguments, imaginary representations and conceptions of all kinds, and maintain itself in the silence of contemplation. Further (and this important feature of St. John of the Cross's teaching may surprise the reader), when the soul perceives itself to be called to the contemplative way, it must not only discard all considerations, but equally cease to rely any more upon miraculous graces or visions, revelations, inner voices, or any similar favours, should any such have been vouchsafed to it. At the time when these blessings were accorded, the soul, without doubt, experienced the salutary effects which these good gifts of God never fail to produce. But far from recalling these favours to mind when the time for receiving them is past, they should be put aside, and the soul should give itself up through prayer to the obscure union of contemplation.

But not at the hour of prayer only, let us add, must the faithful soul mortify its understanding. At other seasons also this too active faculty needs to be restrained. Innumerable imperfections result because pious souls are either over-eager to learn or they cling too tenaciously to their own opinions. A holy indifference for all news and all superfluous information, a complete abnegation of private judgment—this is the aim in

50 dozen, 10 frs. 100.

view. Ever to be ready to admit their faults simply, and when they think themselves in the right to strive always to combine with their love of truth a kindly charity towards those who differ from them.

149. The denudation or *active night* of the memory and the imagination consists in this: that the soul should detach itself "from all knowledge and all acquired forms." "It must labour to destroy all sense of them, so that no impression whatever of them shall be left behind; it must forget them and withdraw itself from them, and that as completely as if they had never entered into it" *(Ascent of Mount Carmel,* iii. i; English trans., p. 242).

St. John of the Cross describes the great detriment done to the soul by these faculties (the memory and the imagination) if they are not mortified. Of how many dangers are they not the cause? For, to begin with, it is these memories, or representations of sensible objects, which give rise to a thousand sensations of "grief and fear and hatred, useless hopes, empty joy or vain glory. All these, at least, are imperfections, and sometimes undoubted venial sins" *(ibid.,* ii., p. 250).

Then, too, it is by means of these faculties that the devil seduces us and that we are lost, while without them he has no sort of hold upon us, being unable to work directly upon either the understanding or the will. And is it not also through these memories and phantoms of the imagination that our peace of mind, that tranquil serenity without which none can experience the Divine union, is always lost?

150. Since it is so important that these two faculties should be mortified by the contemplative soul, it will not be amiss to explain how this mortification should, in our opinion be achieved.

We will speak more particularly of the imagination, for the mind of man is less actively employed in dwelling on the memory of the past than in scanning the horizon of the future, and this principally in two ways. At times the future appears to be all dark, either because of the actual existence of disquieting circumstances, or because the temperament inclines naturally to melancholy. Then everything is seen in sombre hues; we become anxious and preoccupied. Sometimes, on the other hand, everything seems bright and beautiful. We then form innumerable projects, countless happy schemes and castles in the air. Excessive anxiety or wondrous projects are equally harmful when the soul gives itself over to them. In the first case, it will be necessary to practise to the letter Our Lord's words: *Nolite solliciti esse in crastinum* (Take no thought for the morrow). Let us do our duty, certainly; but this once done, commit ourselves with full and complete confidence to the beneficent and fatherly providence of God. "Remember Me," said Our Lord one day to St. Catharine of Siena, "and I will remember thee." As to useless plans for the future, however holy the objects may appear, the mind must on no account be allowed to dwell upon them.

Of course, "we must not omit to think of and remember those things which it is our duty to do and to know; for in that case, provided no selfish attachments intrude, these recollections will do no harm" (*Ascent of Mount Carmel*, iii. 14; English trans., p. 279). But as for other kinds of knowledge and for useless fancies, let us make an entire renunciation of them.

It is true that we may occasionally have perfectly legitimate preoccupations: there are questions which are at the same time both extremely important and complicated; it is very difficult to know how to solve them. Hence arise exceedingly tenacious anxieties, of which it seems impossible to rid ourselves. But even so it would be very desirable to avoid being involved in a multitude of disquieting thoughts and perplexities. Let us reflect and weigh all the pros and cons, but without undue agitation, without losing our peace of mind; let us, above all, pray earnestly, and unless the matter is urgent, reserve judgment awhile. Events frequently dissipate our misgivings and bring light. Then, when the decision is finally taken, leave the success to God with complete confidence, without troubling any further as to the result. "In matters of great importance even," says St. Frances of Sales, "we must be very humble, and not think that we shall arrive at God's will by dint of scrutiny and subtlety of reasoning. But having asked for light from the Holy Spirit and applied our minds diligently to the discovery of His good pleasure, taken counsel with our director, or it may be with two or three other spiritual persons as well, we must make up our minds, and decide in God's name, and never afterwards question our decision, but hold to it devoutly, peacefully, and trustfully. And even although difficulties, temptations, and the various happenings which we shall meet with in the execution of our project, should at times make us inclined to wonder whether we have chosen wisely, we must stand firm notwithstanding, and pay no heed, remembering that we might have found ourselves a thousand times worse off had we decided otherwise. And then, too, how do we know whether it is God's will that we should be exercised in consolation or tribulation, peace or war?" *(Love of God,* viii. 14).

151. This mortification of the imagination is of the first importance for the contemplative soul. Thanks to this constant vigilance it never loses its union with God, and this union, whether it be sensible and full of sweetness, or, on the contrary, arid, persists during the most varied occupations and the most absorbing affairs. This, as we have shown, is an endless source of merit, and the secret of perfection.

And then, "the devil," says Blessed Albertus Magnus,[4] "employs all his care and his strength in order to hinder this exercise, as far as he can He sees in it the prelude and commencement of the life of heaven and is jealous of this happiness of man. He therefore ever seeks to estrange our minds from God, now by means of one temptation or passion, now by another. At one time it will be some unnecessary

---

[4] *Traité de l'Union Intime avec Dieu,* chap. iv.

preoccupation or exaggerated anxiety; at another some disturbance of mind, or by dissipation and life curiosity; or, maybe, the reading of trifling books, frivolous occupations and conversations, various rumours and interesting news; or, again, by difficulties, contradictions, etc.—all these being things which often appear to us to be no faults, or very slight ones, but are none tike less great impediments to the holy exercise of which we are speaking."

§ 3. *The Renunciation of the Will.*

152. With regard to the renunciation of the will, St. John of the Cross wishes the same method to be adopted which he has already described as a means of overcoming the evil tendencies of the sensitive appetite. It consists in the mortification of the four passions of the soul—joy, hope, pain, and fear—"so that we feel no joy except in that which is simply for the honour and glory of our Lord God, nor hope except in Him, nor grief except in what concerns Him, nor fear but of Him only" (*Ascent of Mount Carmel,* in. 15 ; English trans., p. 282).

The Saint would have this denudation of the will carried even to the point of a renunciation of spiritual blessings, which should be sought for and loved not for themselves (*ibid*, 32), but solely on account of God.

153. St. Francis of Sales preaches this same doctrine of the absolute renunciation of the will in another fashion *(Love of God,* Book IX., chaps, iv.-vii.): "This union of our will to God's good pleasure should be by way of holy indifference." And he explains and sums up this indifference by these words: *Ask nothing, refuse nothing.* He goes on to show us all its excellence.

"Resignation gives God's will the preference, but nevertheless it cleaves to many things besides that will. Herein indifference is higher than resignation, for it cleaves to nothing save for the love of that will.

"The indifferent heart is as a ball of wax in God's hands,

equally ready to receive every impress of the Eternal good pleasure. It is a heart without preferences, disposed to all things alike, having no other object for its will than the will of its God, which does not set its love on the things that God wills, but on the will of God which wills them."

The saintly Bishop then goes on to explain how "this holy indifference extends to everything. It must be practised in connexion with the things of *the natural life*, such as health, sickness, beauty or deformity, weakness or strength; in those of *social life*—honour, rank, wealth— as in those of *the spiritual life;* in dryness or consolation, in rapture or aridity, in actions, in sufferings, and, in sum, in all events whatsoever. . . ."

And yet more. "Perceiving that suffering, although uncomely as another Leah, is none the less the daughter, the beloved daughter even, of the Divine good pleasure, the indifferent heart loves it as dearly as it loves consolation, which, however, in itself is the more attractive; nay, it even loves tribulation the most, because it has no attraction other than the stamp of the will of God."

Indifference should dispose the heart to undertake, for God's glory, all which it may be inspired to perform, and if its labours are not crowned with success, to accept the check with quiet, loving submission. "St. Louis was inspired to cross the seas in order to reconquer the Holy Land. He failed, and he submitted meekly. I admire the docility of this acquiescence more than the grandeur of the design," etc.

Finally, "we must practise indifference even where our own progress in virtue is concerned. God has ordered us to do our utmost for the acquisition of the Christian virtues; let us therefore neglect nothing that can contribute to the success of this undertaking. But when once we have *planted* and *watered,* know that it is God only who *gives the increase* (i Cor. iii. 6) to the trees of our good inclinations and habits. This is why we must wait upon His Divine providence for the fruit of our desires and labours. So if we do not find that our progress and advancement in the spiritual and devout life are such as we should wish, let us not be disturbed, but dwell in peace; let peace always prevail in our hearts. It is our duty to tend our souls diligently, and we must apply ourselves thereto faithfully. But as to the abundance of the result, and the harvest, let us leave the care of this to Our Lord. The labourer will be called to account for his careful cultivation, not for the abundance of his harvest."

§ 4. *The Vow of Greater Perfection.*

154. Generous souls, parched with the desire to please God, are sometimes desirous of making an absolute renunciation by way of the vow of doing what is most perfect. Is it well to allow this, and even to counsel it?

First, to make clear what this vow is. A vow that is vague and obscure in its manner of operation would assuredly result in difficulties and scruples, and would be most harmful to the soul. Every vow must bear upon deliberate acts. A vow to abstain from the faults of human frailty would be void, say the theologians, because it is impossible of performance. We may, however, make a vow not to commit some venial fault of deliberate purpose. This vow is valid and binds in conscience, because it is feasible. Acts of a semi-deliberate nature are therefore excluded from the vow of greater perfection. Acts the perfection of which remain doubtful are also excluded. In the chapter on the discernment of spirits we have shown that it would be contrary to perfection to dwell too long on matters of slight importance and to lose peace of mind over trifles. Finally, we must add that this vow does not aim at absolute perfection or any act considered entirely on its own merits without any regard to circumstances, but at the most perfect relatively. In itself it is more perfect to fast than not to fast, but for the great majority of Christians frequent fasts would be an imperfection, because they would be rendering themselves less capable of performing the duties of their state, and often also because it would constitute a culpable singularity.

To bind oneself by vow to a greater perfection is, therefore, to vow that whenever there shall be time to reflect upon the relative advantages of two possible courses of action, we will always choose the one which, after a due consideration of circumstances, is obviously the more pleasing to God.

155. Before permitting, advising, or prohibiting such an action, let the director weight the disadvantages and the advantages of this vow.

The drawbacks to be feared are that souls may be troubled thereby, thrown back too much upon themselves, rendered fastidious and too much occupied in an over-minute self-examination; or, on the other hand, that they should begin to contemplate the performance of heroic actions at the expense of their ordinary duties, or fancy that they have attained to a great height in virtue; and, lastly, that it multiplies the possible occasions of sin.

But, conversely, this vow of greater perfection offers many advantages. It confers fresh merit upon good actions—the merit of the vow—and each one becomes an act of religious virtue. Above all, it confirms the soul in the practice of renunciation. It is pledged to a universal renouncement; it can no longer consent to any deliberate act of self-seeking, or act knowingly for its own gratification; nothing any more for nature, everything for God. This henceforward is its motto. And experience proves that the vow is a far more efficacious support than the simple resolution. It proves also that Our Lord, who never allows Himself to be outdone in generosity, bestows yet more precious gifts of light and strength. He gives an ever holier prudence, a clearer vision, a firmer resolution, to the souls who bind themselves to this practice of perfect love.

156. The drawbacks which we have mentioned should prevent the granting of this permission in the case of narrow-minded persons and those who are subject to perplexities and unreasonable fears and to scruples. Also to those whose judgment is not sound, and who do not understand in what the perfection of their works consists; to the self-complacent, or

those who fail in the practice of self-renunciation, either for lack of courage or because they always find excuses for the justification of their caprices; and, finally, even the very best souls, when God does not vouchsafe them any leanings in this direction.

To the upright, judicious souls who go forward frankly, without entangling themselves in details, having a sincere desire for advancement, realizing their own wretchedness and putting their trust in God—to these it may be permitted, and even, when they feel no reluctance, advantageously recommended.

But though this vow (as is the case with all others—religious vows, for instance), may be the occasion of some slight faults, the benefits which it gives, the glory which it procures for God, the progress which it favours, make it permissible to run these risks. It is always lawful to strive after a great benefit, even when in the pursuit of this object we expose ourselves to some slight and inevitable evils.

A prudent director will, nevertheless, not permit this vow of greater perfection to be taken for any long period at first. Renewed from day to day, or week by week, it will be productive of equally good results. In doubtful cases he will do wisely not to permit this vow at all, or for certain days a week only. He will then be able to see if these souls are more faithful on the days when they are thus stimulated, or whether, on the contrary, they become confused and disturbed, or violate their promise too easily.

157. It will be seen, therefore, that for the guidance of these contemplative souls practically nothing is required but to lead them to the practice of Christian renunciation in all its perfection.

God will do the rest; His purifying action will continue to operate by means of ordeals which the soul must accept in all submission and trust. At the same time the Divine workings which will never be discontinued, in prayer and out of prayer, will not cease from purifying it and sanctifying it yet further, always provided that it is careful not to impede the action of grace. It only remains to describe how it should habitually conduct itself in this state of contemplation when it has become habitual.

CHAPTER III

HOW THE HABITUALLY CONTEMPLATIVE SOUL OUGHT TO MAKE ITS PRAYER

§ 1. *Preparation.*

158. To begin with, does the soul in this condition require preparation?

It often happens that contemplative souls need no sort of preparation for prayer; they find themselves so filled with sentiments of love and conformity to the will of God that they pass into prayer without any effort, and are recollected without seeking to be so.

But this state of recollectedness, which is a favour from God, may become a danger. These souls are, in fact, tempted to trust to the facility which they have so perpetually experienced, and are inclined to dispense with preparation altogether. "They would occupy themselves always," says St. Teresa, "with loving only, without paying heed to any other thing," and this, the Saint says, is because they have experienced the sweet delights of contemplation and desire to partake of them always, without causing the understanding to act at all. But, however much they may desire such a result, it is not in their own power to achieve it. And for this reason : although the will is not dead, its fire has grown cold, so that it needs to be fanned before it can break out into flames again (Sixth Mansion, chap. vii.). "In this case," as St. Jane Frances de Chantal says, "we must not wait for Our Lord to put the honey between our lips." A certain preparation is necessary, and, according to St. Teresa, it is only those who have attained to the seventh mansion who very seldom require it, "To make a practice of discarding preparation," wrote St. Francis of Sales to Madame de Chantal, "this seems a little drastic. It may be useful at times, but that it should be the rule does not, I confess, appeal to me" (*Letter of March* 11, 1610).

159. In what should this preparation, then, consist? It should not be methodical, as for discursive meditation. In fact, as St. Teresa says in the same place, for souls who have reached this point all argument would be useless and fatiguing. Some simple thoughts, a few pious memories, suffice. "For," she says, "discoursing with the understanding is one thing, but merely presenting certain truths to it is quite another thing." The soul, therefore, will not meditate, but will only call to mind some mystery of the Life or Passion of Our Lord. "The sublimest prayer will be no hindrance to this," says St. Teresa again, "and it would be a great fault not to have recourse constantly to this holy exercise" (*ibid.*).

In her Life (chap, xxiv.) the Saint relates that this was the advice which St. Francis of Borgia gave her when he was called upon to pass judgment on her manner of prayer. "He advised me to begin my prayer always with one of the mysteries of the Passion, and then afterwards, if Our Lord should call me higher (to contemplation), without my having attempted to lift myself up to it, I must not resist, but commit myself to His guidance. He thus showed me," the Saint adds, "how far advanced he himself was, giving me both the remedy and the advice, for in these matters it is experience which tells."

St. Paul of the Cross gives the same counsel: "I rejoice," he wrote to a Novice Master, "to hear of the graces which God vouchsafes to His servants, and to Fr. N. . . . in particular. He is beginning to have the gift of prayer. Meanwhile see that he does not neglect the practice of the virtues and the imitation of Jesus Christ. Let him always begin his prayer with one of the mysteries of the Passion, and persevere in a pious soliloquy without making any effort to meditate. And then, if God should will to draw him to the silence of love and faith in His Divine breast, as your Reverence tells me is the case, let him not disturb the peace and repose of his soul with any definite reflections."

160. Some souls have only to think of Holy Communion, or to call the Sacred Host to their minds, and they are at once profoundly moved. Others think how Jesus dwells within them. Some are occupied with the thought of the salvation of souls, or the various ways in which men offend against God, while others take a verse of the Bible. The thought of heaven, the glory and happiness of the Divine Persons, are the means by which the dormant affections of others are aroused. Then, some individuals have recourse in the first place to their heavenly protectors, their guardian angel, or the Saints for whom they have a special devotion, or to the Blessed Virgin. They get themselves thus, as it were, introduced before God; they then feel more confident and more acceptable to Our Lord. We may take any one of these methods, or vary them according to the disposition of the moment.

"Teach me, O Lord," said Blessed Margaret Mary, "what thou wouldst have me say to Thee." And Jesus replied: "Nothing, save these words only, 'My God, my One and my All, Thou art my All, as I am all Thine.'" It is the *Dilectus meus mihi et ego illi* of the Canticles.

"If," said St. Jane Frances de Chantal, "we could utter these words truthfully—'My God and my All'—we should never grow weary in prayer, for if we began to flag, these words, rightly said, would charm away all fatigue." Thus the contemplative soul, when it does not experience the favour of the Divine union, should strive to enter in by having recourse to the understanding or the imagination, but with the greatest moderation, as we have seen.

161. For the better understanding of this doctrine let us give another example which will make our meaning clear. When reciting the Rosary, where it is necessary to meditate on the various mysteries in order to gain the indulgences, the soul which has attained to a condition of habitual contemplation will simply call to mind the mystery in question. If it is the Incarnation, "My God," it will say, "for us Thou hast become incarnate; for us Thou hast made Thyself a Babe; how good Thou art!" And this one thought will be sufficient; no other considerations will be required to move the heart. And so with the other mysteries. For the Visitation the mere remembrance of Mary's charity, or of her modesty, will fill it with admiration, or, rather, will excite in it that vague but ardent feeling of love which, as we have shown, is the foundation of all contemplation.[1]

162. This is what St. Teresa calls setting the *Noria* in motion—that is to say, with little labour and scarcely any difficulty, drawing supplies from the fount of contemplation. The following words of the holy Bishop of Geneva show that this doctrine was likewise his : "It is impossible," he wrote to St. Jane Frances (April, 1606) "to make no use of the imagination or the understanding in prayer; but it is possible to employ them only in order to set the will in motion, and, this once achieved, to rely far more upon the will than upon these other faculties; this should certainly be done. . . . The imagination should be of the simplest, and only utilized as the needle by means of which the thread of the affections is embroidered upon your mind."

---

[1] Some effort may doubtless be required for this preparation; but it will consist in a steadfast act of renouncement of all idle thoughts rather than in any application of the mind to the subject chosen. If dryness still persists, fervour can often be aroused by the reading of some spiritual work, especially the Gospel or the life of a Saint.

§ 2. *On the Way in which a Soul experiencing Sensible Quietude should proceed when at Prayer.*

163. When the soul has once entered into prayer by way of this quiet, simple preparation, it should continue in the loving union, as far as may be, without striving to make any distinct acts, whether of love, contrition, petitions, etc. And this not because the soul never gives birth to these acts, but because it receives them rather than performs them; they come of themselves, unsought. *Eos actus tantummodo faciat*, said St. Alphonsus Liguori, *ad quos se sentit a Deo suaviter impelli*— "The soul should confine itself to those acts to which it feels itself gently drawn by God" (Praxis, 184).

St. Teresa was of a similar opinion. "What the soul has to do at those seasons wherein it is raised to the prayer of quiet is nothing more than to be gentle and without noise. By noise I mean going about with the understanding in search of words and reflections whereby to give God thanks for this grace, and heaping up its sins and imperfections together to show that it does not deserve it. All this commotion takes place now, and the understanding comes forward, and the memory is restless, and certainly, to me, these powers bring much weariness at times; for though my memory is not strong I cannot control it. Let the will quietly and wisely understand that it is not by dint of labour on our part that we can converse to any good purpose with God, and that our own efforts are only great logs of wood, laid on without discretion to quench this little spark; and let it confess this, and in humility say. 'O Lord, what can I do here? what has the servant to do with her Lord, and earth with heaven?' or words of love that suggest themselves now, firmly grounded in the conviction that what it says is truth; and let it make no account of the understanding, which is simply tiresome. . . . for it will often happen that the will is in union and at rest, while the understanding is in extreme disorder. . . . The soul will lose much if it be not careful now, especially if the understanding be acute. . . ."

The soul should be "aware of how near we are to God, and pray to His Majesty for mercies, make intercession for the Church, for those who have been recommended to us, and for the souls in Purgatory—not, however, with noise of words, but with a heartfelt desire to be heard. This is a prayer that contains much, and by it more is obtained than by many reflections of the understanding. Let the will stir up some of those reasons which proceed from reason itself to quicken its love—such as the fact of its being in a better state; and let it make certain acts of love, as what it will do for Him to whom it owes so much— and that, as I said just now, without any noise of the understanding in the search after profound reflections, A little straw—and it will be less than straw if we bring it ourselves — laid on with humility will be more effectual here, and will help to kindle a fire more than many faggots of most learned reasons, which, in my opinion, will put it out in a moment. . . . So, then, when the soul is in the prayer of quiet, let it repose in its rest; let learning be put on one side. . . . Moreover, the understanding bestirs itself to make its thanksgiving in phrases well arranged; but the will, in peace, not daring to lift up its eyes with the publican, makes perhaps a better act of thanksgiving than the understanding, with all the tropes of its rhetoric (*Life*, chap, xv., trans. Lewis, pp. 114-117).

And so, not seeking after fine thoughts, but accepting such pious ones as may occur, and, above all, continuing in union with God in a sweet repose and a silent peace, giving utterance only to such sentiments of love as may offer themselves, and such requests as we feel constrained to make to Him this— according to St. Teresa, is the soul's part in this prayer.

164. The natural anxiety to produce acts is, therefore, one of the dangers against which the contemplative soul should be warned.

Fénelon goes so far as to teach that between active and passive contemplation there is no difference but this: in the first the soul is still disquieted (or occasionally so, at any rate) by the effort to produce distinct acts, its object being to feel its own operation and to furnish itself with a consoling proof of its existence; whereas, in the second, it is wholly and absolutely submissive to the workings of grace, and its only acts are those which God inspires.

"How beautiful," wrote the Venerable Father Libermann, "to see a soul in entire submission to God, abiding in perfect acquiescence before Him, that He may work within it in accordance with the fullness of His holy will. . . . The greatest Saints have certainly served Him after this manner, and they, I think, have described it as the passive way, which, as it seems to me, means merely that in that state we endeavour to do nothing and to still all the motions of our soul, uniting ourselves gently with the grace which is within us, and by which all our actions, both interior and exterior, are prompted" (*Letter of January 22*, 1835).

165. Listen to St. Jane Frances de Chantal, showing how she suffered from this same tendency to produce acts of her own initiative, and the replies of her holy director.

She asks: "Should not the soul, particularly when at prayer, strive to check all discursive action, and, instead of dwelling upon what it has done, will do, or is doing, look upon God, thus simplifying its spirit and emptying it of everything and of all thought of self, continuing in this simple vision of God and of its own nothingness, entirely given up to His holy will, in the effects of which it must rest content and tranquil, without ever departing therefrom for the purpose of making any acts of the understanding or of the will? I even affirm that in the practice of the Christian virtues, and upon the occasions of faults and falls, we should maintain tins attitude, so it seems to me; for our Lord instils all necessary feelings into the soul and gives it perfect enlightenment—in all matters, I say, and a thousand times better than could be accomplished with the help of every one of its arguments and imaginings. You will say: Why, then, depart therefrom? But that, O God, is my misfortune, and in spite of myself, for experience has shown me all the harm of it. Only I am not the mistress of my own mind, which without my leave seeks to see and manage everything. This is why I ask from my dear master the aid of holy obedience to restrain this miserable busybody, for I think it will respect a definite command."

St. Francis of Sales replies: "Since for a long time past Our Lord has called you to this kind of prayer, granting to you to taste the sweetness of its fruits and to know the evils of the contrary method, stand firm therein, and as quietly as you can bring your mind back to this single consciousness of the presence of God and of self-abandonment in Him. And since your spirit desires that I should have recourse to obedience, I say this to it: Dear spirit, why strive to act the part of Martha in prayer, when God shows you that He wills you to take that of Mary? I command you, therefore, to abide simply in God or close to Him, without seeking to do anything or ask anything of Him whatever, save at His inspiration. Do not review your own conduct, only abide in His presence."

It is thus that the contemplative soul should lie passive under God's hand.

$ 3. *On Distractions.*

166. Distractions, however, may come. While the heart is rejoicing in the union of love, the mind falls to arguing, and, still more, the imagination begins to work. What is to be done? We showed above (No. 54) how St. Teresa advises the soul not to be troubled or do violence to the imagination in order to take it captive. "The only remedy," she says, "is to take no more notice of the imagination than one would of a crazy person, and let it go its own way, God alone being able to restrain it and make it steadfast" (Life, chap. xvii.). The Saint repeats this advice frequently, and thus explains the reason of her insistence: "We must guard against allowing ourselves to be troubled or upset by importunate thoughts in prayer. . . . I have suffered much in this way, and thinking that it may be the same

with you, I take every opportunity of speaking about it, desiring, my dear daughters, that you should understand that, distractions being inevitable, you must not be disquieted or distressed by them. Let the imagination (mill-clapper that it is) work away, and you go on with the making of your flour—that is to say, continue your prayers with the assistance of the will and the understanding."[2] The union of love, then, is to be enjoyed as long as it makes itself felt, and the mind is gently and quietly to be led back to God by a swift and simple action of thought; in a word, return again to your prayer in the same way that you entered into it.

Bossuet's teaching is the same. Madame de la Maisonfort places before him the following difficulty:

"It appears from various passages in the writings of St. Francis of Sales that when certain souls were found to be subject to distractions in prayer, he desired them to be satisfied with returning to God by a simple recalling of themselves to Him, and that this bringing of their thoughts back to God was the only effort which he would then allow them to make." And the learned director replied: "This simple return is sufficient. No other act could be more effectual, others being often in the imagination only."

167. We might also fall back, only without any violent effort, upon some holy thought. "Sometimes, when you are conscious of wandering thoughts or levities," writes the Venerable Father Libermann to a seminarist, "you might give your mind some pious thoughts to occupy and amuse itself with, while in the depths of your being your soul is united to God. . . . Your prayer will be an inward uniting of yourself with Him, but as your mind easily wanders away, give it, from

---

[2] "*Y como cosa tan penosa para mi, pienso que quiza sera para vosostras asi, y no hago si no decirio en un cabo, y e n otro, para si acertasse alguna vez a daros a entender como es cosa forzosa, y no os traiga inquietas y afligidas sino que dejemos andar esta taravilla de molino, y molamos nuestra harina no dejando de obrar la voluntad y entendimiento*" (*Fourth Mansion*, chap. i.).

time to time, some good thought, some passage of Holy Scripture, that it may divert itself therewith. But this will not be your prayer, for while the lower faculties amuse themselves with this thought, you will continue in your accustomed manner united to God in your heart. It is like one sitting at table with a little dog barking and fawning because it also wants to be fed, and so it ceaselessly torments him and pulls at his garments. What does its master do? He throws it a morsel, and proceeds undisturbed with his own meal for a time. Do this with your mind. Throw it from time to time some scraps to quiet it, and continue in your inward peace and tranquillity, all undisturbed. Your prayer will consist, not in the good thought which you throw to your mind, but in the secret repose of your soul before God. I know that this plan will not always succeed, but, all the same, never be anxious, go on your own way quietly, and in everything seek God only" (*Letter 76*, 1837).

168. There is one very common distraction of which it might be well to say a word. Often in the middle of our prayer some preoccupation forces its way in. It may be some business that we have to settle and bring to a satisfactory conclusion, or some untoward event which we anticipate and wish to avoid. Then we make plans and calculations and cease to think about God.[3]

The remedy is to say to ourselves at once that we are at prayer, and that consequently it is God's will that we should leave all deliberations and give ourselves completely and with blind trust into His hands. We gain more by thus resigning ourselves to God than by any amount of contrivings and all the

---

[3] There are some priests who profess to prepare their sermons when at prayer. Unless we are great Saints—St. Vincent Ferrer acted thus—able to count on the inspiration of God's Holy Spirit, this is to go about things the wrong way; it is not praying, but looking for distractions. Prayer is prayer; preparing sermons is work. Even where only a short exhortation for the faithful is needed, and a few thoughts will suffice, these thoughts are not prayer. The scheme must be made and the ideas found, and then only we may begin to pray for God's blessing on our ministry.

resources of human prudence. Let us turn once more to St. Jane Frances de Chantal and St. Francis of Sales.

Question: "I come back to my dear Father to ask if the soul, when thus resigned, should not continue to rest in its God, leaving to Him the disposition of all things concerning it, whether internal or external, dwelling, as you say, in His providence and in His will, without any care, attention, choice, or desire whatever, beyond this, that Our Lord shall perform His holy will with it, in it, and through it, without any hindrance or resistance on its own part."

St. Francis: "May God be gracious to you, my dear daughter. The child in its mother's arms needs but to yield itself to her and cling to her."

Question: "And will not Our Lord have an especial care to order all requisite and necessary things for a soul which is resigned thus into His hands?"

St. Francis: "Such souls are dear to Him as the apple of His eye."

§ 4. *Rules for Arid Quietude.*

169. We have hitherto assumed that the soul which has arrived at the union of love in prayer will consequently have experience of sensible quietude, as we have termed it. But this is not always so.

The preparation of which we have spoken is not always sufficient to move the heart and to produce the contemplative union in a sensible manner.

Should we, then, revert to methodical meditation? Not so; for, as we have said with St. Teresa and St. John of the Cross, the repugnance of the soul accustomed to contemplation would be too great.

Now hear Bossuet[4] on the subject: "When God withholds His operation I think that we should recollect ourselves, as do

---

[4] Letter to Madame de la Maisonfort, April 5, 1696.

the rest of the faithful (those who are not contemplatives), only tranquilly and, above all, without anxiety or disquietude, for these are fatal to prayer." "It is quite certain," said Madame de Maisonfort," that M. de Meaux required these souls to use only the very simplest means to stimulate their devotion, and, like St. Francis of Sales, he agreed, and has told me so, that an hour of prayer would be well spent if it were employed only in recalling the thoughts to God whenever they went astray. And when talking to me about dryness and distraction, he said that they gave the opportunty for the prayer of patience."

St. Jane Frances de Chantal's advice to her daughters is identical. "You are at prayer, and God withholds His gifts. If you can do nothing else, adore Him, adore His presence, His ways, His operations. No lofty thoughts are needed for this; you adore Him better by silence than by speech. And if you can do nothing at all, then suffer; if you cannot fray actively, do so by your endurance."

St. Teresa (*Life,* chap, xxii.) recognizes that there are times when, by reason of circumstances, or sorrows, or dryness, the soul cannot meditate or even commune in any way with our Divine Lord. "Then," she says, "all that we can do is to keep the Cross clasped in our arms"— accept the state of dryness, that is to say, with complete resignation.

§ 5. *Resolutions.*

170. How, then, should we conclude these prayers, whether they have been filled with consolations or dryness? Should we make resolutions? Let us turn to Bossuet once more. "I said to him once" (it is still Madame de Maisonfort who is speaking) "that my confessors had asked if I concluded my prayers with resolutions. The Bishop replied: 'You have them in a simple form, you have their essence. There are persons for whom they are not necessary. I do not think they are so for you. You have them in substance.' "

We should not venture to go as far as Bossuet. It seems to

us that the Spirit of God inspires even the most contemplative souls with resolutions, and that those who do not experience His inspirations would do well to formulate them themselves. They can always, besides, confine themselves to a general resolution which need not vary— such as, for example, to seek God only, or to serve Him in all humility, like St. Vincent de Paul, whose life was devoted to this virtue, or in all gentleness, like St. Francis of Sales. In some particular cases they will take special resolutions arising out of the special circumstances.

Athough this seems the wiser course, we do not wish to condemn Bossuet's opinion. It may be that some contemplatives will not require to formulate their resolutions definitely, and will not, for all that, fall into quietism; but, as our illustrious Bishop says, they possess them in substance.

§ 6. *On the Persisting in Quietude throughout the Various Exercises.*

171. This state of the union of love being so desirable, the soul should endeavour to continue therein during all its exercises, or, as Bossuet says, in words which we have already quoted, through "vocal[5] prayers, the recitation or singing in choir, Holy Mass said or heard,[6] and even the examen of conscience, because this same light of faith which keeps us attentive to God will also serve to reveal our least imperfections to us, and make us regard them with the greatest contrition and regret. We must likewise sit down to our meals in the same spirit of simplicity which will make us more attentive to God than to our food.

"And the same disposition must be maintained during our recreations, in order that our hearts and minds may be solaced

---

[5] As to vocal prayers, the habitually contemplative soul should not overburden itself with them. It would be well for the director to diminish their number, simple contemplation being much more helpful.

[6] To the exercises recommended by Bossuet should be added acts of thanksgiving and visits to the Blessed Sacrament.

without giving ourselves up to curious news, immoderate laughter, indiscreet speech, etc. Keeping ourselves pure and detached in our inner lives, without embarrassing others, let us unite ourselves frequently to God by turning to Him lovingly and with simplicity, ever remembering that we are in His presence, that it is His pleasure that we should not at any time separate ourselves from Him and His holy will. . . . And our general conduct should be after this manner, and in the same spirit, maintaining this simple and intimate union with God in all our actions and conduct—in the parlour, the cell, at supper, at recreation. . . . Finally, let the day conclude with this holy Presence, the examen, evening prayer, and retiring to rest; and we shall fall asleep in this loving intention, interrupting our repose when we awake in the night with some few fervent utterances—so many outbursts and cries, as it were, of the heart to God."

"Prayer twenty-fours hours a day," wrote St. Paul of the Cross, in a rule of life for a religious. "That is to say, do all your actions with heart and mind lifted up unto God, remaining in an inner solitude and reposing in God by pure faith."

The Venerable Fr. Libermann gives similar advice to a seminarist, writing January 4, 1838: "For the Rosary do not try to enter absolutely into all the thoughts and sentiments of the prayer which you are reciting. Remain in a state of peaceful union with God or the Blessed Virgin in the depths of your being, or you may unite yourself with the intentions and desires of the Blessed Virgin. Provided that you are really united with God, nothing more is required. If you have distractions and miseries, never mind. In this, as in your prayers, go on just the same. In all your inward or outward actions of the day generally, be as though you were at prayer. This is most important."

CONCLUSION.

172. Zealous and learned priests are sometimes heard to

complain of the difficulties besetting the direction of souls who are far advanced in perfection. As these souls progress in the Divine love, the action of the Holy Spirit growing more powerful and the human activity diminishing, it becomes useless to suggest to them practices which would be rather a hindrance than a help. Again, exhortations such as are applicable to others teach them nothing; hence the great embarrassment to their directors.

But a path must none the less be marked out for these souls, if they are to attain to the degree of perfection to which they are called. There is much truth, if some exaggeration, in the words of Godinez:[7] "Out of a thousand souls whom God calls to perfection, scarcely ten respond to His voice; and out of a hundred whom He calls to contemplation, ninety-nine do not understand their vocation. This is why I say that many are called, but few chosen. Not to mention other difficulties, the failure of many may be attributed to the rarity of a good director, who, with the mariner's compass of Divine grace, guides our souls on this unknown sea which we term the spiritual life."

We have gone to the Saints, the best judges in these matters, for rules for the direction of perfect souls. We have many a time had the happiness of verifying in practice the efficacy of their methods. We should like to see these methods universally known and accepted. We well understand the touching words with which the great Bishop of Meaux concluded his treatise on the prayer of the presence of God, from which we have so often quoted. Since we have done little more than develop his teaching, we may be permitted to repeat them after him.

"Almighty God, who by a marvellous concurrence of particular circumstances hast ordered the manner of this work from all eternity, let not certain souls, whether of the ranks of the learned or of the spiritual, be accused before Thy dread

---

[7] Quoted by Father Faber, *Progress in Holiness*, chap, xviii.

tribunal of contributing in the least degree to bar Thy entrance into hearts, because the simplicity with which Thou hast willed to enter in has offended them and the door, which the Saints throughout all the ages of the Church have thrown open, was not yet sufficiently familiar to them.

"Grant, rather, that, becoming as little children, as Jesus Christ has commanded, we may enter in once for all by that little door, so as to be enabled to point out the way afterwards to others with greater certainty and efficacy."

BOOK VI

SIXTH DEGREE—HEROIC SOULS

CHAPTER I

ON HEROISM: ITS DEFINITION AND EXAMPLES

173. WE class in the sixth degree souls who practise virtue after a heroic fashion. Before virtue can be called heroic it is necessary, says Benedict XIV. *(De Canonizatione Sanctorum),* (1) that the matter should be arduous, and that the practice of virtue in those special circumstances should argue an energy above the ordinary power of humanity; (2) that the acts of virtue should be accomplished promptly and unhesitatingly; (3) that they should be performed joyfully and enthusiastically; (4) and this not on one occasion alone, but habitually and whenever the occasion offers.

This quickness and enthusiasm in the performance of arduous undertakings are properly attributed by the learned Pontiff to the influence of the gifts of the Holy Spirit. Thus, he attributes heroic faith to the gift of understanding, heroic hope to the gift of the fear of the Lord, heroic charity to the gift of wisdom, heroic prudence to the gift of counsel, etc.

"With the aid of these gifts of the Holy Spirit" says Father Lallemant, "the Saints arrive at such a pitch of perfection that they accomplish without difficulty actions which we should not even dare to contemplate, the Holy Spirit making all their rough ways smooth and causing them to overcome all obstacles" (*Doctr. Spir.,* 4 principe, chap, iii., article 2, $ 5).

It will not be amiss to give some examples, borrowed mostly from Benedict XIV., of the heroic virtues.

The Theological Virtues.

174. *Faith.*—It was heroic faith which gave St. Pius V., when still in minor Orders, the courage needed to perform the functions of Inquisitor—both at Como, against a noted heretic, Planta by name, who, supported by a large and powerful party, was about to be raised to the Episcopate; and at Bergamo against the Bishop himself who was tainted by the poison of heresy, and against a certain George Medolaco, whose popularity and reputation had daunted all previous Inquisitors and prevented their taking proceedings against him. The danger which he ran (both life and liberty being imperilled) did not influence the young Dominican, or hold him back from the successful accomplishment of his duty, such was his zeal for the purity of the faith.

When St. Cajetan learned that the city of Naples had rejected the tribunal of the holy Inquisition, and that the Council of Trent had been compelled to suspend its sittings, his grief was so extreme that he thought that it would actually be the cause of his death. During the process of his canonization the judges rightly saw in this circumstance a proof of his heroic faith.

175. *Hope.*—Heroic was the virtue of hope in St. Louis Bertrand, whom the gravest dangers left unmoved, and who even on one occasion when he had swallowed some poison continued undisturbed, leaving himself entirely in God's hands. It was also heroic hope that enabled him so patiently to endure the ill-treatment to which he was subjected by the enemies of the Church as well as the cruel maladies from which he suffered, during which illnesses he took pleasure in repeating, *Domine, hic ure, hic seca, ut in aternum parcas* (Lord, let me be burned, torn, tortured here, that I may be spared hereafter).

It was also the virtue of hope, carried to the point of heroism, which threw so many of the Saints into transports of joy at the approach of death, and caused them to repeat with full hearts those words of David, *Laetatus sum in his, quae dicta sunt mihi: in domum Domini ibimus.*

Heroic, also, is the hope of the Saints when, a prey to the agonies of conscience, or even at times pursued by the thought of eternal perdition, they do not lose their hope of attaining to the life of the blessed; or, again, when, stripped of everything, weighed down with trials, confronted with a thousand difficulties, they continue to trust in God with unshaken constancy. Heroic were St. Francis of Assisi and St. Cajetan in their perfect confidence in God, when they insisted that the houses of their Orders should hold no possessions, but trust in Providence alone for their needs.

176. *Charity.*—During St. Teresa's process of canonization her heroic charity was proved by the continuity of her outbursts of love (for the thought of her Well-beloved never left her); by the laboriousness of the undertakings in which she engaged with the object of gaining hearts for Him and making them share in her devotion; by her zeal for the conversion of souls; by her admirable vow to choose always in all things that which should be most pleasing to God; by the keenness of her suffering at remaining separated from Him—suffering which was the eventual cause of her death.

St. Magdalen of Pazzi was at times possessed by such transports of devotion that she was wont to run hither and thither through the gardens and cloisters, rending her garments, stopping the Sisters whom she met, and inquiring of them anxiously whether they also experienced this Divine fire of love, embracing them if the reply were in the affirmative, and addressing burning exhortations to such as she found to be too cold. She was at times constrained to bathe her breast and limbs with cold water in order to temper the ardours which consumed her.

Examples of heroic love for their neighbours abound in the

lives of the Saints. St. Stephen praying for his murderers, St. Paulinus of Nola selling himself as a slave to ransom the poor widow's son, St. John Gualbert pardoning the murderer of his brother, St. Vincent de Paul supporting whole provinces and coming to the assistance of all in misfortune, St. John of God casting himself into the flames to save the lives of the sick.

The Cardinal Virtues.

177. *Prudence.*—The cardinal virtues, like the theological virtues, can be carried to the point of heroism. St. Teresa, in the opinion of the postulators of her cause, gave proof of a prudence greatly in excess of ordinary wisdom, and amounting to actual heroism, in the difficult works which she undertook. She was, in fact, able to bring them to a happy conclusion in spite of the most disconcerting obstacles, foreseeing opposition, baffling the wiles of the devil, surmounting all difficulties, giving her spiritual daughters and sons rules wherein austerity and suavity were admirably blended, and, finally, governing all her houses with the most consummate wisdom.

Heroic, too, was the wisdom with which St. Charles Borromeo ruled his diocese, that of St. Francis of Sales, etc.

178. *Justice.*—Obedience is one of the virtues related to justice. Benedict XIV describes the obedience of Isaac as heroic. The unfailing obedience of so many of the Saints to their rule was heroic also: their admirable deference to their Superiors, forestalling their least wishes, never questioning their orders, carrying out their most difficult and sometimes—in appearance, at least—unreasonable commands without comment.

179. *Fortitude.*—Heroic fortitude is shown by a contempt for death, which is braved, not with the fiery, unreflecting ardour of hot-headed men or enthusiasts, but with a calm and tranquil mind in the fulfilment of duty. St. Charles Borromeo, basely attacked by an assassin at the moment when he was at

evening prayers with his servants, was shot at from an arquebus at close quarters. Two bullets struck him, but by the miraculous protection of God he was not wounded. The Saint never moved, he went on quietly with his prayers, and did not exhibit the least emotion.

Heroic fortitude is also shown in laborious works undertaken for God's glory, or, again, in superhuman austerities. The Venerable Jeanne Delanoue, that humble saleswoman of Saumur who became the foundress of the Congregation of St. Anne, carried the virtue of mortification to the point of heroism. She took, when still quite young, a resolution never again to sleep in a bed, and she chose for her resting- place a chest in which, with the eyes of faith, she saw our Blessed Lord's cradle represented. It was so short and narrow that it could hardly have accommodated a child of five. There being no place for her head, it reposed on a big stone which served her as a pillow. When her confessor would not allow her to prolong this martyrdom, she then, much to her regret, consented to take a few hours' rest in a chair, her head leaning against the wall or some article of furniture, and this, in good or ill health alike, up to her last breath—that is to say, for forty-two years.

180. *Temperance.*—Amongst the virtues related to temperance are included sobriety, purity, and humility. Heroic was the sobriety of St. John the Baptist in living in the desert upon locusts and wild honey; of St. Basil, subsisting on bread and water; of St. Benedict at Subiaco, whose only food was the bread brought to him by the monk Romanus.

As to chastity, it need not be preserved at the risk of life, or at the expense of all worldly advantages, in order to be heroic, says Benedict XIV. Those who, in the face of violent and frequent temptations, resist them, instantly and without any weakness; who, for the sake of gaining the victory, do not shrink from resorting to means from which ordinary human nature would turn aside in terror—these have attained to heroic chastity. Such was St. Benedict's chastity, such also that of St.

Francis of Assisi, plunging into the thorns or the snow for the sake of overcoming temptations against holy purity.

Heroic, also, was the chastity of St. Henry, Emperor of Germany, and of St. Cunegund, his spouse; of St. Julian, St. Basilissa, St. Boleslas V., King of Poland, and Cunegund Bela, his wife, who preserved their virginity in the marriage state.

181. With reference to humility, we should never come to an end, said Benedict XIV, were we to enumerate all the heroic acts of this virtue which the lives of the Saints supply. St. Jerome, speaking of St. Hilarion, thus expresses himself: "Let others wonder at his miracles, his incredible abstinence, his knowledge, his humility. As for me, nothing so fills me with astonishment as that he was able to trample underfoot glory and honour. Bishops, priests, flocks of derks and of monks came, Christian matrons also (a great temptation), the common people from city and countryside, as well as powerful magistrates and judges, that they might obtain a little oil or bread blessed by him. And all the time his one desire was solitude" *(Vita St. Hilarionis,* 30).

And was not the holy Archdeacon of Evreux, M. Boudon, humble to the point of heroism when, being accused of a horrible crime, and deposed by his Bishop, he cast himself on his knees before his crucifix, thanking God and considering himself all undeserving of such a grace? What can we think of the great St. Augustine, who, with the object of lessening the esteem with which he was regarded by those about him, drew a picture of all his faults and wretchedness in his *Confessions?* of St. Dominic, counting contempt as the world's most desirable offering, and at the gates of the cities into which he was about to enter, falling on his knees and calling upon Heaven, with tears, to refrain from launching the thunderbolts of the Divine justice upon walls which were about to harbour so great a sinner?

182. These examples suffice to show the great distance which separates these heroic souls from all who have hitherto been in question, including those whom we have spoken of as

perfect souls. Heroism does not, we repeat, consist in one single act of supreme virtue, but in an habitual disposition to perform difficult actions, with a good grace and enthusiasm, whenever the occasion for them arises. And this supposes a degree of perfection far beyond any which we have yet seen. Even perfect souls are still—for the most part, at any rate—marked by a certain languor of action. They are sometimes slow to accomplish the sacrifices which present themselves. But it is not so with heroic souls. They do not walk; they fly forward upon the path of renunciation and perfection.

CHAPTER II

HOW SOULS ATTAIN TO THIS HEROISM

GENERAL SURVEY.

183. ALL through the spiritual life the soul's progress is due, on the one hand, to its prayers, its affective aspirations, its efforts and its sacrifices; and, on the other, to the illuminating action of the Holy Spirit and the trials vouchsafed to it by Providence. These means of advancement, which we have already seen operating in the inferior degrees of the spiritual life, will be encountered here again. But, although not novel, they are now growing ever more and more perfect and effective. Prayer which has become contemplative illumines the soul with yet brighter rays, and causes it to produce acts of love with far greater frequency and intensity. Its trials and acts of renunciation, too, now take effect upon the noblest faculties of the soul; they penetrate into the innermost recesses of its being, and this is why the resultant purification, described for this reason by St. John of the Cross as the night of the spirit, is the more profound and complete.

Let us sum up briefly what we have already said as to the dispositions of the perfect soul. Detached from all worldly frivolities, freed from useless preoccupations and purely human desires, emancipated from all that is inordinate and ill-regulated in the natural affections, willing only what God wills, knowing but one desire—that God should dispose of it according to His good pleasure—the perfect soul tastes the happiness and peace of loving naught but God and of knowing itself to be beloved of Him.

184. Many souls thus pass the remainder of their lives with but little variety,[1] and without any particular struggles or severe ordeals.

Others, however, undergo a more rigorous process of purification and progress farther in love, and this either because God's designs upon them are higher, or because they ask it more insistently, or show themselves more prompt to die unto themselves in all things, by a more unbroken state of recollectedness and a more generous self-sacrifice.[2] "When God," says St. John of the Cross, "does not find sufficient strength in a soul, He does not follow up His work of purification" *(Living Flame,* stanza ii., verse 5).

These generous souls, whose secret martyrdom is so agonizing, have mostly gone through trials of exceptional severity before reaching the perfect state. "To my mind," said St. Teresa, "it is far better that these venomous beasts (temptations of every kind) should break into the fourth mansion, and wage war upon the soul which has attained to this state of prayer (quietude); for should it not have been thus

---

[1] Father Surin, *Cat. Spir.,* vol, i,, part, vi., chap. via.

[2] "My dear daughters," said St, Jane Frances de Chantal one day to the nuns of the Visitation, "the majority of our holy Fathers and pillars of the Church did not suffer martyrdom. Can you tell me why?" And when all had replied, "And I," she said, "think it is because there is a martyrdom called the martyrdom of love, wherein God, while preserving the lives of His servants, causes them to be at the same time both martyrs and confessors. . . . *But this refers to those generous hearts* who, without ever looking back, are faithful to their love. As for weaklings, *Our Lord does not think of martyrdom for them.* He is content to let them pursue their quiet way at their own pace, lest, if He should urge them on too fast, they should fail Him altogether." One Sister asked in what the martyrdom of love consisted. "Give your will to God," the Saint replied, "and you will feel it" (*Histoire de Ste. Chantal,* by Monseigneur Bougaud. chap. xxxii.).

tempted, the devil might mingle poisonous sweets with the delights which God vouchsafes to it, or, at any rate, lessen its reward by keeping from it things which would be occasions of merit" (*Fourth Mansion*, chap. i,).

St. John of the Cross describes similar conflicts. "God," he says, "often permits that angel of Satan, the spirit of fornication, to trouble them by violent and abominable, disturbances of the senses, agitating their minds with horrible thoughts and their imaginations by pictures a thousand times more painful to them than death. And," the Saint adds, "God, as a rule, sends these tempests and agonies of the purification of the senses to such souls only as He intends should penetrate into the second night" (*Obscure Night*, i. 14).

These conflicts, which were already so violent when the souls were still in the fourth mansion, were yet further prolonged in the fifth, and served to establish them in a more lasting and profound perfection. Their love has become more ardent; convinced of their own frailty, they are now more enamoured of solitude and prayer, more faithful in that self-denudation which we have described, and in active mortification. These also are the souls who have experienced more vividly that condition which, following St. John of the Cross, we have called *the anxiety of love*, a sensation at once distressing and sweet, caused by their burning desire to love God more, and by the spectacle of their own helplessness.

SOME PRELIMINARY REMARKS.

§ 1. *Feelings which are Simultaneous, but Conflicting.*

185. We have just referred to the two simultaneous but contrary feelings which occur in the anxiety of love, and this is a very common phenomenon in the souls of which we are now speaking. How strange a thing is the heart of a Saint![3] They

---

[3] Something very similar happens with fervent souls, and still more with

suffer and are happy; their lives are an incomprehensible mingling of griefs and joys which blend and coexist without putting an end one to another.

It would often be hard to say whether the joy or the sorrow predominates. *Superabundo gaudio in omni tribulatione,* said St. Paul. They feel their trials keenly, and yet these trials are to them a source of great joy. They are a prey to agonies that torture them cruelly, and they know that at its centre the peace of the soul continues all the while undisturbed.

186. The human soul, simple as it is, is none the less complex. Theologians and mystical writers divide it into two parts, which they term the superior part and the inferior part; and they recognize that the latter may be the seat of the sharpest pains and anxieties while the superior part remains calm and happy. What, then, are these two parts of the soul? First, in order to prevent any misconceptions, let us say, with St. Francis of Sales (*Love of God,* i. xi.): "The inferior part of the soul is not identical with the sensitive nature, nor is the inferior will the same as the appetite of the senses." It is really the spiritual faculties—the intellect and the will—which are divided thus. There is a superior intellect that judges and reasons in accordance with the highest ideas which it attains to of itself, and there is an inferior intelligence that acts upon knowledge which it derives directly from the senses. And to this twofold mode of intellectual operations corresponds a twofold tendency of the will. "In the soul," says St. Francis of Sales again, "*in so far as it is reasonable,* we clearly see the two degrees of perfection which the great St. Augustine and all the theologians after him have called the two parts of the soul—the 'inferior' and the 'superior,' of which that styled 'inferior' acts and reasons in accordance with the experience of the senses, and that styled 'superior' reasons and acts according to its intellectual acquirements, which are based, not on the

---

perfect souls. But the further the soul progresses, the more the contrast between these opposing sensations is accentuated, and in the case of the Saints it is very striking.

experiences of the senses, but upon the perceptions and judgments of the spirit" (*Love of God*, Book I., chap. xi.). The holy Bishop illustrates his theory by the example of Our Lord, who was all-perfect, even from His Mother's womb, "and was subject, nevertheless, to sadness, sorrow, and grief of heart. And He cannot be said to have suffered in the body only, nor yet merely in the soul, in so far as it was sensitive, or (which is the same thing) in the senses; for He Himself says that before He suffered any outward affliction, even before He saw His executioners, His soul was sorrowful even unto death."

187. Were there here in reality two parts only, and would it not be more accurate to make a further subdivision? Our Divine Saviour suffered, doubtless, in the inferior part of the soul. In the agony in the garden the representation of the torments which He was to suffer, and during the scenes of the Passion the actual presence of these torments, caused the most acute suffering to the senses; but the whole reasonable portion of His Humanity, which saw all these evils, could not fail to suffer most keenly also. And Our Lord had other sufferings more bitter still. These were caused by the vision of all the offences committed against His Father, by the ingratitude of mankind, by the foreknowledge of the multitudes of the lost. Can we say of these sufferings that they affected the inferior part of the spiritual faculties?

Without presuming to question St. Francis of Sales's teaching, it may be allowable to amplify it on one point. In our own opinion Our Lord, during His Passion, suffered through the senses, through the inferior part of the spiritual faculties but in their superior part also; and at the same time He was happy—happy in the accomplishment of His Father's will, and in making a reparation for the outrages done to His Divine Majesty; happy in procuring our salvation. And over and above all these feelings He experienced in the supreme part of His Being the ineffable joys of the intuitive vision.

The perfect servants of Jesus Christ, in this as in all else, bear some resemblance to their Divine Master. We do not pretend to determine the precise number of strata (if it is permissible to speak thus) which are superimposed in the human soul, but a certain number must be conceded. In the superior part of their being—there where the contemplative operations take place—the Saints experience the peace, the happiness, the joy, which are born of love satisfied and the vision of the ineffable majesty of God. And, further, and, as it were, in another part of the soul, the consciousness of their inability to serve this great God, the thought of their sins and those of their brethren and other like motives, cause them the keenest suffering.

§ 2. *Of Supernatural Gifts which are Miraculous and of those which are Non-Miraculous.*

188. Another notable point is the double character of those eminent graces which God bestows upon these chosen souls, causing an important distinction between them. "There are," says Father Surin, "two kinds of supernatural blessings—one entirely extraordinary, such as visions, inner voices, ecstasies, raptures, and phenomena, altogether outside the region of faith; the others, which are within the region of faith, consist of illuminations and feelings" *(Traité de l'Amour de Dieu,* iii. i).

We have already had occasion to remark this (Nos. 31 and 32). In contemplation the truths which the soul grasps, and into which it penetrates in a wonderful manner by the aid of the gifts of understanding, are the truths of faith, which are accepted on the testimony of the Church. This is manifestly not the case with visions and inner voices, which are quite "outside the region of faith." We think Father Surin is right in saying the same of ecstasies and raptures. In raptures new truths, which faith would not teach, are revealed; and thus, usually by means of intellectual visions, God communicates marvellous secrets to the soul.

This last condition appeared essential to St. Teresa. "I am convinced," she says *(Sixth Mansion,* chap, iv.), "that if the soul is not the recipient in its raptures of these Divine secrets, they are not true raptures, but natural conditions caused by some weakness of constitution such as women are liable to."

189. But because they belong to another order of things these non-miraculous supernatural gifts are none the less precious.

"There is this difference," says Father Surin again, "that extraordinary occurrences, such as visions, ecstasies and miracles, are things which take us by surprise, and are outside the ordinary processes of grace acting upon free will, while the others result from the ordinary causes which God places in the economy of faith and grace which He gives to His children. And even although these latter results are consequent upon an ordinary co-operation with grace, and though they are promised by the Prophets and described by the Apostles, they are of such a nature— based, that is, upon such an exalted faith, such a strong hope, such a lively charity—that the man who possesses them is no less convinced of the supernatural and raised to a height above and beyond reason and human understanding, and enters, none the less into the knowledge of the world to come than if he had received those extraordinary gifts which God vouchsafes to those for whom He reserves these privileges."

No; God does not grant to all, even to the most intimate of His friends, the miraculous gifts which are outside the region of faith—apparitions, visions, whether of the imagination or the intellect, or rapture. St. Vincent de Paul had arrived at a very high state of sanctity before he was favoured with any visions-—of the imagination, at all events—for he declares that previously to the vision in which the death of St. Jane Frances de Chantal and her meeting with the soul of St. Francis of Sales in heaven was revealed to him, he had never received any similar favour.[4]

---

[4] It should be noted, however, that this is no proof that this great servant of God had not received other extraordinary favours, such as inner voices, intellectual visions, miraculous revelations, etc. No Saint ever concealed

St. Teresa teaches us not to judge of the worth of a soul by favours such as apparitions of Our Lord, etc. "There are many saintly persons," she says, "who have never received them, and others, not at all Saints, who have" (*Sixth Mansion,* chap. lx.).

190. And still more is this the case where rapture and ecstasy are concerned. They may at times be "marks of imperfection or some remnants of impurity when they occur, for the very reason that the soul is not accustomed to the things which ravish it" (Lallemant, *Doct. Spit.,* 7 principe, chap, iv., article 16). As the soul purifies itself the spirit becomes strengthened and more capable of enduring the Divine operations without any emotions or suspension of the faculties. " Our Lord, the Blessed Virgin, the Apostles and other Saints were always occupied in spirit with the sublimest things, and they enjoyed marvellous inner transports without any outward manifestations such as raptures and ecstasies" (Lallemant, *ibid.,* article 1).

"Rapture and ecstasy," says this same writer again *(ibid.),* "occur, as a rule, chiefly with women and those whose work is of a less active character, because their lives rather predispose them for these phenomena, and also because in their cases health, which becomes greatly impaired as a result of this kind of favour, is not so necessary for giving glory to God. The devotion of apostolical men, on the other hand, who have to labour for the salvation of souls, is less sensible, more spiritual, more solid. God, as a rule, does not grant them the grace of ecstasy, unless (as sometimes happens) He purposes thus to stamp their ministry, as in the cases of St. Vincent Ferrer and St. Francis Xavier. But He communicates Himself to them chiefly by way of the understanding, which is capable of receiving the fullest illumination, rather than by that of the imagination, where the Divine rays are more sensible and the results more perceptible from without."[5]

---

more jealously than he the graces with which Heaven dowered him.

[5] *Cf.* St. Teresa (*Life,* chap xx). For the same reason raptures and ecstasies become much more rare in the state of transforming union, which is the

191. With regard to eminent graces which, however, to use Father Surin's expression, are *within* the order of faith, graces of such sublimity that man, as the same writer says, is thereby "admitted into the outer courts of eternity and to the foretaste of glory," God denies them to none of these saintly souls. "These are the things to which all those who correspond to ordinary grace may aspire; they are the fruits and rewards of Christian endeavour; and in one sense we may say to each individual soul that it may expect them, and that if, possessing the aids which God gives in His Church, and the efficacy of the Blood of Jesus Christ which He has shed in order to purchase those treasures for mankind, it fails to receive them, the fault is its own" (Surin, *VAmour de Dieu,* iii. 1).

§ 3. *On the Further Illumination vouchsafed to the Chosen Souls, and the Acts of very Perfect Love which Result.*

192. The soul, therefore, that is wholly and constantly faithful, receives ever more and more precious graces, which cause it to advance rapidly along the path of perfection.

The lights communicated to it by the Holy Spirit bear especially upon the Divine greatness, the majesty of God, His mercy, His infinite benevolence, the perfections or the love of Jesus, the Word Incarnate, the sufferings which He endured for us in His Passion, His sweetness and tenderness in the Eucharist, etc. On all these things the faithful soul of which we speak possesses conceptions which, if not very distinct and easily formulated in precise and definite terms, are at least of a very high order, and such as to impress it profoundly. It has also a far truer understanding of the Blessed Virgin than is the case with the imperfect souls, and feels a much more tender and ardent devotion for this good Mother. Finally, as we shall presently show, it has a much more perfect knowledge of itself and its own wretchedness.

---

supreme degree of perfection (St. Teresa, *Seventh Mansion*, chap. iii.).

193. Many and varied are the ways of which God makes use to illuminate the soul, St. John of the Cross first describes[6] those created beings in which, according to the expression of the theologians (S. Th,, I., q, 45, a, 7. 0), God has left traces (*vestigia,* literally "footprints") of His perfections. "The soul," he says, "in the light of contemplation, and in the resultant keen understanding of created beings, sees that they so abound in the graces and perfections given to them by God that they all appear as though clothed in a wonderful beauty and a supernatural virtue . . . and thus it is that creatures bring home to the soul something of the beauty and excellence of its Beloved by the traces which His passage has left in them."

To this, the least perfect of the ways in which we may come to a knowledge of God, a way which, nevertheless, increases the Divine love within us and accentuates the grief which His absence causes (the anxiety of love), are added others of a higher order and greater efficaciousness. These are the knowledge of the Incarnation of the Son and of the mysteries of the Faith (*ibid.,* stanza 7), The angels by their inspirations[7] and men by their teachings, direct the soul's

---

[6] *Spiritual Canticle*, stanzas 4, 5,6. The order followed by the Saint is evidently based on the grades of perfection of these various ways of attaining to knowledge. As to the sequence in which they succeed each other, there is no fixed rule, and it may vary in different cases.

[7] The angelic inspirations, like human suggestions, are distinct and definite, and appear to act upon the minds of men solely by means of sensible ideas and with the aid of the imagination, while the Holy Spirit can act directly upon the will, and without any intermediary. "God alone," says St. Ignatius, "can impart consolation to the soul without any antecedent cause, because God only can enter into the soul in order to produce and excite within it inner dispositions which shall turn it wholly to the love of His Divine Majesty. I say *without any cause*—that is to say, without any antecedent sentiment or previous knowledge of anything which might have given birth to this consolation, by way of acts of the understanding or the will" (*Spiritual Exercises : Discernment of Spirits*, second week, rule ii.). St. John of the Cross also appears to be in agreement with St. Ignatius in attributing to angelic inspiration certain definite thoughts, ideas, or new ways of regarding the mysteries of the faith, and in attributing to the action of God

attention to these marvels of Divine grace and compassion, revealing to it new aspects; and these fresh lights which have come to it in contemplation, "by increasing its love, serve only to augment the pain of its wound." Finally and especially, there is a third and indefinable grace which is productive of still more marvellous results, both in the heart and the mind. "It is something, as it were, beyond knowledge, and which words are powerless to express, a comprehension of God so high and so wonderful that it cannot be conveyed by human speech. . . . Souls far advanced in perfection are at times conscious of this impress of grace. It means that in all that they see, hear, or know, and also sometimes independently of these channels, God grants them the favour of a wonderfully exalted conception of His goodness and greatness. When a soul experiences this grace, God vouchsafes to it ideas of such magnitude that it realizes with absolute clearness that it has not yet so much as begun to know Him. He causes it so to appreciate the Divine immensity, that by this sublime consciousness of Him which God imparts to the soul, it sees with equal distinctness its own inability ever to know Him perfectly."

194. St. Catharine of Genoa, in her *Dialogues,* also gives us an account of the graces of enlightenment, which become more abundant and more vivid at this stage of the spiritual[18] life.

Himself the third order of graces of which we shall speak presently. Moreover, illuminations derived directly from God are more general and more brilliant. A star lights up one point of the sky only, and so the angel makes only one truth luminous, or a few at most. The sun, on the contrary, makes visible every object upon which its rays fall. If we do not perceive them all, the weakness of our sight is the only cause. So Almighty God opens out vast horizons to the soul, and nothing but the feebleness of our human vision prevents us from seeing all that He illumines.

[8] We say "at this stage of the spiritual life" because, in her *Dialogues,* - where the itinerary of the soul's journeying towards sanctity is recorded, this great Saint shows us how, after a period of struggles and generous efforts, the soul come at last to perfect renunciation (chap, vii.), putting its entire trust in God, and giving itself up without reserve to the Divine will. Now,

"God sheds His Divine love upon the soul," she says, "and reveals to it a spark of the pure love[9] which He bears us, and the great things which He performs and has performed by this love." According to the same Saint, He further illumines the soul with regard to the value and abundance of the graces which have been granted to it, showing side by side all the greatness of the Divine mercy and the blindness and malice of the sinner. He further enlightens it with regard to the mysteries of the life and death of Our Lord, wherein God's love for us is so strikingly manifested.

195. So much light cannot fail to produce good results, and in the heart of the contemplative a perfect blaze of love is kindled thereby. It loves God, it thinks of Him unceasingly. Love holds all its thoughts captive, and ever leads them back to God, from whom it can only separate itself by violence. This is what Richard of St. Victor calls *caritas ligans,* the captivity of love. The more it loves the more it craves to love, and hence in all the conduct of life there follows a more vigilant attention, more generous efforts, and especially a thirst for self-sacrifice, which goes on ever growing, leading it to a joyful acceptance of the most painful ordeals and to the accomplishment of the most arduous and meritorious works.

§ 4. *Purifying Trials*

196. But all the proofs of devotion which it gives to its Well-beloved fail to satisfy the soul wounded by the Divine love. The obstacles which it encounters, whether from within or without, and which hinder its union with God, cause it the most cruel sufferings while increasing its devotion. The

---

this state of perfect renunciation constitutes, as we have already said, the fifth degree, and it is then, according to St. Teresa, that, when God desires to lead the faithful soul still further in the paths of self- sacrifice, He bestows on it the enlightenment of which we are speaking (Part i., chap. vili.).

[9] St. Catharine of Genoa, *Dialogues*, part i., chap. viii.

necessaries of life for which it is bound to provide (St. John of the Cross, *Spir. Cant.,* stanza 8), its unavoidable dealings with the world (*ibid.,* stanza 10)—all, in a word, which distracts it and prevents it from devoting itself to its love—are a source of real torment to it. It is resigned, however, because God's will is dearer to it than any other thing, but it suffers greatly notwithstanding. Temptations, which now frequently redouble their strength, are a still more fruitful source of anxiety and distress; and should such a soul chance to be guilty of some act of unfaithfulness, how great is the bitterness of its self-reproach!

197. Let us hear Blessed Margaret Mary upon her own conflicts. Towards the age of eighteen, after being favoured for a long time with the grace of perfect contemplation and being carried to a high state of perfection, she had to fight against a temptation to serve the world, and to give herself up overmuch to its pleasures. What she is about to tell us will give us some idea of the pains and anguish which these fierce conflicts cause to the loving soul.

"In the midst of my amusements God would transfix me with such burning darts that they pierced and consumed my heart from every side, and this suffering astounded me. But as this was not sufficient for a heart as ungrateful as mine to compel me to turn to Him, I felt myself, as it were, bound and dragged so forcibly, as with cords, that I was at length constrained to follow Him who was calling me aside into a place apart. There He would rebuke me with great sternness, for He was jealous for my wretched heart which was undergoing terrible persecutions; and after having implored His pardon, prostrate on my face at His feet, He made me take a severe and prolonged discipline. And then I fell back as before into my resistance and my follies. And then at night, when I divested myself of those liveries of Satan—I mean my vain attire, the instruments of his malice—my Sovereign Master would come to me as He was during His flagellation, all disfigured, uttering the strangest upbraidings: how it was my vanity, He would say, which had brought Him to this state, and that I was losing time of the utmost value and of which He would exact a full account at the hour of my death; that I was betraying and persecuting Him, when He had given me so many proofs of His love and of His desire that I should conform myself wholly to Him. All this made such a deep impression upon me and so pierced me to the heart, that I wept bitterly; and I should find it difficult to express what I endured and all that went on within me.

"In order to revenge upon myself the wrongs which I had done to my Master, and to conform myself again to His likeness, while assuaging my own grief which weighed me down, I used to bind this miserable, criminal body with knotted cords, drawing them so tightly that I could scarcely breathe or eat. I used to leave these cords so long that they became embedded in my flesh which began to close over them, so that violence was required to remove them, causing me great pain; and the same with the little chains which I wore round my arms, the skin coming away with them when I took them off.

"But greater than any other torment was my fear of offending God, for my sins seemed to me to be perpetual. After *several years* passed in agonies and struggles and many other sufferings, my only consolation being my Lord Jesus Christ, *who had made Himself my Master and my Governor,* the longing for the religious life gained such strength in my heart that I was resolved to accomplish it, at no matter what cost. But, alas! this could not be *for another four or five years, during which time my troubles and struggles were redoubled from every side*, and I strove also to redouble my penances in so far as my Divine Master permitted it."

198. It may surprise some readers to see these frailties in such great souls.[10] They ask themselves whether these souls

---

[10] St. Teresa reproached herself bitterly by reason of an over-compliance, which caused her during one period of her life to frequent the Parlour oftener than her conscience approved, considering this frailty a great act of infidelity; and all the time these interviews were innocent in themselves.

had already attained to a high level of virtue when they fought all these battles with varying success. Can they be said to have already made a sincere offering of themselves to God? Do they not seem to be still below those dispositions which we have attributed to simple fervour?

We have described the fervent soul as one in dispositions to refuse nothing to grace. In entire sincerity it repeats its desire to belong unreservedly to God. Meanwhile it is very far from being as virtuous as Blessed Margaret Mary at the time of the struggles which she has just described. God proportions His inspirations to the strength of His children. From fervent souls He asks less, knowing their weakness. He removes many occasions of sacrifice from their paths, nor does He reveal to them all which they might accomplish; for even such tasks as He leaves for their performance already seem so hard to them, and yet He often makes them easier by means of sensible graces.

In spite of its longing for perfection, the fervent soul has many faults of frailty with which to reproach itself. It commits them unconsciously, too, and falls into many imperfections, deceiving itself with regard to them, and failing to realize all the extent of the renunciation to which it is aspiring. A merely fervent soul would never have reproached itself with those conversations and friendships which St. Teresa lamented, nor those goings out into the world and that probably quite simple and unpretending attire for which Blessed Margaret Mary did such heroic penance.

199. When the perfect soul says to its God: "I am wholly Thine," there are no reservations in its gift of self. God, who requires more of it than of the fervent soul, does not urge it on to such heights as in the case of the heroic soul.[11] It should

---

[11] In a chapter of his *Treatise of the Love of God* (Book X., chap, xiii.), entitled "How God is jealous of us," St. Francis of Sales relates the following trait: "One day St. Catharine of Siena was in a rapture which did not take away the use of her senses. While God was revealing wondrous things to her, a brother of hers passed by her and attracted her attention by

refuse nothing to grace, but it must not outrun it and act through human zeal. If it is constantly faithful, the Divine inspiration will become more frequent and more urgent. If the desire for advancement slackens, if the soul does not show itself eager to do ever more and more for God, then the grace will cease to increase in light and strength. 'But whosoever wills to attain to the summit of love, not counting the cost, will receive ever more light and more powerful impulses to good. The more the soul gives to God, the more He will ask of it again, and at the same time He allows the temptations and trials to redouble in order that the victories may be multiplied. He it is who orders the new conditions which will be the occasions of unexpected sacrifices, often revealing to the soul some hidden ties, some remnants of self-love, or else some defect of courage and generosity which it had not perceived.

200. A rich landowner gives his vassals some land to till, a sterile soil which requires much cultivation. Some, out of idleness, only really cultivate a portion of it; the rest lies fallow, and remains overgrown with briers, brushwood, and weeds. These stand for faithful but imperfect Christians, who do not aim at complete self-abnegation, retaining many defects alongside of their real virtues. Others there are who are more industrious, and will not permit a single foot of ground to remain infertile. But these for the most part use the spade or plough only for turning up the earth, and as under a thin layer of good soil many rocks lie concealed, the result is that only plants with surface roots can thrive, while forest trees and fruit-trees cannot grow. Such are the fervent souls who banish sin from their hearts, labouring after true renunciation, leaving no fault uncombated, but whose virtues do not attain to any great

---

the noise he made, so that she turned to look at him just for one little moment. This slight distraction, so sudden and unforeseen, was neither a sin nor an infidelity, but simply the shadow of a sin, and a mere semblance of infidelity. And yet the most holy Mother of the Divine Spouse so reproved her for it, and the glorious St. Paul gave her so great confusion thereat, that she nearly burst into tears"

height. Other servants there are— a small band only—who are not afraid to delve deep into the bowels of this infertile soil. They penetrate to a great depth and extract the rocks which prevent its productiveness. Their master, seeing their good-will, comes to their aid, employing mining operations and blowing up the heaviest and hardest of the blocks of stone, which his servitors, with all their labour, would have been unable to dislodge. In the place of these boulders they lay down a rich vegetable soil, and on this renovated ground they succeed in the cultivation of the most useful plants and the most magnificent trees. Thus, on the land committed to them are to be found rich crops, gardens full of profitable plants, orchards, vineyards, and parks with shady alleys. These industrious servants are the faithful Christians of indomitable courage who have waged a merciless war with nature, and the Saviour has crowned their work by sending them the severest trials, and henceforth all kinds of heroic virtues germinate and grow in their souls.

201. The soul, then, is greatly the gainer by passing through these purifying ordeals. The further it feels itself removed from God, the more it yearns for Him; harassed by temptations, it redoubles its efforts to free itself from the toils of Satan, and to become one with its God. Hence its strife with itself—a deadly and unremitting warfare waged against the tendencies to self-love, sensuality, etc.; hence, also, great victories, stupendous acts of mortification.

202. The biographies of the Saints—those, at least, with whose inner lives we are familiar—show ordeals such as those to which Blessed Margaret Mary was subjected, and which, like hers, extended over many years, during which their onward progress was continual. When by a prolonged and constant fidelity to grace they have overcome the resistance of nature, and have submitted themselves unreservedly to Our Lord, who has "become their Master and their Governor," we might fancy that their warfare would be ended. But, on the contrary, from all sides the strife and conflict are redoubled.

The fact is that the soul is now capable of a more complete purification, and the phenomena which we have just described become daily more accentuated, attaining finally to a frightful intensity. The soul in this condition feels itself borne towards God with a rapidity only comparable to the velocity with which a falling stone approaches its centre of gravity" (*Spiritual Canticle,* stanza 12). The Divine attraction becomes ever more and more powerful, but the soul's distress becomes more acute thereby, owing to its inability to unite itself with God in accordance with its desire, and because it estimates more and more correctly the power of the obstacles which separate it from Him.

God causes it to realize with the utmost vividness the nothingness of the creature and all the hideousness and ingratitude of sin. At the same time He impresses it with a no less powerful conviction of His holiness and dread justice. It is impossible to form an idea of the condition to which the soul is then reduced. "It seems to it as though this state would endure for ever" (*Obscure Night,* ii. 6), and it is racked with inexpressible anguish.

203. This is the crisis which St. John of the Cross calls the "night of the spirit," and it is brought about by way of a high and interior contemplation. It is apparent that neither the arguments of meditative prayer nor the ordinary sentiments of the affective life could give the Saints this humility, this love of sacrifice, this forgetfulness, this hatred of self, which astonish and stupefy us. A much more powerful action of grace is necessary, and one which the gifts of the Holy Spirit alone can exercise.

It is, then, an interior light which God sheds upon these souls for their illumination and purification. "By the rays of this pure light which penetrates it, dispelling all impurities, the soul sees itself as it is, all wretched and unclean. It seems as though God had risen up against it, and it had risen up against God. This is a most terrible experience. Thanks, then, to the luminous beams which enlighten it, it realizes its own unworthiness before God and His creatures" (*Obscure Night,* ii. 5).

§ 5. *The Chief End of this Spiritual Purification.*

204. But Almighty God is not satisfied with revealing all its unworthiness to the faithful soul; He reduces it to a state of grievous helplessness. His aim is to bring home to it the fact that of itself it can do nothing, and to *render it more and more passive under the action of His grace.* The ordeals to which it was subjected in the inferior degrees, in the fourth and fifth mansions particularly, were not of the same stamp. Designed to wean it from the false joys of this world and to attach it to spiritual blessings, these, when endured in the right spirit, only make it more and more eager in the pursuit of those means and practices which bring it nearer to God—frequentation of the Sacraments, recourse to direction, religious books, and especially the careful practice of the Christian virtues—charity, apostleship, obedience, penance. Thanks to all these aids to perfection, the faithful soul made the most satisfactory progress; but a remnant of human activity was too often mingled with the operations of grace.

We have said that this eagerness was very usual and, as a rule, perceptible in fervent souls, and less so in perfect souls, who practise the Christian virtues with more strength and courage but also with a greater repose, although this characteristic has not quite disappeared in them. Their actions are all for God, but nature still finds some satisfaction in the virtues which they exercise and in the practices to which they have recourse. They like humbling themselves before a Superior or a Director, because they can then rest in the assurances and encouragements which they receive. The most difficult virtues are also the most beautiful, and this beauty delights them; it gives birth in them to ardent and enthusiastic desires, and is a powerful incentive to good.

It is sweet to them to spend themselves in apostolic works,

and the hope of success sustains their courage. If they do not shrink from the most arduous undertakings, if the prospect of a life of perpetual struggles, of incessant self-sacrifice, does not appal them, it is because the thought of the harvest gives them renewed strength. They even find consolations in their penances and trials, remembering that these sufferings and sacrifices are offered for the souls that they love, and this perfectly legitimate affection sustains and animates them. If in many ways nature is opposed to grace and is the cause of distressing cross-conflicts, in others, again, it acts in concert with it, and influences the soul towards the same actions. The virtues are then practised with extreme ardour, and the soul, if faithful, gains much merit and rises to a great height of perfection.

205. And then there comes a day when God, seeing that it is sufficiently established to allow of its undergoing a more rigorous purification successfully and attaining to a more exalted love, causes all that is human about this soul to die in it. "In order to arrive at being everything," says St. John of the Cross, "you must aim at being nothing" *(Ascent of Mount Carmel,* i. 13). But this necessary annihilation would never be realized by the soul did not God Himself work within it. For a time, therefore, He deprives it of all its supports, He reduces all its faculties to a state of void, of nakedness, of entire abandonment *(Obscure Night,* ii. 6). The imagination is, as it were, fettered, the intellect in darkness, the will arid and constrained, the heart reduced to inaction (*ibid.,* iii. 16) ; the soul feels forsaken, unable to find comfort in books or in the counsels offered to it (*ibid.,* vii.). At times it is even powerless to make distinct acts of faith, hope, and charity. But none the less it truly possesses these virtues and does not cease to have merit, because it continues freely in a disposition of entire submission to the Divine will, and in this disposition these three virtues are embraced. It yields itself up, in fact, into God's hands, and waits to produce distinct acts until He gives it the power to do so.

216

206. When this severe purgation is generously accepted, the soul is established thereby in excellent dispositions. Then in very deed it desires only what God desires; it suffers for whomsoever God may will it to suffer, as readily for those who persecute it as for those whom it loves. Its natural inclinations have lost nearly all their power; its repugnances have almost disappeared. It is no longer as subject to the senses as was formerly the case. The longing to perform some service for God possesses it so entirely that it has lost, as it were, the habit of forming other desires. If formerly, before embarking upon any action, it took into consideration the Divine good pleasure, it also considered the worldly point of view, going carefully into the matter in question, weighing the advantages and difficulties. Now it looks steadily at the heavenly aspect of all things, and will not pause to consider anything other than the will of God. And although the Divine will should be about to require of it new sacrifices, to hang it upon the Cross, or to raise it up on Mount Tabor, it takes no thought of this, because its sole concern is to accept all that Providence ordains for it, to carry out any commands that it receives and to follow up every motion of grace. Moreover, the supreme part of its faculties— that which the masters term the soul's summit—is so concentrated upon God, so firmly attached to the object of its love, that it feels powerless, as it were, to turn away from Him. It is not, of course, safeguarded from every fault, but in the case of a soul whose ordinary dispositions are such as we have described, faults can be but infrequent and slight.

207. The Venerable Mary of the Incarnation explains very clearly how and why, in the case of generous souls, God purges all the faculties successively.

After speaking of the curtailment of sensible consolations, she says: "Nature being, in the first place, annihilated by penance, and then again by the deprivation of all spiritual delights (the sensible). . . . it is humbled to an unspeakable point, while the superior part is in a state of real contentment at seeing itself freed from the things which stood in the way of the true and unalloyed purity of its rejoicing in its sovereign good." The soul, freed from the things of sense, enters, then, into a superior state —that of contemplation. " But the Spirit of God, desiring to possess it wholly, and seeing that the understanding, however purified, still mingles something of self and its own interests with the Divine operations (which constitutes an impurity and a notable defect), checks it abruptly; so that it is, as it were, suspended and rendered wholly incapable of performing its ordinary and natural functions." These, however, freed from sensible influences, were of a very high order and did not tend to nourish self-love, for the understanding "did not regard them as its own, seeing that their simplicity made them almost imperceptible. . . . Then the will, having been caught up into God, enjoys His embrace, and having no further need of the understanding to supply fuel to its fire, but finding it rather harmful by reason of its abundance and fertility, it abides, like a Queen rejoicing in her Divine Bridegroom, in a liberty of which seraphs with their tongues of fire are more fitted to speak than are mortal men of unclean lips. Years pass thus, but the Holy Spirit, who is the endless source of all purity, desires to triumph yet further over the will; for even although He Himself was the cause of these divine motions, the will, none the less, had apart there in. And this He cannot suffer. As though jealous of its beauty, He desires to be its absolute Master. And He purifies it, therefore, of this last remainder.[12] And so upon this loving but yet delicate activity, which surpassed all other delights in the Bridegroom's embrace. . . . the arresting touch is also laid, as was the case with the understanding and the memory. . . . Such is the victim-like condition to which the Holy Spirit, in His infinite zeal for the purity of souls, the spouses of the Son of

---

[12] We quote the complete passage because it shows the extent to which God proposes to lead the soul that is constantly faithful. But we should remark that when it is as wholly purified as in the case to which the Venerable Mary of the Incarnation refers, it would seem to have attained to the seventh degree, that of transforming union.

God, reduces them, in order that they may be brought to the state in which He desires them to be, that He may take His delight therein" (*Vie,* by Dom Ch. Martin, iv. 2, pp. 647, 648).

§ 6. *Examples of Purifying Ordeals.*

208. Some examples drawn from the lives of the Saints will show us better than any theoretical explanations those paths, so arduous but also so full of love, by which God leads the most faithful of His servants.

We will first quote St. Veronica Juliani, to whom our Lord showed, through a vision, the value of this dolorous purification, but she learned to realize it chiefly through her own personal experiences.[13]

"Being one morning at prayer, I was lifted up into an ecstasy. Here the Lord showed me a wonderful place in the form of a castle. . . . The Lord appeared to me, and led me up to it. 'This castle' He said, 'represents the castle of the soul. I desire that thou shouldst take possession of it. Pure suffering is its name. Outside it is built of stones all graven with crosses, but within there is one single cross only, but this one is of greater worth than a multitude of the others. This cross which is within, is named the Naked Cross. It is the heaviest of all those that it is given to the soul to bear. Give thy consent, then, to accept, to possess to the uttermost all that I have shown to thee and explained'. . . . At this moment I was conscious of a generosity so great that I would have accepted not only all that was before my eyes, but more also.

"God revealed to me that this naked cross is such a precious thing that no diamonds can compare with it in value. As He showed it to me it was of an indescribable beauty; nothing could be more admirable, more beautiful, more to be appreciated, more delightful, more dear, more to be desired. It

---

[13] The following is translated from the Saint's Diary, published by Father Pizzicaria, S.J.

is the treasure of all treasures, the greatest gratification that the soul could desire. But it is enough to say that it is the door through which we must pass in order to go to God.

"When I had given my consent, Our Lord took me into the beautiful castle in which was this solitary cross. The mere sight of it terrified me, for in my heart I saw and perfectly understood what this pure suffering was. While undergoing it we do not know its worth. It appears then like some tyrant who desires to slay the soul, and the soul seems to be treading the winepress of the most terrible and indescribable sufferings. We can then only exclaim: *Manus Domini tetigit me*—The hand of the Lord hath touched me (Job xix. 21).

"In this hour, when the Lord causes the soul to endure this pure suffering, I think it would die did it not receive supernatural strength. This pure suffering resides in the innermost centre of our being; it extends throughout the noblest faculties—to the intelligence, which it obscures; to the memory, which becomes, as it were, crazed with regard to all that concerns these sufferings, although not to other things; and to the will, which becomes incapable of action. If it accomplishes anything, it is the very opposite of that which it desires. It suffers violence, it seems as though all that was passing within it were in opposition to God. Alas, what pain! what torment! And then, in a flash, all the senses and the inferior appetites rebel. They are like hounds, lions, seeking to devour the poor soul. And with them the world, the devil and the flesh ally themselves. All take up arms to fight against the spirit, which finds itself abandoned and without any to succour it. 'Oh God,' it exclaims, 'to whom should I turn ? If I desire to cry unto Thee I cannot; I am as one that is dumb, unable to utter a word. If my soul would wing its way towards Thee, it finds itself chained to the earth, unable to take its flight. If it calls Thee, Thou hidest, Thou withdrawest Thyself still further.' All this achieves and completes its pure suffering. Whosoever would understand this torment, it suffices to say that the soul feels as though it were utterly deprived of its only and sovereign good, which is an agony equivalent to all the torments of Purgatory, Hell, and every imaginable suffering. Verily, it were better to be silent than to speak of these things, for it is a pain even to refer to them. What, then, is it to suffer them?" (April 3, 1694).

209. Again, a little later on, speaking of the calls to suffer which God makes to the soul, the Saint thus expresses herself: "If these loving invitations to suffering invigorate and enkindle the spirit, the desolations and aridities which follow are too agonizing for description. The soul finds itself suddenly in the very presence, in the sight of its God, learning the lessons of Paradise, and then, in a flash, this presence is taken away, and it remains surrounded by thick darkness, encompassed with tortures, assailed on every side.

"No matter in which direction it may look, it sees only the ministers of hell. They encircle it that they may overwhelm it with outrages, now under the form of giants, now of brutes, now of unclean beasts, now of serpents, now of young men. They assume all kinds of shapes. In these conflicts the soul passes through many different conditions. At times, in its innermost centre, it is conscious of some remainder, as it were, of the presence of God, in which it formerly rejoiced, and this makes it generous and strong. At others, on the contrary, this recollection only redoubles its sufferings, for it grieves to find that it is deprived of Him, and that a myriad hells have taken the place of its Paradise, for each of these demons is like a hell to it. It can do nothing; it only calls on these evil spirits to perform all that is permitted to them by God with regard to it, for it desires nothing but the accomplishment of the Divine will.

"The final sentence of reprobation is all that it now expects, and this is a pain surpassing every other pain. And then it becomes aware of a light, the conception of which I know not how to convey. It seems to the soul that it sees and understands the great good which it has lost. The mere thought of this separation from God is an agony such as I cannot describe; no one can understand it but those only who experience it. I have experienced it in the past and I experience it still.

"Formerly there was some slight degree of comfort and consolation in this ordeal. Now, on the contrary, one suffering only seems to be a prelude to another. I have no leisure to draw my breath. All is bitterness. Blessed be God! for His love's sake all is as nothing. Thank God for suffering! thank God for the Cross!"

210. "The soul," says St. Catharine of Genoa (it is her own story that she is relating), "remained for some time all absorbed in this vision [the spectacle of its faults and irregularities], and this was such a source of inward distress to it that it could think of nothing else nor make a single act of cheerfulness. Plunged into a profound melancholy, it knew not what to do with itself, for it found no place of repose: not in heaven, for there it felt that it would be out of its proper sphere; not on earth, for it deserved rather to be swallowed up therein. So, too, it seemed as though it were not permitted to appear before men or to retain the least recollection of anything which concerned its own convenience or inconvenience. It understood that of its own act it had done nothing but evil. . . . It was then in a state of profound desolation. It seemed that it could never satisfy or have recourse to God's mercy. It found nothing within it that could give it confidence. It tortured itself; unwilling wholly to give up hope, it was at the same time bowed down by the weight of despair, and recognized all the enormity of the evil which it had committed. Its heart was racked with a great agony and shaken with inner tears, while all the while it was unable to weep; it sighed in secret, consuming its life. It could neither speak, eat, sleep, smile, nor look heavenwards. It had no longer any tastes, neither of the body nor the spirit; it knew not where it was, and was like a creature that is stunned and senseless. Willingly would it have hidden itself that no one might find it, and that it might not be compelled to associate with anyone whatsoever" (*Dialogue,* Part I., chap. xi.).

211. The picture which Blessed Angela of Foligno draws of

her trials is no less terrible (chap. xix.). But, first, we should say that she had already attained to a tolerably high state of perfection. She had sold her estates and all her possessions in order to distribute the proceeds to the poor. She had enjoyed great spiritual delights, and had arrived at such a sublime sense of the Divinity of God that the Name of God, merely uttered in her presence, was sufficient to send her into an ecstasy. She had been favoured with many visions and revelations, and yet she was still on the threshold of the heroic life, when, in order that she might be more completely purified and fitted for still higher favours and a sublimer sanctity, God plunged her into the crucible of tribulation.

"My frame is racked by innumerable torments, and these are due to the action of demons, who cause them in a thousand ways. I do not think that my bodily sufferings can be described. There is not one of my members but is a prey to horrible sufferings.

"And as to the incomparably more numerous and more terrible torments of the soul, the fiends inflict them upon me almost without intermission. I can only compare myself to one who, suspended by the neck, blindfolded, with hands bound behind his back, continues thus upon the gibbet, and lives on without succour, without redress, without support. And my fate at the hands of these demons seems to me to be even more cruel and desperate; for they have hanged my soul, and even as the victim has nothing upon which to rest, so my soul hangs without any support, and all my faculties are overthrown in the sight of my spirit. When my soul sees this overthrow and abandon of all my faculties and is unable to offer any resistance, its suffering is such that by excess of grief, rage, and despair, I am almost beyond tears. And then, again, I weep helplessly. Sometimes my wrath is so great that it is all I can do not to rend myself in pieces. At times I am unable to refrain from raining upon myself blows of such violence that my head and my every limb become swollen.

"And I endure yet another torment, and this is the return,

apparently at least, of former vices. Not that my soul actually submits to their empire, but they torture me cruelly. . . .

"When I remember that God was afflicted, despised, and poor, I wish that all my sufferings were redoubled.

"And sometimes an awful and hellish darkness, in which all hope disappears,[14] envelops me, and this night is full of horror. And the vices which I feel to be dead within my soul come to life again in my body. But the demons awake them, apart from the soul, and excite others also which were never there before. I then suffer in the body especially, after a threefold manner. The fire of concupiscence is such at those times that, before I was forbidden to do so, I have burned myself with material fire in the hope of extinguishing the other thereby. Ah! sooner far would I be burned alive. I cry aloud; I call upon death— death no matter in what guise; and I say to God: 'If I am to be damned, well, then, let it be *now:* let there be no delay. Since Thou hast abandoned me, finish Thy work, and let the abyss receive me!'

"And then I understand that these vices do not touch the soul, because it never consents to them, the body only suffering violence from them. And then weariness links itself with suffering, and were this prolonged the endurance of the body would be exhausted. The soul sees itself despoiled of its powers, and though it does not consent to the evils, it lacks the strength to combat them. *It sees itself deplorably at variance with God*; it perceives its own downfall and suffers martyrdom. A vice from which I have never suffered makes itself felt, by a special permission, within me. I am dearly conscious and know

---

[14] In this state into which souls are at times plunged there is nothing of the despair of sinners. It is true that hope is no longer sensibly experienced; it seems to have disappeared, but at bottom it endures more steadfastly than ever. This is proved by the behaviour of all the souls who are tried thus. They have a dread of sin; they appeal to the Divine mercy. They press ever closer to God, as He seems to withdraw Himself. A soul in despair, however, ceases to struggle; it yields and gives itself up to evil without resistance.

that it comes by a special permission. I think that it exceeds any of the others in magnitude. The virtue by which I combat it is manifestly a gift of God, my Deliverer; and if amidst the destruction of all my beliefs, my trust in God were to fail, the realization of this gift would give me back my faith. Therein lies an assured hope and peace, and doubt is an impossibility. This force gains the day; it holds me suspended above the abyss, and vice is worsted. Such is this force and such the power which it communicates, that all men and demons and all the wiles of the world and hell are powerless to move me in the smallest degree. . . .

"Within my soul a certain humility and a certain pride are painfully at variance, and everything palls upon me. This kind of humility, which causes me to see myself as void of all goodness, virtue, or grace, which reveals to me the multitude of my sins and all the barren places in my soul, robs me of all hope and cuts me off from mercy. I see myself then as a habitation of the devil—his dupe, his child and his agent—far from all rectitude, all truth, worthy of the lowest place in the lowest hell. This wretched humility is not that other—the true—which overwhelms the soul by the realization of the Divine goodness. False humility brings all other evils in its train. Engulfed therein, I see myself surrounded with demons. In body and soul alike I perceive only defects. God is a closed book to me. His might and His grace are alike hidden from me; even the memory of my Saviour is denied to me. The conviction that I am damned does not even disquiet me. I am not concerned about my sins, which 1 would not have committed for all the good and all the evil that the world can offer. . . .

"In the abyss into which I have fallen I contemplate my superabundant iniquities. I make a futile search for some way of revealing them and making them known to the world. Would that I could go naked through the towns and open spaces with meats and fishes slung about my neck, crying out: 'Behold this wretch, so full of malice and falsehood! Behold the seed of vice! Behold the seed of evil!' I did well in men's eyes. They said: 'She abstains from both meat and fish.' Listen! I was gluttonous and a drunkard; I feigned to dispense with everything but the necessaries of life. I was playing with exterior poverty. . . . Oh, that I had around my neck a collar or a noose, whereby I might be dragged about the open places and the towns! And the children would follow me, crying out: 'See the prodigy—the prodigy which God has wrought! The malice which she so carefully concealed during her whole life she herself has now made public.'

212. "But all this is but little, and nothing makes amends; and herein is the source of a fresh, an unsuspected, despair. I have despaired absolutely with regard to God and all His goodness. It is finished, settled—settled between me and Him. I am utterly convinced that nowhere in the whole world does hell possess another victim so deserving as I am of damnation. All God's graces, all His favours, were merely to deepen my despair and my hell. Oh, of your charity, pray for me, that God's justice may make my heart manifest to all! My head is racked, my knees faint, my eyes are blind with tears, my limbs are out of joint, because I can no longer show forth all my untruth. Know, O thou that writest, that all my words are as nothing in comparison with my sins, my iniquities, and my deceits. I was quite a little child when they first began. This is what I am constrained to say in the depths of my abasement; and then pride steps in!

"I become all anger, haughtiness, chagrin, bitterness and elation. All God's good gifts become transformed into an infinite bitterness within my soul. They serve no good purpose, they remedy nothing; they only provoke me to a melancholy admiration that seems like an insult offered to my despair. Why should there always be this negation of all virtue within me? Why has God permitted it? And then I begin to doubt, and I say: Has He deceived me? This temptation obstructs and conceals all good within me. Anger, pride, grief, bitterness, elation, and woe—no words can describe it fully. Though all the sages in the world and all the Saints in Paradise were to overwhelm me with their consolations and their promises, and though God Himself should load me with His gifts, yet, did He not change my nature and begin a new work in me from the beginning, far from its doing me any good, the sages, the Saints, God Himself, would only inflame my despair, my fury, my grief, my pain and my blindness beyond all power of expression.

"Ah! could I but exchange these tortures for all worldly ills, and take all the infirmities and all the pains which the whole body of mankind are suffering; they would be lighter and less. As I have often said: would that my torments could be exchanged for martyrdom, no matter of what kind!

"My tortures began some time before the Pontificate of Pope Celestine (1294). They continued for more than two years, the paroxysms being frequent. I am not yet wholly recovered from them, although the attacks are now slight, and exterior only. Conditions having changed, I now understand that the soul, ground between false humility and pride, undergoes an infinite purgation and that I have thus acquired a true humility, without which salvation is impossible ; and the more complete the purgation of the soul, the greater the humility; the more deeply the soul is afflicted, denuded, and humbled, the more it attains to purity and an aptitude for the heights. The heights to which it now become scapable of attaining, correspond with the depths of the abyss wherein its roots and its foundations are established."

213. "O God," says St. Teresa, "how great are the sufferings, both outward and inward, which we have to endure before we can enter into the seventh mansion! It seems to me sometimes that if the soul could see them all beforehand, there would be good ground, knowing its natural weakness, to fear that it would never make up its mind to endure them, no matter how great the benefits to be derived." And then, after enumerating the various trials, the Saint adds: "So many troubles all coming together result in an interior torture, so

sensible and insupportable that I can only liken it to that which the devils themselves undergo."

214. "I am writing to you, and cannot refrain from so doing," wrote St. Jane Frances de Chantal to St. Francis of Sales, "because I feel more disgusted with myself than usual this morning. I find myself in the anguish of my spirit, wavering about everything, and this by reason of *my* inner deformity, which is so great that I assure you, my good lord and only father, that I lose myself in this gulf of misery. *God's presence, which used to afford me such unspeakable delight, now leaves me trembling in every limb and shivering with fear.* The Almighty Eye, which I adore with all the submission of my heart, seems to pierce my soul through and through and to contemplate all my works, thoughts, and words with indignation ; and this fills me with such grief of heart that death—as it seems to me—would be less hard to bear. And everything appears to have power to harm me. I am afraid of everything; I am apprehensive about everything—not that I fear any injury to myself, but that I may displease God. Alas! it is as though His succour had withdrawn itself from me. This has caused me to pass the night in great bitterness of spirit. 1 can only exclaim: 'My God! my God! alas! why hast Thou forsaken me? I am Thine; dispose of me as a thing that is wholly thine.'

"At daybreak God vouchsafed to me, although almost imperceptibly, a little ray of light in the highest, the supreme, point of my mind. The rest of my soul and its faculties had no part in it. It lasted about half the duration of the *Ave Maria,* and then my distress once more overpowered me, and all again was darkened and obscured.

"Notwithstanding the length of time that this dereliction continued, my dear Lord, I still said (only without any feeling): 'O God, do what seemeth best unto Thee. I am willing. Annihilate me; I am content. Overwhelm me; it is also my desire. Rend me, wound me, burn me, as Thou dost please; even so, I am Thine.'

"God has taught me that He does not set a high value on faith when it has been arrived at by way of the senses or feelings. This is why, in the face of all my distresses, I reject sentiment. No; I will not have it, because God is sufficient unto me. I hope in Him, notwithstanding my infinite misery. I trust that He will aid me still. In any case, His holy will be done."

215. In the Life of St. Paul of the Cross (Book II., chap, xxiv.) we read: "These lessons (humility, resignation, and faith) Father Paul practised scrupulously amidst the harassings of hell, to which were allied the persecutions of men and the ordeals of grievous ill-health.

"But all this, if the truth were told, constituted only the least part of his sufferings. His greatest affliction, and one which caused him mortal distress, was the fear that he had lost God, and would never behold Him. The Lord had withdrawn that abundance of light with which He had formerly favoured him. Paul, who for the love of God had left all, and who would have given a thousand lives to please Him, seeing now, so it appeared to him, that God's anger was kindled against him, that He had withdrawn Himself from him and was lost to him, could find neither consolation nor rest in his grief. His heart yearned after God with all its strength, but an iron hand ever seemed to be thrusting it back. . . . This is how he described his condition to his director. "Picture some poor shipwrecked man clinging to one of the planks of his vessel; each wave, each gust of wind, seems to threaten him with death. Or, again, think cf an unhappy wretch condemned to the gallows. His heart throbs agonizingly as he awaits the moment when he shall be led out to die. Such is my state."

This is why, writing to one of his religious, he says: "I am encompassed about with conflicts, but God allows no sign of this to appear outwardly. Often even in sleep (I say this to you in confidence; do not speak of it) I suffer, and I awake all trembling, I have been in this melancholy condition for years past. But all this is nothing, however, because of another cross which for a long time past has weighed me down without any consolation. I compare it to a hail-storm which ravages everything. I am like a man cast into the deeps of the sea during a storm, and to whom no one offers a plank of rescue, neither from heaven nor yet from earth. A ray of faith and hope, however, still remains with me, but so faint as to be hardly perceptible."

These quotations could be multiplied, and a very slight familiarity with the lives of holy persons will suffice to show us that these souls, whose heroism so astounds us, have not arrived at this point until grace has performed a great work in them, and they have experienced the salutary but most rigorous operations of the Holy Spirit upon their souls.

§ 7. *Of the Essential Part of Spiritual Purification and of the Varying Accessory Circumstances occurring therein.*

216. "Some Saints there are," says Father Surin, "of whom such occurrences are not related; but," he adds, "this deficiency is often atoned for by great labours undertaken for the salvation of souls, or in some other way; and, besides, biographers have but little knowledge of these things, which are of a most intimate character" *(Cat. Spir.,* vol. i., part iii., chap. iii.). This last reason seems to us to be the true explanation, for, as a rule, these experiences are kept secret by the souls who have undergone them. Those about them are under the impression that they are perfectly at peace in their minds, while all the time they are undergoing some terrible crisis.

Let us give an example taken from the life of the Venerable Fr. libermann. One day in Paris he was crossing a bridge in company with a seminarist, who was just then going through a period of great agony of mind. With all the charm of his winning manner and smile, the Father endeavoured to comfort him; but his companion, in increasing agitation, answered brusquely: "It is all very well for one who is calm and happy to talk in that way. It is easy to see by your voice and expression that you have never known these agonies, or you would not smile like that." "My dear boy," his comforter frankly replied, "I do not wish you to go through the crucible in which I have been tried. I pray God that your life may never be as burdensome as mine is to me. I scarcely ever cross a bridge that the thought does not occur to me of throwing myself into the river to end my sufferings. But the sight of my Jesus supports me and makes me patient" *(Vie,* by Cardinal Petra, chap. iv.).

The silence of their biographers on this point does not, therefore, prove that in the life of this or that Saint this purging crisis may not have occurred, for it may have been hidden from the eyes of their closest companions.

217. In these phenomena described by the mystic writers it is necessary, besides, to make a careful distinction between the *essential features*—those which are common to all chosen souls—and the *circumstances,* which vary greatly between one case and another.

The common basis, which is never absent, consists in the revelation that God makes to them with regard to His infinite greatness, the nothingness of the creature, the deformity of sin;[15] the feeling of impotence which the soul experiences, losing all its supports and finding no refuge but in the power and mercy of God; the absolute denudation, brought about either by great suffering or by the removal of all that delighted and consoled the soul.

218. I. Amongst those circumstances, which vary in each case, we will first take the time when this second process of purification is accomplished. In some instances it is early, in others later, but it is always (and the examples already given, with many more which might be added to them, prove this) when the soul is already sufficiently established in perfection.

---

[15] "Knowledge of God, knowledge of self; therein lies man's perfection. This double knowledge produces grace upon grace, light upon light, vision upon vision" (Blessed Angela of Foligno, chap. lxv.). *Noverim te, noverim me,* prayed St. Augustine.

Might it not be that the purification of the spirit is closely allied to that of the senses, so that there is no interval between them? Possibly so. But the general rule—one to which we find no exception in the lives of the Saints—is that between the two purifications there is an intermediate period, which may be extended over several years.[16]

II. The duration of the night of the spirit varies, similarly, according to the individual. Cardinal Bona[17] quotes a large number of cases of Saints who underwent terrible trials for years before attaining to the higher degrees of contemplation. But we do not believe that all these experiences belonged to the night of the spirit. Some of the instances selected by this learned writer seem to include the whole of the purifications, both sensible and spiritual, which led the soul to sanctity. Their enumeration is not, however, any the Iras instructive, for they show how the trials, which are a preparation for higher favours, may, according to the subject, have a different duration. He quotes Ubertino of Casali, who continued for fourteen years in these dire conflicts; St. Teresa, eighteen years; St. Francis of Assisi, two years (Father Surin gives it as three); Blessed Clare of Montefalco, fifteen years; St. Catharine of Bologna, five; St. Mary of Egypt, seventeen; St Mary Magdalen of Pazzi, five at first, and then sixteen more; Blessed Suzo, ten years; Father Balthazar Alvarez, sixteen years; Thomas of Jesus, over twenty years. Father Surin also cites St. Eligius, who was two years in this state. To these might be added Blessed Angela of Foligno, who, as we have already seen, was two years. St. Catharine of Genoa was more than fourteen months in the condition, her description of which we have borrowed, and after this period the bitter memory of her faults, which had hitherto clung to her day and night, was wholly removed, so that she had no more recollection of her sins than she would have had if they had been cast into the sea.[18]

---

[16] *Obscure Night,* Book II., chap. i.

[17] *Via comp., Ad Deum,* Cap. x., No. 6.

[18] Later on, the Saint, as we shall show, had to undergo another ordeal of

III. Sometimes these purgations of the spiritual faculties are continuous; at others the same phenomena only recur at intervals, and periods of consolation and sweetness succeed to times of anguish and purification.

IV. The ways which God employs for bringing home all its wretchedness and impotence to the soul, and for detaching it from itself, are also very various. With some, God resorts to visions, interior voices, etc.; with others, less startling graces, not of the miraculous order, are employed. St. Teresa describes all the soul's sufferings which are caused by uncertainty as to the paths by which God is leading it—the fear of being mistaken, its director's doubts concerning it, which redouble the poor soul's anguish, the murmurs and criticisms of its neighbours, the terrible bodily sicknesses which sometimes overpower it.

St. John of the Cross also speaks of desertion and general contempt, and that even of intimate friends, as a very common trial incident to the night of the spirit.

Speaking to St. Teresa, St. Peter of Alcantara, so noted for his passionate love of penance, says that of all other vexations the most distressing are those which we suffer at the hands of good people. This is a very common trial of the Saints. St. Teresa knew all its bitterness, and St. John of the Cross perhaps still more, while St. John Baptist de la Salle and the Blessed de Montfort were blamed and condemned by those who ought to have supported them. Nearer to our own nineteenth century, would those admirable women, the Venerable Mother Mary of St. Euphrasia Pelletier, foundress of the Central Mother House of the Good Shepherd, or Mother Javouhey, foundress of the Congregation of St. Joseph of Cluny, whom God made use of for the accomplishment of such great works—would they have attained to the heroic height of virtue to which they arrived if they had not been forced to undergo similar ordeals?

---

trial and purification, lasting ten years.

Others may not suffer in the same way, but they will experience the difficulties which have to be surmounted in all exterior works, the bitternesses of the apostolic life, and especially the extreme grief which they feel at the spectacle of the iniquities of all those souls that they long to win over for God at all costs. It was this thought which drew tears from the Curé of Ars. To see God so little loved, so shamefully and universally offended, was a bitter sorrow to him.

There is another trial of a different kind which St. Vincent de Paul had to undergo. Taken prisoner by the Turks, he remained enslaved at Tunis for many months, surrounded by barbarians and infidels, without any of the aids of religion, and his ardent zeal was reduced to a state of helpless impotence. All this helped to complete the work of denudation and heroic submission to the Divine will which had already been so well begun in him.

So the state of extraordinary helplessness to which M. Olier was reduced some time after his conversion was evidently designed to complete his detachment from self, and to bring his spirit of self-sacrifice to the point of heroism.

V. From all that we have said, this other difference also follows—that certain souls concentrate all their experiences within their hearts, so that no outward sign betrays the work of purification which is going on within them. Others, on the contrary, and especially in the case of women, are unable to conceal from those about them the extremity of anguish to which they are reduced. St. Catharine of Genoa, referring to herself, says that "she was so overwhelmed and crushed by the spectacle of her sins against God that she had more the air of a terrified wild creature than a rational being" *(Dialogue,* part i., chap. xi.).

219. *Remarks.*—Not all the sufferings that the Saints endured must, however, be attributed to that salutary crisis which St. John of the Cross calls the night of the spirit. We should be inclined to class amongst the purifications of this night, such trials only as are designed to establish the soul with

a view to leading it on to heroism. Later on, when the soul has become well grounded in sanctity and inflamed with love, the trials, though they will not disappear out of its life, will no longer have that character of anxiety and distress, that sensation of being abandoned and forsaken, which commonly distinguished them at the entry into the heroic life.

CHAPTER III

ON THE INNER DISPOSITIONS OF HEROIC SOULS

§ 1. *The Effects of Spiritual Purification.*

WE have explained the object of this dolorous crisis which St. John of the Cross calls the night of the spirit. We must now give examples of the marvellous effects which it produces.

220. *Despoliation.*—In the first place, this stripping of the soul comes very near to being absolute. St. Jane Frances de Chantal, with touching simplicity, describes the state of denudation to which she had arrived. "I am very glad," she wrote (August 9, 1619) to St. Francis of Sales, who was ill at the time, "of anything which preserves your solitude, because you will employ it for the good of your dear soul. I have not said 'our,' for I no longer seem to have any share in it, to such an extent do I find myself stripped and despoiled of all that I held most precious.

"Oh, my true Father, *to what a depth has the knife Penetrated* ! . . . I was remembering to-day how you were once telling me to practise renunciation, and I replied that I did not know what I had left to renounce. You answered: 'My child, did I not tell you that I should strip you of everything?' Oh, how easy it is to leave all that is round about us! But to part with our skin, our flesh, our bones, to penetrate even unto the marrow (which is what we have done), that, so it seems to me, is a grievous thing, difficult and impossible, but by the grace of God. To Him, then, alone be the glory, and be it rendered for ever more!"

And the holy Bishop encouraged her in this complete self-sacrifice. "Think no more of friendship, or of the unity which God has made between us, nor of your children, nor of your heart, nor of your soul, nor, in fact, of anything whatsoever, for you have given back everything to God. Reclothe yourself in Jesus Christ crucified, love Him in His sufferings, have recourse to ejaculatory prayers thereupon. What you have to do, do it, not because of your own inclinations, but purely because it is the will of God" *(Letter of August* 10, 1619).

St. Catharine of Genoa relates that, after passing through the severe ordeals of which we have spoken, "a ray of light was shed within her heart, and this ray was so burning and penetrating, so completely did it transfix her innermost soul, that it made an end of all the affections, appetites, joys and love of possessing which ever had been or might have been hers in this world" (chap. xii.).

221. *Passiveness.*—The Venerable Mary of the Incarnation repeatedly states that she had made such a complete surrender of her will to God that He had possessed Himself of it, and had, as it were, chained it to His own. "I cannot say whether it would be possible for the soul, thus taken possession of, to escape from its sufferings, for it seems as if it then had no power of action or even of volition, no more than if it had no free will. Love appears to have possessed itself of everything when the gift was made to it through the acquiescence of the superior part of the spirit" *(Vie,* by C. Martin, chap, xxviii., p. 154). "The soul learns in what true poverty of spirit consists, being able to will only what the Divine will wills within it" *(Lettres,* cii., p. 237).

This taking possession of the human will by God, which is not, however, continuous, does not in any wise destroy liberty or detract from merit, because it has been earnestly desired and continues to be joyfully accepted. It manifests itself especially in the time of prayer. "In my prayers," wrote the Venerable Mary again to her son, "I speak to God according as He moves me. If I am drawn to consider His greatness and my own nothingness, my soul speaks to Him in conformity with this. If it should be of His sweetness, how He is love itself, I speak as to my Bridegroom, and it is not in my power to do otherwise. . . . At other times I am, as it were, crucified; my soul contemplates God, who, however, seems to take pleasure in holding me captive. I long to embrace Him, and to be with Him after my customary manner, but He holds me bound. In my bonds I see that He loves me, but none the less I am unable to embrace Him. And what a torment this is! But my soul acquiesces, however, because it is impossible that I should desire any condition other than that which His Divine Majesty chooses for me."[1]

222. *Peace.*—This great despoliation and this annihilation of the will are accompanied by a profound peace. Let us take St. Jane Frances de Chantal's testimony again.

"My spirit feels free, and *tastes a deep and infinite consolution at finding itself thus in God's hands.* It is true that the rest of my being continues, as it were, in a state of bewilderment, but in following out your directions, my only father (as with God's help I shall doubtless succeed in doing), things will go on improving." And in another note of the same date she again says : "I have not said that I have but little light or inward consolation ; I am merely quite at peace" (August 9, 1619).

"When God," says Father Surin, "has brought the soul through labours or by the dark defiles of the mountains, and

---

[1] Even in this sublime state of prayer distractions are possible, but they are slight. The Ven. Mary, in fact, says: "As nothing material is to be found in this inner preoccupation, my imagination torments me at times with trifles, which, having no foundation, vanish as they have come" *(Letter* cxxxii,, pp. 301, 302).

begins to show it the lights of the sublime country of its love, He causes an abundant peace to overflow upon it as a mighty river. *Declinabo super eam quasi fluvium pacis* (Isa. ixvi. 12), Torrents of peace. Not a calm merely, like the stillness of the sea or the quiet flow of great rivers, but this peace and this Divine repose inundate the soul like torrents, so that it experiences, as it were, actual floods of peace after the past storms" *(Amour de Dieu,* iii. 2).

223. *Humility.*—Another fruit of this deep purification is a truly heroic humility.

"The extreme love from which the soul suffers causes it to feel with bitter regret how little its works correspond with its aspirations; for it longs, and would find it sweet, to die a thousand times for God. It looks on itself as a useless being, whose whole life is sterile. And there is also another admirable result of humility. Love first reveals to it all its debt to God, and then causes it to understand the defects and imperfections of its works for Him, so that it regards itself as the vilest of creatures" *(Obscure Night,* ii, 19).

"If, when in this state of mind, anyone attempts to praise it, the effect upon it is that of a stupid jest" (Blessed Angela of Foligno, chap. liv.).

"Seeing clearly, then, that if it possesses any virtue at all it has received it from God, and no wise as a result of its own actions, it suffers, more especially at first, intolerable anguish upon hearing itself praised" (St. Teresa, *Sixth Mansion,* chap. i.).

One of the principal results, therefore, of these purgative trials is to lead the soul to realize its wretchedness, or, rather, it is the light of self-knowledge communicated to it by God which produces in it these purificatory pains.

"On one occasion," says Blessed Margaret Mary, "having given way to some movement of vanity when speaking of myself, oh the tears and lamentations which this fault caused me! For when we were alone He called me to account thus with a severe countenance: 'Oh, thou dust and ashes, what hast thou wherewith to glorify thyself, since thou hast naught of thine own but nothingness and misery, which thou shouldst ever bear in mind, nor depart from out of the abyss of thy nothingness. And lest the magnitude of My gifts should make thee misconstrue and forget what thou art, I am about to reveal thy likeness to thine eyes.'

"And then, immediately unveiling this horrible picture, He showed me an epitome of all that I am, which so amazed me and filled me with such a horror of myself, that if He had not upheld me I should have fainted with grief, not being able to understand the superabundance of goodness and mercy which had abstained from already plunging me into the abyss of hell, but had continued to bear with me, seeing that I could not endure myself. This was the torture with which He punished the least stirrings of vain complacency in me, so that I was obliged sometimes to say to Him: 'Oh, Lord, either let me die or hide that picture from my eyes, because I cannot see it and live,' For it aroused in me unbearable agonies of hatred and self-vengeance; and as obedience did not allow of my executing upon myself the severities to which these feelings prompted me, my sufferings were indescribable."

And then these great servants of God are so profoundly convinced of their abjectness, that God's most marvellous gifts do not inspire them with any vain complacency. We see them performing the most wonderful acts, working miracles, and still preserving their humility.

Blessed Angela of Foligno is a good example of this profound humility of the Saints. "Our Lord said to me: 'Oh, My beloved, My spouse! . . . I will accomplish great things in thee in the sight of the nations. I will be known in thee, glorified, manifested in thee. The name that I bear in thee shall be adored before all nations.' He added many other things also.

"But I, while I listened, remembering all my sins and defects, said within myself: 'Thou art not worthy of this great love.' Doubt laid hold of me, and my soul spoke thus to Him who addressed me: 'If Thou wert the Holy Spirit, Thou wouldst not utter these unsuitable words, for I am weak and liable to pride.' He answered: 'Try, then—try to draw vanity from My words. Make the effort. Try; strive to think of something else.' I strove with my whole strength to conjure up a feeling of pride, but all my sins crowded into my memory, and 1 felt an access of humility such as I had never before in all my life experienced"[2] *(The Visions and Instruction,* chap. xx.).

224. *The Power of Love.*—In these humble and denuded souls the Divine love has not failed to assume unexampled proportions. The acts of charity which they produce are far more intense and meritorious than those of the perfect souls themselves. "When God leads a soul into this mystic night," says Father Lallemant, "He enlarges the understanding and the will, making them capable of producing acts of a high perfection."

According to St. Thomas and numberless other theologians, the good angels have merited eternal beatitude by a single act of love and submission to God, even as the wicked have deserved hell by a single act of sin. Their merits, however, are very diverse, the angels of the first choir, the Seraphim, being enormously superior in merit and glory to those of the lowest choirs. It is further believed, and it is the general opinion, that the elect in their entry into their true country will have their portion in the hierarchy of the blessed amongst the angels with whose merits theirs have corresponded, the holiest only attaining to the higher choirs.

It would follow, therefore, that the angels of the superior degrees, the Cherubim and the Seraphim, would have been able to produce as much love in one single act as the perfect man could do in the whole course of a life of heroism and sanctity.

---

[2] Humility is truth. We see from all that has been said how they deceive themselves who take the humility of the Saints for madness. Madness has its home in pride. Humility is the true wisdom; it is the perfect knowledge of God and of ourselves.

Who would question God's power to create beings who in one single act gain as much merit as others in a million acts?

The difference amongst men could never, of course, be as great as in the angelic world; men have all the same nature, whereas the angels of the various choirs are specifically different. But very great varieties may exist even amongst men. Some penetrate much more deeply than others into the meanings of Divine things, and devote themselves with more intensity of will and energy to the love of supernatural truths, and more especially to the love of God Himself.

225. It is this growth of the spiritual faculties which Father Lallemant desires to express in the words just quoted. Blessed Angela of Foligno had said it before him. "When the Lord unveils His face He *expands the soul,* and into *this suddenly enlarged capacity* He pours unknown joys and treasures. . . . I see," she says later on, "how, since the days gone by, the Lord has *increased my capacity for knowing Him*" (chap, xxvii.).

"Amid the dark shadows," says Father Surin on his side, "into which this state of affliction plunges them, a great light shines in the soul, and in virtue of this light, and by the power of its resultant grace, these persons *perceive the truth of the faith* and the things of the spirit *more clearly* than ever before, having a knowledge of the inner condition of their souls and all their defects, everything being made plain to them. Thus, when the daylight breaks in upon the night, objects scarcely perceptible before become distinctly visible." Then, a little further on, he says again: "God pours into these souls treasures of wisdom and knowledge, very exalted perceptions of Divine things, an abundance of counsels and of lights, as much for themselves as for others. First, they realize the mysteries of religion in such a lofty and special manner that they seem to penetrate into them profoundly, although still falling short of their actual grandeur. And this by such a sublime illumination that, without exaggeration, it may be said that their conceptions concerning the mysteries of the Incarnation and the Passion, the communication of graces and of all that relates to the economy of Christianity generally, are so high that there is no more proportion between their knowledge and what is commonly known by theology and science than there is between the knowledge of children and that of philosophers in natural things. . . ."

As to the graces of the will vouchsafed to these souls, they consist in loving communications with the celestial Bridegroom such as cannot be uttered. For they know the *inconceivable ardours,* joys, and caresses of this same Bridegroom, *surpassing all that our imagination can depict or humanity bear up under, which, indeed, of itself could not endure* did not God Himself sustain them. This is why it is said, *Quae est ista quae procedit deliciis affluens, innixa super Dilectum?*

"But of such graces it is better to be silent than to speak. Suffice it to say that they consist generally in a perpetual application of the soul to God, and a reciprocal interchange of benefits conferred and homage rendered. So that the soul's experience of these supernatural joys leads it to prefer one moment of this converse with God to all earthly delights, and to all that God is capable of creating and giving outside this way of conversation" *(Cat. Spir.,* vol. i., part iv., chap. vii.).

§ 2. *On the Favours which are granted to such Souls as have undergone the Rigorous Purification of the Spirit.*

226. It is impossible, therefore, to describe the degree of faith and love to which those souls are raised after passing through this bitter purgation—impossible, even, to understand how a single act of charity on their part outweighs in value and merit many of our own, no matter how great the disinterestedness and perfection which we strive to put into them.

227. The spiritual joys and delights which God causes them to experience do not fail to lift them above the level of ordinary Christians. They themselves can only say: "These experiences

which bring so much knowledge to the understanding have no words worthy of them. It is as if a traveller who, coming from the East, where he had eaten of the fruits of those countries, might in no wise be able to explain in what way they differed from other fruits, however definite his knowledge of them might be, because there are no words suitable for the purpose. Even so any* one wishing to describe the difference between the muscat grape, the apricot, and the melon, would find it very difficult, and would be unable to do so without gestures or some expression of admiration, although inwardly his knowledge of these fruits, whereby he distinguishes one from another, should be very extensive. So in supernatural things the sentiments and knowledge that we possess of them are so different that no words can be found to explain them : *Non licet homini loqui*" (Surin, *loc. cit,*).

This is especially striking in the book of *The Visions and Instructions of Blessed Angela of Foligno.* She is striving to describe the joys and delights which God vouchsafed to her, and she can only find words like the following, which constantly recur: "And this joy is unspeakable, and quite different from all joys of which I have already spoken." Then she waxes indignant with herself for the weakness of these expressions, which are so far removed from the reality. Let us quote some passages of her writings:

"When the soul is taken out of itself, illuminated by the presence of God, when God and the soul have met within each other's breasts, it knows, it rejoices, it reposes in the Divine joys which it cannot describe. They annihilate all speech and all conception." Later on she says again: "Often my soul is caught up into God, unto such overpowering joys that their continuance would lie insupportable to the body, which would straightway forsake its senses and its members. . . . Delectation, pleasure, joy, all succeed without resembling one another. Oh, do not compel me to speak further. I do not speak, I blaspheme; and if I open my mouth, instead of making God manifest, I shall betray Him."

The difficulty experienced by those who have known these delectable emotions when they attempt to describe them shows how far they surpass all imagination. This is the explication of St. Ignatius's saying "that the written biographies of the Saints do not relate the highest things in their lives, and that what he himself had received from God surpassed all that he found recorded in their histories" (Surin, *loc. cil.*).

228. The favours which God accords to these souls may not, as we have already said, be outside the order of faith; they are then admirable and sublime without being miraculous. They may, on the other hand, be invested with such a character of the strange and marvellous as to be truly miracles. Such are ecstasies, flights of the spirit, revelations, visions, etc. We find them described by St. Teresa (*Sixth Mansion,* chap. iii. *et seq.)* and by St. John of the Cross *(Spiritual Canticle,* stanza 13), etc.

Of these latter gifts we will only say that, in our opinion, a very large number of heroic souls are favoured with them. These souls have become so dear to God that He uses the most tender familiarity with regard to them. He admits them as a matter of course, as it were, to a knowledge of His secrets and to the privilege of Divine communications. And yet only a very small proportion of them are known, for the humility of these servants of God causes them to guard the secret of the King of Kings. If the Blessed Curé of Ars had not been constrained for the good of souls to make known the truly miraculous gifts which enabled him to penetrate into the secrets of the heart, and by which he often knew the faults of his penitents better than they knew them themselves, who would have been aware that God had accorded such high favours to him?

229. But none the less, as St. John of the Cross says, before enumerating the various favours vouchsafed to these betrothed souls—for the Saint calls the state which we have just described the spiritual betrothal—"we are not to suppose that all souls thus far advanced receive all that is here described, either in the same way or in some degree of knowledge and of consciousness. Some souls receive more, others less; some in

one way, some in another; and yet all may be in the state of spiritual betrothal" *(Spiritual Canticle,* stanza iv.).

But however this may be, we will conclude the matter by quoting St. John of the Cross's summing-up of the marvellous blessings which God vouchsafes in a greater or less degree to these perfect souls: "In this Divine union the soul has a vision and foretaste of abundant and inestimable riches, and finds there all the repose and refreshment it desired; it attains to the secrets of God, and to a strange knowledge of Him which is the food of those who know Him most; it is conscious of the awful power of God beyond all other power and might, tastes of the wonderful sweetness and delight of the spirit, finds its true rest and Divine light, drinks deeply of the wisdom of God, which shines forth in the harmony of the creatures and works of God[3] it feels itself filled with all good, emptied and delivered from all evil, and, above all, rejoices consciously in the inestimable banquet of love which confirms it in love" *(ibid.,* stanza xiv., xv., p. 244).

230. Some writers have attempted a methodical classification of the Divine favours which God vouchsafes to these chosen souls and to give the order of their sequence. To our minds this is an impossible task; and more, it would be a manifest error to pretend to establish a regular and systematic order in phenomena, whether miraculous or not, which follow one another in this state. Transports, Divine contacts, the melting or flowing away of the soul into God, agonies of love, languors of love, wounds of love, ecstasies, raptures, flights of the soul, visions of the imagination, intellectual visions,

---

[3] These revelations, which afford it much delight, revealing to it God's wisdom through His works, cause it also acute sufferings when it sees creatures turning away from the Divine scheme and not giving to God, who is so great and so good, the glory which they owe to Him. Hence its distress at the sight of the wrongdoing of sinners, and also of its own wretchedness and powerlessness to glorify God in accordance with His merits.

apparitions of Our Blessed Lord, revelations, etc.—all these graces are susceptible of a thousand different combinations. In one case they may all occur in the same subject, while another may experience a few only; they may also intermingle in very various fashions.

"In the order of grace," wrote Father Libermann, "there are many things which work together, and which consequently prevent us from tracing up the plan and sequence which occur in God's operations, because we are not always cognizant of all the things which combine together, nor of their several degrees. These things are—(i) The eternal predestination of God as regards each soul, both as to its degree of glory and its degree of grace. (2) Man's malice (the degree, I mean, of the malice), opposing itself to this grace. (3) The human will, with its various predilections and affections, which respond more or less to this Divine grace. (4) The character, the temperament, and the inner dispositions of the individual, whereby the actions of grace are largely modified. (5) The external circumstances of the subject's environment. All these have a great influence upon souls and bring about innumerable variations in their interior condition. . . . Arrived at contemplation, the soul passes through different stages, for the prayer perfects itself as the soul progresses, but that any order and regular sequence is followed I do not believe. This depends solely upon the perfection with which it goes forward, combined with God's designs upon each. Beware of writers who want to know and regulate everything" (Libermann, *Letter of August* 9, 1842).

Father Lallemant is of the same opinion: "In God's various dealings with the soul, in His gifts and visitations, there is no certain and defined rule, so that one can say, 'After this manifestation, for instance, such another one will follow.' "

St. Teresa gives this same advice, and says "that the sequence in which she sets down the favours that she received from God concern her case only, and merely specify what she herself has experienced."

§ 3. *The Slight Imperfections of Heroic Souls.*

231. Does it not seem as though nothing were lacking in the heroic souls, and that they have attained to as high a state of perfection as is possible here below? But when we come to treat of the seventh degree we shall see that there is a yet higher state of sanctity. The imperfections of these souls are very small and difficult to detect; in the eyes of the all-holy God, however, something is still wanting for their perfection.

Thus, they may perhaps consent to gratify certain almost imperceptible natural inclinations, preferring one thing to another; they will cling, however slightly, to some spiritual[4] consolations, or in their relations with their neighbours they will be actuated occasionally by a too human compliance.

"I rejoice, Lord," said Suzo, in his *Colloquy of the Nine Rocks,* "to perceive the perfection of the inhabitants of this rock" (the eighth); "these at least must be united to their end.

"*Jesus Christ.* You are mistaken, Henry. It is true that God loads them with marvellous graces. Angels reveal Divine things unto them under forms and sensible images. Their souls are adorned with admirable virtues, and they approach the perfect union more nearly than any of the others; but they have not yet attained to the summit of the mountain and to the last degree of perfection.

"*Henry.* How is it that they are not yet in possession of the Divine union, and that they have such difficulty in arriving at their end and reaching the mountain-top?

"*Jesus Christ.* There are two obstacles, wherein are the enemy's most perfect snares. The first is that when they receive the Divine illumination they attach themselves to it ardently, and desire to depart from the rock in order to soar higher. This is an imperfection which to a certain extent retards their attainment to the perfect union. They are unaware of this

---

[4] *Cf. Spiritual Canticle,* stanzas xxvi. and xxviii.

hidden defect of the will, and because they have not entirely eradicated even the desire for Divine consolation from their hearts, they cannot advance further. The second obstacle is that they unconsciously take delight in the extraordinary ways by which God leads them, and in the celestial secrets which He makes known to them by means of visions and ecstasies. God perceives this defect, but as He knows how difficult it is to overthrow nature, He pardons them, and maintains them in this same degree of sanctity and grace."

"It seemed to me," said St. Veronica Juliani, "that Our Lord shed a special light upon the faults which I commit daily. He rebuked me on account of certain idle words and many useless thoughts, also for not having done everything only for the sake of pure love, but having mingled a little self-love in my undertakings" (*Diary,* May i, 1694).

232. These, doubtless, are slight blemishes, since the souls themselves, whose love is all the time so delicate and perspicacious, scarcely perceive them. But it is nevertheless true that the sensible part is not wholly conquered within them, nor is their nature entirely overcome. The devil therefore succeeds in harming them to a certain extent, and, at any rate, he brings all his animosity to bear upon them.

"The devil," says St. John of the Cross, "beholding this prosperity of the soul, and in his great malice envying all the good he sees in it, now uses all his power, and has recourse to all his devices, in order to thwart it, if possible, even in the slightest degree. He thinks it of more consequence to keep back the soul, even for an instant, from this abundance, bliss, and delight, than to make others fall into many and mortal sins. Other souls have little or nothing to lose, while this soul has much, having gained many and great treasures; for the loss of one grain of refined gold is greater than the loss of many of the baser metals" (*Spiritual Canticle,* stanza xvi., pp. 261, 262).

§ 4. *The Merit and Sanctity of these Chosen Souls.*

233. In spite of these slight blemishes, imperceptible to mortal eyes, the perfect soul leads a wonderful existence. It courageously undertakes the most burdensome and arduous works; it bears the severest trials calmly. Thanks to the sublime strength communicated to it by the Holy Spirit and to its trust in God, which its purification, faithfully borne, has still further strengthened, these trials no longer cause it the same anguish, the same cruel doubts. They no longer deserve the name of suffering, St. Teresa tells us, because the soul, while undergoing them, knows them to be high favours from God, of which it is not worthy *(Sixth Mansion,* chap, i.).

What must not be the sum of merit amassed by hearts thus disposed! How dear must they not be to God! The more we reflect on the power of their intercession (which is as the measure of their holiness), the more we understand the words which Our Lord spoke to Suzo: "If the Church possessed many of these great servants of God, the affairs of Christendom would go much better than they do now."

§ 5. *The Direction of these Souls.*

234. Arrived at this point of the spiritual life, the soul is evidently under the constant influence of grace and the continual direction, so to speak, of the Holy Spirit. The rôle of the spiritual father should therefore be confined to making the soul follow this Divine direction and preventing its going aside from it. There is no longer any need for exhortations, suggestions, or the imposing of new practices; but rather for surveillance and for giving an exterior recognition to inspirations of grace, supplying to its actions the merit of obedience and preserving the soul from imprudent flights.

And what a delicate task is this! In the case of certain souls practising the heroic virtues, natural activity still mingles its impulses with the motions of grace, and may lead to ill-considered sacrifices and harmful austerities. But also, and more frequently, the Lord, who directs these souls, has designs very different from the designs of man, and we should be grossly mistaken in desiring to submit all their actions to the inadequate tribunal of human wisdom. A director condemning some enterprise, even one which is apparently unreasonable, in a saintly soul might be thwarting God's work. This would have been the case with anyone wishing to prevent St. Teresa from undertaking her reforms, or Blessed Margaret Mary from propagating the devotion of the Sacred Heart. So God at times requires extraordinary and seemingly imprudent mortifications from generous souls. The Blessed J. B. Vianney's fasts were certainly absolutely contrary to the rules of human wisdom. If a director had wished to arrest him in this path, he would undoubtedly have been in opposition to the designs of God, and would have injured the sanctity of his penitent.

235. The art of direction is the most noble, but also the most delicate, of all arts—*ars artium regimen animarum*— and he who is called to exercise it should pray ceaselessly to Our Lord for the necessary illumination. But if this duty of prayer is imposed upon every director, even were he to have none but ordinary souls to guide, it becomes all the more imperative when the souls confided to his care are far advanced in perfection.

To direct an elect soul, called by God to the practice of the heroic virtues, is a heavy responsibility. He who has received it should redouble his efforts in the work of his own sanctification, applying himself to the practice of absolute renunciation and Divine love in all its perfection. In fact, the more perfect his own dispositions, the better will he understand the inner dispositions of perfect souls and God's dealings with them. Those who are not themselves fervent, however learned they may be, cannot understand what takes place in the hearts of tire Saints, and their entire inexperience of the mystical operations of grace renders their task of direction much more difficult.

For the rest, God takes more readily as the interpreters of His will those who are the most loving and the most holy. He enlightens them, He inspires them, He finds in them docile instruments. Negligent or imperfect hearts, on the contrary, present many obstacles to the lights which He wishes to communicate.

236. When a director has under his care a soul which appears to him to be heroic, he should first satisfy himself that it has really attained to this degree; for God has great designs upon these holy souls, and the director should further them. The true sign will be the superhuman practice of the virtues. First, humility. The spiritual father has the right to prove his penitents. When he has occasion to do so, he may rebuke them severely, even roughly, rebuffing them and ignoring their words, acts, and persons. This should be but rarely, however, and not as his ordinary habit, for must he not remember that he represents Our Lord; and if the Divine Master put the faith of the Canaanite woman to the test, if one day He called St. Peter "Satan," He was none the less in His habitual conduct full of kindness and goodness to all. Still more, the director must not, under pretence of trying the generous soul, drive it out of the path into which God is calling it.

Two other virtues must also serve as a criterion— fidelity to the duties of its position, and charity towards its neighbour. Even when certain virtues appear to be in excess of the ordinary forces of humanity, if the others— particularly charity and faithful devotion to the duties of its state—are not also cherished and practised to perfection, heroism must not be assumed to be present.

237. Heroic souls still require to watch over their temperament, which has not yet lost all its influence. If naturally ardent, they are inclined to bring to their enterprises and their thirst for sacrifice a certain overhuman zeal, and they must be checked. If naturally inclined to melancholy, it will not

do to attribute solely to humility all their anxieties, their desire to examine themselves incessantly, their fears of not acting for God alone, or of spoiling the Divine work by their co-operation, and they must be taken to task for their distresses, and urged on to an entire abandonment and a saintly boldness.

However, the director has only to assist the work of grace, which in these chosen souls operates incessantly towards the destruction of any remains of the natural defects. The Spirit of God, by His secret admonitions, teaches them to know what is still defective in their conduct, and the avowals which they readily make enlighten their directors.

BOOK VII

SEVENTH DEGREE—GREAT SAINTS

PROLOGUE

238. "Now raise the eyes of thy soul and scan the summit of the mountain," said Jesus Christ to Suzo.

Then he perceived the last rock, which was of such a height that the eye could scarcely attain to it, and suddenly found himself caught up and set down among the heavenly inhabitants of this enchanting region. He noticed several amongst them who were striving to climb up to it from the eighth rock, but nearly all soon relinquished the attempt, and two or three only succeeded.

We now desire to make known to our readers this ninth rock, which was thus shown to Blessed Suzo. From the standpoint of our spiritual poverty, how dare we cast our eyes so high, and attempt to unveil the marvels of this supreme abode of sanctity! Had we our own light alone upon which to rely, the essay would be more than rash, it would be madness; but here, again, we confine ourselves to reproducing the teachings of the Saints who have experienced these Divine favours, well content if we have understood them aright, and are able to transmit their doctrines accurately.

Let not the reader be astonished if he encounter certain sayings of the Saints, certain expressions which may strike him as forced, or comparisons (such as that of marriage as a symbol of the intimate union between God and the soul) which at first sight may seem strange to him. Human speech is powerless for the purpose of showing the marvels of God's love for His faithful creature and that of this creature for its God. Words and analogies can but imperfectly shadow forth the sublime truths which it is sought to convey. But these expressions and symbols are sanctioned by the example of Holy Scripture, notably in the Canticle of Canticles, and the holy Doctors cannot be blamed for having employed them.

CHAPTER I

THE WAY LEADING FROM HEROISM TO PERFECT SANCTITY

§1. *The End which is to be attained—The Transforming Union.*

239. WE have already explained the state of union, and have shown that it consists in a habitual identity of will between the soul and God. But the holy writers describe another and a much more perfect species of union—the transforming union, or the transformation of love. "Love," said St. John of the Cross, "arrives at its full perfection only when the lovers are so closely united that each is transformed into the other" *(Spiritual Canticle,* stanza ii.).

The inferior union is effected by way of the will, which forms itself in the habitual disposition of desiring only what God desires. But there will be more than this in the transforming union. The Divine action takes possession of the soul in its innermost being, in its most secret centre, by a more particular cohabitation of God within it; this great God making it more like unto Himself, vouchsafing unto it a more perfect communication of His Divine perfections— in a word, deifying it after a more complete and marvellous fashion than in the preceding states.

The transforming union, which, in fact, is merely sanctifying grace in its highest degree, seems to absorb, or rather to "penetrate without destroying them, all the soul's energies; and then all—or, at least, nearly all—this soul's works are wonderfully supernaturalized, and its entire life is, as it were, made Divine.

"The nature of the two spouses (God and the soul) is different, it is true, but the supernatural beauty of their physiognomy and the glory with which they shine seem to identify them so completely one with the other that it is as though a transformation of the soul into God, and of God into the soul, were effected" (*Spiritual Canticle,* stanza xxxi.).

Blessed Angela of Foligno also says: "The third degree is the fullness of perfection and the transformation of the soul into God. The elect of this third degree seem to me to be transformed into God, so that in them I no longer see anything but Jesus, now suffering, now glorified; it is as though He had transubstantiated them and engulfed them in His depths" (chap, xlvii.).

§ 2. The Length of the Way leading to this Supreme Degree of Perfection.

240. During the course of this work we have already constantly pointed out how the various halting-places of the spiritual life are separated one from another by long stretches of unremitting and generous efforts. The higher we climb upon the mystic ladder, the farther apart are the steps and the greater is the difficulty in surmounting them. Many are the works of piety which must be accomplished before we can become pious; and then what endeavours, and how much time must elapse before we pass from ordinary piety to fervour, and from fervour to the state of perfection! By what struggles, by what a course of generous self-sacrifice and quite exceptional trials, must the perfect soul advance to heroism! Finally, what heroic actions must be performed before heroism has become a habitual condition and an ordinary disposition!

Having once attained to this degree, the soul travels on with giant strides in the paths of sanctity. God endows it with the most precious and sanctifying graces; its life abounds in admirable works, its daily progress is marvellous, and we can scarcely form an idea of the sum of merits and graces which it incessantly acquires.

And yet in the lives of the Saints we find that long years often pass thus before they are raised to that culminating point of perfection which is called the transforming union.

241. St. Teresa was about forty years old at the date of the termination of the bitter agonies of the purification of the spirit, in the course of which, by her fidelity and unshaken constancy, she had formed herself in heroism. The years which followed were an uninterrupted series of holy works, sublime fervours, of labours and trials, which enormously increased her merit. At forty a seraph appeared to her, and transfixed her heart with a flarning dart, signifying the burning ardour of her love. At forty-five she made the vow of perfection. Then she undertook the reform of her Order and that of the Carmelite Friars; she established numberless foundations. She was already a Saint of rare sanctity, and yet it was not until she had reached the age of fifty-seven that she was raised to the dignity of a spouse of Jesus Christ, and brought to that degree of the mystic life which she describes in the *Seventh Mansion.*

242. St. Catharine of Genoa, after passing through the experiences that we have described, and that brought her to such a profound pitch of humility and such vigorous self-hatred, gave herself up to the practice of the virtues, especially that of charity towards the sick, mortifying herself after a most heroic fashion. Her first probation was only of fourteen months' duration, but her laborious works and incessant penances stood in the stead of those inward trials which, in the case of other Saints, carried on and completed the work of spiritual purification, "I have known and made trial of the two ways," she says *(Dialogues,* part 1, chap, xx.), "and however great and horrible the sufferings which I encountered" (caring for sick persons who were filthy and covered with vermin, whom she tended with superhuman devotion—chap, xix.), "I

think I would rather live with them than under the attack of the Divine ray" (revealing her faults to her). She persevered for three years in these heroic acts,[1] without any inner consolation. "At the end of the time," says her biographer, "no vestige of her natural appetites remained. She had become so established in the habits of virtue that the practice of perfection seemed to have no difficulties for her, and she was free from all temptations" *(Life and Doctrine of St. Catharine of Genoa,* chap. v.). She was then about one-and-thirty.

But she had not yet attained to the degree of sanctity for which God destined her, so that He caused her to undergo a new and still more woeful purification (*Dialogue,* part ii., chap. x.). Her body was afflicted with terrible physical sufferings; without God's special aid "human nature could never have survived these martyrdoms, which were so many and so severe as to be indescribable in ordinary language, and which, if told, would not be understood, not even if actually witnessed. The inward martyrdom was infinitely greater than the exterior one, and nobody knew by what means or in what manner to apply a remedy. Sometimes for several days God gave her rest from the bodily sufferings, and she would continue free from pain and apparently well, although the inner oppression was always increasing. She would then go to and fro in the house, consumed with distress, while no one understood what she was enduring, so subtle, hidden and penetrating was the Divine action. . . . She continued for *ten years* in this condition, her knowledge and consciousness of these secret operations by which God held her bound to Him diminishing daily."

At the conclusion of this fresh purification the Saint was about forty-one or forty-two years of age. What the sublimity

---

[1] It was at this time that she repeatedly performed that act of mortification which is to be found in the lives of many of the Saints —St. Elisabeth, Blessed Angela of Foligno, Blessed Margaret Mary, etc.—swallowing unclean things and vermin the better to overcome the repugnances of her nature.

of her sanctity could have been during the remaining eighteen or twenty years of her life it is impossible to imagine, but we have no doubt that she was thenceforward established upon the last step of the mystic ladder which writers call the transforming union. She tells us that "towards the close of this purifying operation God at times revealed to her a ray of the glory to which she was drawing near, because the affections of the soul and the bodily sensations were consumed. . . . She then perceived that God held the spirit so wholly fixed and rooted in Himself that He did not allow it to turn aside for a single instant" (part ii., chap. xi.). This was the commencement of the perfect union which was the Saint's condition until the end of her life.

243. The period of heroic labours which precedes the perfect union is not always so prolonged as was the case with these two great souls; for other Saints, snatched away early from this world, like St. Catharine of Siena or St. Aloysius Gonzaga, who died still younger, were also raised to these supreme heights of perfection. God can make other graces supply the place of these long years of labours. He can also increase the capacity for love in those whom He intends to leave for a shorter time in the world, and can make up for brevity by intensity. The way may also be curtailed for another reason—namely, that *the transforming union is,* as we shall explain, *susceptible of very various degrees;* so that a shorter and less rigorous preparation may suffice for a transforming union of a less exalted kind.

But whether it be brief or of long duration, a preparation is necessary, for many are the steps which must be taken before these heights are attained. St. Teresa and St. Catharine of Genoa have given us an account of their own spiritual journeyings, and yet they have not been able to lay bare to us more than a small fraction of their inner lives. And then think of all those other and no less wonderful operations which take place in the hearts of Saints whose exterior lives alone are known to us. What went on in the heart of St. Martin, St.

Benedict, St, Bernard, St. Dominic, St. Francis of Assisi, St. Antony of Padua, St. Ignatius, St. Francis of Sales, etc.? How did they reach those heights of sanctity that astonished the world? These are some of the impenetrable secrets the revealing of which will not be amongst the least of the joys of Paradise. In spite of our great unfitness to describe the phenomena whereby the ascent of the holy soul to perfection is effected, we will attempt a few words on the subject. But these operations of God are so sweet, so Divine, that even our stammering utterances will, we trust, in spite of their incompleteness, afford interest and edification.

§ 3. *The Purification of Love.*

244. Before going further, let us, with St. John of the Cross, call to mind a point of great importance.

"In the state of the spiritual betrothal—the sixth degree — the soul does not *fully* enjoy the delights of the repose belonging to its condition, in which, however, the Well-beloved communicates to His spouse all that it is possible to bestow during this life; but the superior part of the soul alone experiences these favours, for until it has attained to the spiritual marriage the sensitive part still suffers pain, and cannot wholly vanquish nature."[2]

Thus, in the sixth degree, in spite of the high perfection of the soul, the sensitive part has, as yet, no share in the Divine union, and while the superior part receives the favours of the Divine Bridegroom, it, on the contrary, suffers from not being freed from its natural tendencies, with their anguishes and griefs.

245. In order to dissipate this remnant of human infirmity as far as is possible here below, God has recourse to those anxieties of love, which are often of terrible intensity in this

---

[2] *Spiritual Canticle,* stanza xiii. ; *cf.* stanza xviii. St. Teresa makes a similar remark *(Seventh Mansion,* chap, i.).

state. In fact, the consciousness of the Divine presence is far from being constant, the soul experiencing it at intervals only. God draws near, then again hides Himself, in order to return and then withdraw Himself once more. "This alternation of visits and absences is doubtless a device of a love which has no other aim than that of leading these souls to the highest possiblestate of perfection" *(Dialogue of St. Catharine of Siena,* chap, lxxviii.), but it is none the less painful to the heart which is so athirst for the Divine union.

"We must keep in mind that the absence of the Beloved, from which the soul suffers in a state of spiritual betrothal, is an exceeding great affliction, and at times greater than all other trials whatever. The reason is this: the love of the soul for God is now so vehement and deep that the pain of His absence is vehement and deep also. This pain is increased also by the annoyance which comes from intercourse with creatures, which is very great; for the soul, under the pressure of its quickened desire of union with God, finds all other conversation most painful and difficult to endure. It is like a stone in its flight to the place whither it is rapidly tending: every obstacle it meets with occasions a violent shock. And as the soul has tasted of the sweetness of the Beloved's visits, which are now more desirable than gold and all that is beautiful, it therefore dreads even a momentary absence" (*Spiritual Canticle,* stanza xvii., pp. 267, 268).

246. St. Teresa enters still more fully into this anguish of the betrothed soul, and her descriptions are truly terrible (*Sixth Mansion,* chap. xi.).

"In proportion as her knowledge of God's attributes grows, while she sees herself still so far from Him, her desire of Him grows even stronger and stronger. Her devotion is more fervent as she learns more fully how this great God and Sovereign deserves to be loved; as, year by year, her yearning after Him gradually becomes keener, she experiences the bitter suffering I am about to describe. . . . These longings, tears, sighs, and violent and impetuous desires and strong feelings, are yet as nothing compared with what I am about to write of; for these seem but like a smouldering fire, the heat of which, though painful, is yet tolerable. Often while the soul is thus inflamed with love, by a passing thought or a spoken word of how death delays its coming, the heart receives, it knows not how or whence, a blow as from a fiery dart. I do not say that this actually is a 'dart,' but, whatever it may be, decidedly it does not come from any part of our being. Neither is it really a 'blow' though I call it one, but it wounds us severely—not, I think in that part of our nature subject to bodily pain, but in the very depths and centre of the soul, where this thunderbolt, in its rapid course, reduces all the earthly part of our nature to powder. At the time we cannot even remember our own existence, for in an instant the faculties of the soul are made captive, so as to be incapable of any action, except the power they retain of increasing our torture. Do not think I am exaggerating; indeed, I fall short of explaining what happens, which cannot be described. This is a trance of the senses and faculties of the soul, for everything else combines, as I told you, to make the agony more intense. His understanding realizes acutely what cause there is for grief in separation from God, and His Majesty now augments the sorrow by a vivid manifestation of Himself, thus increasing her anguish to such a degree that the sufferer gives vent to loud cries, which she cannot stifle, however patient and accustomed to pain she may be, because this torture is not corporal, but attacks the innermost recesses of the soul. The person I am speaking of learnt from this how much more keenly the spirit is capable of suffering than the body; she thought this resembled the pains of Purgatory, where the absence of the flesh does not prevent the torture from being far worse than any we can feel in this world. . . . I know by experience that under these circumstances no bodily suffering is felt, be it great or small, nor do I think the person would care if she were torn in pieces" (*Interior Castle*, pp. 244-246).

St. Teresa does not tell us how long this martyrdom was prolonged in her own case; she merely says that each one of these transports of Divine love lasted but a short while— three or four hours at most. "If this agony were longer protracted," she adds, "I do not think that poor humanity could endure it without a miracle."

We have purposely omitted from St. Teresa's description certain details, such as the dislocation of the bones and the cry which escapes involuntarily. These are obviously accessory circumstances. They were present in St. Teresa's case, but many Saints have been able to undergo the acute anguish of the purification of love without these external symptoms.

CHAPTER II

THE LAST DEGREE OF SANCTITY: THE FINAL AND PERFECT UNION

§ 1. *The Spiritual Marriage.*

247. BEFORE explaining the nature of the transforming union an important point has to be elucidated. Is this supreme union to be identified with the mystical marriage? Those who read only St. Teresa and St. John of the Cross will answer in the affirmative. We were of this opinion before studying the lives and writings of other saintly souls who likewise received the favour of the spiritual marriage. The Saints in their writings speak more especially of their own personal experiences. With St. Teresa and St. John of the Cross the favour of the mystical marriage seems to have coincided with their entry into the seventh degree, and they refer to the transforming union under the name of spiritual marriage.

But this term spiritual marriage, although always signifying a close union between God and the soul, does not necessarily apply to the seventh degree. That it refers to various degrees is proved by the fact that many holy persons received the favour of spiritual marriage more than once.

St. Veronica Juliani had gone through the experiences which we have related (No. 208), when, on April 11, 1694, she being then thirty-one years of age, the mystic marriage took place. She has given us an account of this touching ceremony (vol. ii., pp. 244 *et seq.).* Three years later (April 7,1697) Our Lord, who had more than once renewed these holy espousals with St. Veronica, gave her to understand that He was about to contract a new alliance with her, which should be perpetual and indissoluble—*vincolo di legame unttivo perpetuo ed indissolubile.* At the moment of Communion, drawing a ring from His sacred side,[1] He gave it to her, saying, "This is now a true marriage. Those that went before were but the means of arriving at this perfect union which I shall now make with thee."[2]

It was the same with Venerable Marina Escobar.

248. Between God and His creatures unions of such an intimate nature exist that they cannot be better explained in human speech than by the symbolism of marriage. But who can say what graces of ever closer union may be brought about by Him whose love is infinite; whose power unlimited; what favours He may grant to His chosen ones, blessings of greater and greater worth, which bring the soul ever nearer to God, knitting it still more straitly in the union which is bom of love, by an assimilation of wills and the communication of blessings?

Such, as it seems to us, are the elements which always occur in the case of the mystic marriage: Love, carried to the point of heroism; the habitual subordination of the human will to the Divine, the former awaiting those motions of grace which the latter manifests to it; and community of spiritual riches. This love operates in the innermost sanctuary of the soul. "From that moment" (the time of her spiritual marriage),

---

[1] He had already given her a ring at the time of the first marriage, three years previously.

[2] *Ora e vero sposalizio. Gli altri che tu hai fatti meco sono stati mezzi per arrivare a questo perfetto che ora faro con te.*

says Venerable Mary of the Incarnation, "my soul has dwelt in its centre, which is God; and this centre is within—a secret place, uplifted above all sensation. It is something so simple, so delicate, that it cannot be expressed. One can desire anything, read, write, work, and do all that one wills, and yet this fundamental preoccupation persists, and the soul never ceases to be united to God. . . . The tempests of temptation (which may none the less be extremely strong) cannot penetrate thither, and nothing can drive the soul from its happy abiding-place" *(Vie, by* C. Martin, i. 28; *Additions,* p. 152).

The inspirations of grace have become so frequent that the soul knows, so to speak, under all circumstances, what God requires of it. "The soul," says the Venerable Mary again, "constantly experiences this gracious Prompter (the Holy Spirit), who has taken possession of it in the spiritual marriage" *(Vie,* i. 23, p. 107). And this action of the Divine Spirit which holds it in such a close union with God does not allow it to forget the interests of the Bridegroom, or to show itself indifferent to them.

The union has at length become so close that the creature possesses nothing which is not God's, nor God anything which is not also His creature's. "Love belongs to the soul," says the same servant of God, "and the soul belongs to God, and (if I dare so say) all goods are in common; there is no longer any distinction between mine and His" *(ibid.,* i. 25, p. 121). For the creature makes a sacrifice to God of all its tastes, desires, will and works; it no longer takes any action on its own account; it does not belong to itself any more. In return, Jesus gives it a lien, as it were, upon all the riches which He has acquired, upon all His merits. It can draw upon them as a bride draws upon the bridegroom's treasures. When Our Lord accorded the favour of the spiritual marriage to Jeanne Bénigne Gojoz, the holy Visitation nun of the seventeenth century, He said to her: "To-day, at this very instant, thou enterest into the participation of My infinite possessions."

These dispositions are even to be met with in the sixth degree—not always, it is true, in the first phase (that of great purifying trials), but, at any rate, in the state of heroism which succeeds to this acute crisis. And we believe that the mystic marriage may be met with in this degree.

249. The reader may perhaps be wondering what difference exists between the sixth degree and the seventh. The difference is a vast one, but it is very difficult of appreciation by us who are so far removed from it. To us the stars of a constellation seem in close proximity to each other, but were we on the one nearest to us we should then see what an enormous distance lies between it and the others.

The most notable differences thus escape us, but here are some which may be mentioned. This annihilation, so freely desired, of nature before grace, this lovingly accepted captivity which knits the human will to the Divine, is subject in the sixth degree to a considerable number of interruptions; in the seventh it is almost continuous, but at the same time less violent. The human will, although closely united to the Divine, is no longer so sensible of its chain nor kept in such a state of rigorous subjection as hitherto; for the soul participates much more fully in the lights, in the desires, of God Himself. Nor does it suffer from that weariness which used sometimes to overpower it in the sixth degree. Then the fight was often so fierce that the poor soul had need of a respite; the mountain ascent was so toilsome that it was forced from time to time to stop and rest, and then to gather itself together and take heart again. The soul which has reached the seventh degree is in a much more stable condition.

In the sixth degree slight lapses into self-interest still occasionally, although rarely, occur, and these are at once promptly atoned for by acts of self-abandonment which are full of love, the soul going out towards God and calling the Divine justice down upon itself for the destruction and annihilation of its faults. In the seventh degree the transforming action of grace is so abundant, so powerful, that it inundates the soul, and absorbs, and, so to speak, overwhelms the natural passions. The first movements of their human passions are usually so weak as to be powerless to shake the will, and these remain in this latent condition only, being imperceptible to the outside world. Onlookers are led to believe that in these holy souls no conflict between nature and grace exists any more.

§ 2. *On the Closeness of this Union with God.*

250. The sublime operations, the special graces of which we have spoken, illuminate and purify the soul to a supreme degree. It becomes wonderfully enlightened, and detached as far as is possible in this world from all which savoured of imperfection within it, and is indissolubly united to God. It is now established on the heights of perfection.

Let us listen to the words of those who have had the happiness of being raised to this state.

"All that can be said of this state," says St. Teresa, "is that this is mysterious and hidden; the favour is sublime that God thus bestows in an instant on the soul, which feels a supreme delight, only to be described by saying that Our Lord vouchsafes for the moment to reveal to it His own heavenly glory in a higher way than by any vision or spiritual delight. I can only say that, as far as one can understand, the soul—I mean the spirit of this soul—is made one with God, who, as He says Himself, is a spirit, and has been pleased to show certain persons how far His love for us extends, that we may praise His greatness. Thus, He has been pleased to unite Himself to His creature, and has bound Himself to her as inseparably as two human beings are joined in wedlock. Spiritual espousals are different, and, like the grace of union, are often dissolved; for though two things are one by union, still separation is possible, and each part then remains a thing of itself. We generally find this favour passes quickly, and afterwards the soul, as far as it is aware, remains alone. This is not so in spiritual marriage with Our Lord, where God always remains in the centre of the soul. Union may be symbolized by two wax candles, the tips of which touch each other so closely that the wick, the wax, and the light become one, but the one candle can again be separated from the other, so that two distinct candles remain, or even the wick may be withdrawn from the wax. But spiritual marriage is like rain falling from the sky into a river or stream, becoming one and the same liquid, so that the river-water and the rain cannot be divided; or it resembles a streamlet flowing into the ocean, which cannot afterwards be dissevered from it. The marriage may also be likened to a room into which a bright light enters through two windows—though it passes through the two, the light is one" *(Seventh Mansion,* chap, ii., pp. 264, 265).

251. "The two natures are so united," says St. John of the Cross ; "what is Divine is so communicated to what is human, that, without undergoing any essential change, each seems to be God—yet not perfectly so in this life, though still in a manner which can neither be described nor conceived" *(Spiritual Canticle,* stanza xxii,, p. 298).

"What God communicates to the soul in this intimate union is utterly ineffable, beyond the reach of all possible words—just as it is impossible to speak of God Himself so as to convey any idea of what He is, because it is God Himself who communicates Himself to the soul now in the marvellous bliss of its transformation. In this state God and the soul are united, as the window is with the light, or coal with the fire, or the light of the stars with that of the sun, yet, however, not so essentially and completely as it will be in the life to come" *(ibid.,* stanza xxvi., p. 320).

"God Himself is here the suitor, who, in the omnipotence of His unfathomable love, absorbs the soul with greater violence and efficacy than a torrent of fire seizes upon a single drop of the morning dew which resolves itself into air" *(ibid.,* stanza xxx., p. 351).

252. "This mysterious union," says St. Teresa, "takes place in the innermost centre of the soul." And St. John of the Cross

explains how this expression is to be understood. "The innermost centre of the soul is there where its being, power, and the force of its action and movement penetrate and cannot go further. . . . The centre of the soul is God. When the soul shall have reached Him, according to its essence, and according to the power of its operations, it will then have attained to its ultimate and deepest centre in God. This will be when the soul shall love Him, comprehend Him, and enjoy Him with all its strength. . . . The love of God will then wound it in its inmost depth or centre, and the soul will be transformed and enlightened in the highest degree in its substance, faculties, and strength, *until it shall become most like unto God*" (*Living Flame*, stanza i., p. 417).

253. In the life of St. Catharine of Ricci we read of a touching miracle in which Our Lord sensibly manifested His union with the soul which He had espoused and showed to what a point He makes it like unto Himself. One of St. Catharine's sisters in religion could not believe in her ecstasies. Finding her one day in this condition, and being without witnesses, she threw herself upon her knees before the Saint, imploring Our Lord to take pity upon her and to root out of her heart the obstinacy which prevented her believing in the ravishments of His holy spouse. Then, raising her eyes to St. Catharine's face, she beheld only the face of Jesus, with long hair and bearded. Terror-stricken at the sight, she wished to fly. But without coming out of her ecstasy, the Saint, laying both hands upon her shoulders, and holding her, said, as she gazed at her: "Who do you now think that I am, Jesus or Catharine ?" The poor child, yet more terrified, uttered such a cry that a number of her companions heard her and came running thither from all parts, and answered: "You are Jesus." Three times to the same question she made the same reply, "You are Jesus." And instantly a great joy filled her soul. She naively related to her companions that "never had she seen any beauty comparable to the countenance of Jesus which had replaced

that of Catharine" (F. Bayonne, *Vie de St. Catharine de Ricci,* vol. i., chap. ix,).

The same thing had happened in the case of St. Catharine of Siena. Her confessor, B. Raymond of Capua, saw the Saint's features suddenly disappear one day to be replaced by those of Our Saviour. "Who is He that looks at me thus?" he exclaimed, trembling. "He who is," replied the Saint.

§ 3. *The Permanence of the Perfect Union.*

254. The soul thus deified does not readily lose the close union which it has contracted with God and the ineffable consolations which result. The absences of the Beloved have hitherto been a source of great distress, as He alternately showed Himself and then again withdrew for the purpose of heightening its desires and enflaming its love. But now, at this last stage of perfection, God will "desist from this device of love," and the soul will never more lose the consciousness of His presence" (SL *Catharine of Siena).* It "departs no more from that centre where it abides together with God" (*Seventh Mansion,* chap. ii.). "Even amidst the heaviest crosses and the most trying surroundings the principal part of the soul never stirs from this inward dwelling-place" (*ibid.,* chap, i.) where God dwells.

And then *"the distinguishing mark of the seventh mansion is that spiritual dryness is but rarely present" (Seventh Mansion,* chap. iii.). "Those who have the happiness of entering therein scarcely ever, or very seldom, find themselves obliged to resort to considerations for the sake of inflaming the will. They walk perpetually, and in a wonderful way, in the company of their Lord, His Divinity and His humanity being alike and simultaneously visible to them" *(Sixth Mansion,* chap. vii.).

"Hence a soul that is disposed may elicit many more, and more intense, acts in a brief period than another soul not so disposed in a long time, for this soul spends all its energies in the preparation of itself, and even afterwards the fire does not wholly penetrate the fuel it has to burn. But when the soul is already prepared, love enters in continuously, and the spark at the first contact seizes on the fuel that is dry" *(Living Flame, stanza i., verse 6, p. 425).*

The anxieties of love are therefore ended. The soul is happy. "It is in possession of a marvellous fullness of God's presence" *(Spiritual Canticle,* stanza xxii.). "It is clothed with God, and bathed in the Divinity itself; not outwardly only, but in its innermost being it swims in an ocean of Divine joys and in the spiritual waters of eternal life" *(ibid.,* stanza xxvi,).

255. This sensible presence of God, this beautiful union, extends sometimes to an explicit consciousness and an intellectual perception of the three Divine Persons. It was thus with St. Teresa[3] *(Seventh Mansion,* chap. i.).

"By some mysterious manifestation of the truth the three Persons of the most Blessed Trinity reveal themselves, preceded by an illumination which shines on the spirit like a most dazzling cloud of light. The three Persons are distinct from one another; a sublime knowledge is infused into the soul, imbuing it with a certainty of the truth that the Three are of one substance, power, and knowledge, and are one God"[4] *(Seventh Mansion,* chap. i., pp. 257, 258).

From this moment, without, it is true, retaining such a clear conception of this supreme mystery, the Saint never ceased to

---

[3] There is no question here of an intuitive vision, but a purely intellectual knowledge similar to that which the angels in a state of probation might possess of this mystery. But even for the angels (who by nature, and without a revelation, can only know the existence and unity of the Divine nature, and not the Trinity of the Persons) it is supernatural knowledge.

[4] It was before uniting Himself with the Saint by the bonds of spiritual marriage and as by way of preparation, that God accorded to her this marvellous vision. It is often thus with the souls whom the Lord calls to this sublime favour. Is it not proper that the soul should thus acquire a more intimate knowledge of the God whose spouse it is about to become?

feel the Divine Persons present within her, and to be conscious of this adorable companionship; rather "as one who, finding himself with several other persons in a very light room, would certainly no longer see them if the room were darkened, but would not cease to be assured of their presence."

256. But we regard this distinct consciousness in the light of an extraordinary favour, and it would be a mistake to generalize from it. Other great Saints may have been as closely united to God, and as constantly and as perfectly so as St. Teresa, without her clear consciousness of the great things which were wrought in them. In the *Dialogue of the Nine Rocks* we read: "God at times, by a special grace, shows Himself to them" (the inhabitants of the ninth rock) "face to face. But this favour is very rare, and, like St. Paul's ecstasy, lasts but a few moments. *The greater number*[5] are called to contemplate the incomprehensibility of God in a divine obscurity, and to unite themselves to Him, spirit to spirit, without any intermediary, in the fullest intimacy of love."

Not to all of these saintly souls does Our Lord reveal the fact that He is conferring upon them the dignity of the spiritual marriage, or, at least, that He intends to treat them as His spouses. But, whether He accords this title to them or no, cannot God grant the same precious favours to His faithful ones and work in them the same wonders of His love? So we believe that the greater number[6] learn only in heaven that God raised them to this supreme degree of grace and sanctity.

---

[5] We make the same reservation here as above. We do not believe that these words refer to the intuitive vision, but rather to a purely intellectual consciousness, giving a highly exalted idea of the Divinity.

[6] "Do the inhabitants of the ninth rock know," inquired Suzo of Our Lord, "that they are made one with God and their end?" "They do not know positively," Our Lord replied. In fact, it seems more in accord with the ordinary conduct of Providence to hide from the elect souls the excellence of the gifts which are imparted to them.

§ 4. *The Ineffable Peace of Saintly Souls.*

257. The natural and necessary consequence of this sensible and beatifying presence of God in the soul is an indescribable peace. "God," says St. Angela of Foligno, "has established my soul in a state which is almost immutable. My heart, my flesh and my soul, have been caught up upon the mountains of peace, and in all things I am content."

If in the unitive life, as we have already shown, a profound peace is enjoyed and one which can persist even amidst conflicts and trials, this is even more true in the case of those who have attained to the supreme degree of this unitive life.

258. But the happiness of the Saints is now greatly heightened by the fact that disturbances and troubles very rarely occur. Formerly the senses constantly rebelled, and caused acute anguish to the spirit. The faculties of the soul, especially the imagination, "when the will is tranquilly enjoying the sweet converse of the Beloved, produce weariness, and in their swift flight quench its joy." *(Spiritual Canticle* stanza xx., p. 285). Henceforward the contrary tendencies are largely diminished, a much greater harmony reigning between the inferior and the superior parts. "The soul is so penetrated with God that it does not even suffer from the first movements of opposition to what it knows to be God's will. The imperfect soul finds itself often inclining to evil, if it be only by unpremeditated movements which are due to the understanding, the will, the memory, or to its own desires and imperfections. But when it has come to that degree of perfection of which we are now speaking all its powers and all its inclinations, in an exactly converse way, tend habitually towards God, even by their first instincts" *(ibid.,* stanza xxix.).

259. The natural appetites are not perpetually stifled, it is true, nor the faculties always thus in participation with the Divine union. "It must not be imagined," said St. Teresa, "that the powers, the senses, and the passions are always thus at peace" *(Seventh Mansion).*

"Do not fancy," she says again, "that these souls always experience the effects of which I have spoken to such a high degree. *It is only usually* thus. Sometimes the Lord leaves them in their natural condition, and then it is as if all the venomous beasts from the outer enclosure and the other mansions of the castle were combining to avenge themselves upon these souls, because of the times when they were unable to molest them" *(ibid.,* chap, iv.),

260. Not only are the evil inclinations modified and stilled, so that they no longer force the soul to many painful conflicts, but sorrow does not touch it as deeply as before; so ardent is the charity, so intimate is the union with God, that there is no longer any place for natural griefs and anxieties.

The life of St. Francis of Sales furnishes us with some beautiful examples of the perfect indifference of the Saints. It had got abroad that he would be obliged to bid good-bye to his beloved diocese of Geneva, where he had laboured so long and where his affections were naturally entwined, in order to be transferred to the See of Paris. This is how he writes to St. Jane Frances de Chantal on the subject: "Whether Providence sends me elsewhere, or leaves me here, *is all one to me.* . . . I can say nothing about my soul beyond this, that it becomes more and more conscious of the ardent desire to esteem nothing but the love of Our Saviour crucified, and that I find myself so proof against the events of this world that scarcely anything affects me" (February 26, 1620).

This was not the first time that the Saint gave proof of his wonderful detachment. Some years previously, when the Order of the Visitation had just come into being, he had seen his plans as founder thwarted and radically changed. He had wished to establish an Institute of unmarried women who, combining the active with the contemplative life, should go about the world alleviating suffering. The Archbishop of Lyons, on the other hand, insisted that the Visitation should be an enclosed Order. The Saint cheerfully accepted a plan which was the opposite of what he had desired. "I acquiesce in this," he said, "calmly and tranquilly, and with an unparalleled satisfaction; and not my will only, but my judgment also, has rejoiced thus to render homage to this great and worthy prelate. Believe me, my dear daughter, that I love our poor little Congregation devotedly, but without any anxiety, an element which love is not accustomed to dispense with. But mine, which is no common love, lives, I assure you, entirely without it, with the help of a very special trust which I feel in the grace of Our Lord Jesus Christ" (October, 1617).

This complete self-possession, which put him out of the reach of the natural emotions, made fear an unknown sensation to him. Every one knows how he passed one day through the town of Geneva, where his life would have been in serious danger had he been recognized. Some ill-disposed people had seized upon this journey as a pretext for accusing him to the Prince of Savoy of holding communication with the enemy. The saintly Bishop paid no heed to their calumnies. "Do not think," he wrote to St. Jane Frances de Chantal, "that I am troubled, because I am not so the least in the world" (December, 1609).

In this same letter he describes the heroic actions which he had just performed at Geneva, speaking quite naturally about them as though he saw no special merit in them. "These who know me are aware now that I never thought of holding any communications with the inhabitants, and that I performed a thousand acts of courage, not certainly in simplicity of mind (for I will not speak otherwise than openly to you), but by simplicity of faith. But this is all nothing, and I relate it only to you, from whom I can keep back nothing that concerns me."

261. Such is the calm of these saintly souls! They seem to be above conflicts and sorrows, so perfect is their indifference, so completely does their whole being participate in the Divine union and the exquisite peace which results.

"The Beloved adjures the affections of these four passions—desire, joy, fear, and grief—compels them to cease and to be at rest, because He supplies the bride now with force, and courage, and satisfaction, by the soft lyres of His sweetness, and the sudden strains of His delight, so that not only they shall not domineer over the soul, but shall not occasion it any distaste whatever. Such is the grandeur and stability of the soul in this state, that, although formerly the waters of grief overwhelmed it, because of its own or other men's sins, which is what spiritual persons most feel, the consideration of them now excites neither pain nor annoyance; even the sensible feeling of compassion exists not now, though the effects of it continue in perfection. The weaknesses of its virtues are no longer in the soul, for they ate now constant, strong, and perfect. As the angels perfectly appreciate all sorrowful things without the sense of pain, and perform acts of mercy without the sentiment of pity, so the soul in this transformation of love" (*Spiritual Canticle,* stanza xx., p. 289).

But we must take care not to carry this doctrine too far, or to forget that an entire absence of sorrow is reserved for our celestial home.

"It is true," said St. John of the Cross *(ibid.),* "that God, however, dispenses sometimes, on certain occasions, with the soul in this matter, allowing it to feel and suffer, that it may become more fervent in love and grow in merit, or for some other reasons, as He dispensed with His Virgin Mother, St. Paul, and others. This, however, is not the ordinary condition of this state of spiritual marriage."

262. It may be thought that even with this limitation St. John of the Cross goes a little far in his picture of this cloudless happiness. Sanctity is in no way insensibility. The death of Lazarus and the grief of Mary and Martha, the calamities about to overtake Jerusalem, did not these call forth the tears of Jesus? That at times even the spectacle of sins committed should cause neither distress or affliction to the saintly soul (as in the case of our guardian angels) is very probable. But that this should be, so to say, its regular disposition is more debatable. We believe that in the presence of sin it will often experience a deep anguish, similar to that which Our Saviour

suffered during His Passion. In this case, however, peace and joy would still persist in the superior parts, or, rather, in the supreme point of the soul, without being in any way affected by the sorrows and agitations of the inferior parts.

"The world," said St. Catharine of Siena, "when it metes out injuries, persecutions, and reproaches to My perfect servants"—it is God the Father who is speaking—"can find no vulnerable spot in them, because the gardens of their souls are closed, and the dart recoils upon the sender, poisoned by his own evil deed. It cannot wound these perfect ones in any way, because, although attacking the body, it cannot touch the soul, which remains at the same time both *happy and sad*—sad because of its neighbour's sin, and happy because of the love which it possesses.

"And so It imitates the Lamb without spot, My beloved Son, who upon the Cross was both happy and afflicted—afflicted by reason of the cross of bodily suffering, and the cross of His longing desire to expiate the sins of mankind. And He was happy because His Divine nature, united to His human nature, was incapable of suffering and ravished His soul with joy by revealing itself all unveiled. He was both happy and afflicted, because the flesh indeed suffered, but the Divinity could not suffer, neither the soul in the superior part of the understanding. And so with My beloved children, when they have attained to the third[7] and fourth degrees, they are afflicted

---

[7] These lines refer, not only to the fourth degree, which, in the classification adopted by the Saint, is supreme perfection, but also to the third, which is a condition of inferior perfection. But as she recognises the fact that the peace of which she speaks flows from the state of beatitude, and as she elsewhere states that with souls of perfect sanctity, beatitude is more continual than with those of a lesser sanctity, it follows that the peace which souls of the third and fourth degree are here spoken of as possessing must be much deeper and more unalterable in the case of the latter. In the former degree the soul went through intoxicating periods of peace and happiness, but these were intermittent. There were times when the Beloved withdrew Himself. The anxieties of love came, if not to destroy, at least to cloud, to lessen, its peace. But now it is no longer thus, and the peace is far more continuous.

with spiritual and bodily crosses; they suffer in the body as I permit, and are tormented with regret for the offences committed against Me and the sorrows of their neighbours; but they are happy because the treasure of love which they possess cannot be taken away, and is to them a source of joy and beatitude" *(Dialogue,* chap, dxviii.).

St. John of the Cross, in painting his exquisite picture of the condition of these saintly souls, was really giving us his own history. After causing him to pass through the terrible experiences which he has analysed so beautifully in the book of the *Obscure Night of the Soul,* God had been able to communicate to him a cloudless peace which the most distressing exterior trials were powerless to disturb. The Saints and many spiritual writers are quite naturally inclined to portray themselves in the pictures that they paint for us concerning the phenomena of the inner life. When giving an account of states of which they have had personal acquaintance, how should they describe them but according to their own experiences? Their testimonies are only so much the more valuable, but they do not always apply to every analogous case.

Other great servants of God who seem to have climbed as high upon the ladder of sanctity—St. Alphonsus Liguori, for example—have endured inner sufferings to the very end of their lives. St. Veronica Juliani and Venerable Mary of the Incarnation suffered acutely after receiving the favour of the spiritual marriage. If Mary, the Mother of Sorrows, bore the most agonizing inward martyrdom at the foot of the Cross, the great Saints, also, may undergo bitter interior tortures. If Our Divine Saviour died uttering that piercing cry, "My God, My God, why hast Thou forsaken Me?" those who are called to continue His life of immolation and expiation upon earth may also suffer pains like unto His, whatever the height of sanctity to which they may have attained.

§ 5. *The Joys of Saintly Souls*

263. While St. Catharine of Siena seems to draw a distinction between joy and beatitude, St. John of the Cross makes a formal distinction between the substantial beatitude which results from the union with God and the accidental joys that accrue to it. These last are many and various, but the first is so full and so powerful that it undergoes no modification.

"The affections of joy, also, which were wont to move the soul with more or less vehemence, are not sensibly diminished, neither does their abundance occasion any surprise. The joy of the soul is now so abundant that it is like the sea, which is not diminished by the rivers that flow out of it, nor increased by those that empty themselves into it. . . . Accidental joys and sweetness are, indeed, no strangers to this soul—yea, rather, those which it ordinarily has cannot be numbered; yet, for all this, as to the substantial communication of the spirit, there is no increase of joy, for that which may occur anew the soul possesses already, and thus what the soul has already within itself is greater than anything that comes anew. Hence, then, whenever any subject of joy and gladness, whether exterior or spiritually interior, presents itself to the soul, the soul betakes itself forthwith to rejoicing in the riches it possesses already within itself, and the joy it has in them is far greater than any which these new accessions minister, because, in a certain sense, God is become its possession, Who, though he delights in all things, yet in nothing so much as in Himself. Thus all accessions of joy serve to remind the soul that its real joy is in its interior possessions, rather than in these accidental causes, because, as I have said, the former are greater than the latter. It is very natural for the soul, even when a particular matter gives it pleasure, that, possessing another of greater worth and gladness, it should remember it at once, and take its pleasure in it. The accidental character of these spiritual accessions, and the new impressions they make on the soul, may be said to be as nothing in comparison with that substantial source which it has within itself; for the soul which has attained to the perfect transformation, and is full-grown, grows no more in this state by means of these spiritual accessions, as those souls do who have not yet advanced so far. It is a marvellous thing that the soul, while it receives no accessions of delight, should still seem to do so, and also to have been in possession of them. The reason is that it is always tasting them anew, because they are ever renewed, and thus it seems to be continually the recipient of new accessions, while it has no need of them whatever" *(Spiritual Canticle*, stanza xx., pp. 290, 991).

§6. *On the Light that is accorded to Saintly Souls.*

264. "But if we attempt to speak of the marvellous illumination with which the soul, abiding thus continually in God's embrace, is sometimes dowered . . . all our words will be powerless, and would fail to convey the least idea of the truth" *(ibid.).*

Here, again, we think that a double element should be noted. The saintly soul is blessed with a kind of substantial and, so to say, permanent illumination, supplemented by other accidental lights.

It was the essential and fundamental illumination which enabled St. Teresa to see herself as standing in the perpetual presence of the Three Persons of the Blessed Trinity. It was also this substantial illumination, though less dear and definite in his case, which Blessed Henry Suzo describes, and which he calls the last degree of union with God.

"The soul that is faithful in the imitation of Jesus Christ may meet with Him in the depths of His Divinity, since He has given us this promise: 'Where I am, there also shall My servant be.' This is a meeting-place full of joy and happiness. The spirit loses its activity, and disappears in the ocean of His Divine Being, and precisely in this lies its safety and happiness. . . . The spirit of the perfect man can be raised even unto the abyss of the Divinity, that ocean of the unknowable. It can plunge therein and swim in the infinite depths of the Divine Essence, and there, detached from all worldly thoughts, can rest motionless in the secrets of God. Man then strips himself of the darkness of his natural light and reclothes himself in a superior light. God attracts him into the simplicity of His Unity, wherein he loses himself to be transformed into God, not by nature, but by grace. And in this infinite sea of light which encompasses him he attains to the fruition of a silence which is perfect peace and joy. He understands the Eternal and living Nothing which is the Divine, incomprehensible Being, the Nothing which is called Nothing because it has no place amongst created things and the human mind can find nothing that can contain it. He sees that this Nothing surpasses all intelligence, and is for all men incomprehensible.

"When the spirit begins to be established in the darkness of the light, it loses all interest in itself, all action. It no longer understands itself, because it is absorbed, swallowed up in God. And as in the loftiness of this contemplation it receives into its own substance a beam which radiates from the unity of tire Divine Essence and from the Trinity of Persons, it loses itself in these splendours; it dies unto itself and to the use of its powers and faculties. It is enwrapt and, as it were, all astray in a Divine ignorance; it is absorbed in the ineffable silence of the infinite light and the supreme unity. This is the highest point to which the spirit of man can attain.

"St. Dionysius the Areopagite calls this state 'the unknown and luminous height, the deep glooms of dazzling splendour, the ray of Divine darkness,' because the soul unites itself to the Divine Essence and in this ocean of light beholds, contemplates, and possesses it. It understands in this ecstasy that the Infinite surpasses its reason and remains beyond the reach of every intellect; but it attains to the enjoyment of this unknown athwart the darkness and obscurity of a light that reveals the immensity and incomprehensibility of God" (*Traité de l'Union avec Dieu*, § 6, ed. Cartier).

265. This wondrous contemplation does not always take possession of the soul with equal strength. At times the impression will be less distinct; but there will remain a deep consciousness of the Divinity, a light which, though milder and less dazzling, will be no less penetrating and which will maintain a mode of perception of God exceedingly precious and desirable.

It is from this contemplation of the Divine Being, more or less definite but exceedingly exalted and fruitful, that the essential joy, which St. John of the Cross describes above, proceeds. This it is that begets those sublime acts of the love of God of which we shall treat later on, and that make the merits of the Saints of such marvellously high worth.

Then the influence of the Divinity acts upon them most powerfully, kindling in their hearts a thirst, so to speak, for the infinite. Each of the Divine attributes produces its proper operation within them. In the presence of the Divine Holiness they are vividly conscious of their own impurity. Their realisation of God's glory and splendour makes their own deformity stand out in sharper contrast; in the light of the Omnipotence, the Immensity, the Eternity of the Most High they see their own impotence, littleness, and nothingness.

266. The accidental lights which God deigns to grant to the espoused soul come to it very commonly by the way of pure intelligence, which is the mode of perception of angels and disembodied spirits (see above, No. 33}.

"The fourth (and supreme) degree of contemplation," says Father Lallemant, "is when the soul's actions are no longer inspired by the imagination, which is wrought upon in raptures and ecstasies, but when God enlightens it by species or revelations which are intellectual and independent of the imagination and of phantasmata. The highest point only of the soul is then the actor, or rather the recipient of God's action, for this Divine operation in no wise hinders the external activity of the senses. . . .

"At this stage God gives them, sometimes for a time, sometimes for always, such keen perceptions that they are enabled to perceive with their spiritual vision persons who are not before their bodily eyes, and to be cognizant of what is about to be said before the speaker has opened his lips. They know what they ought to answer on all occasions and with regard to any matter, and are the recipients of supernatural lights so as to be led always and in all things by the Holy Spirit.

"This was the degree of the Divine Union in which the Apostles habitually dwelt even when they were going about in the world engaged in their most laborious undertakings" *(Doct. Spir.,* 7 principe, chap, iv., article S).

267. Such accidental illuminations may become very frequent in the case of these great servants of God, and they bear especially upon the fundamental truths of religion.

"When the soul has been raised," says St. John of the Cross, "to the high state of spiritual marriage, the Bridegroom reveals to it, as His faithful consort. His own marvellous secrets most readily and most frequently, for he who truly and sincerely loves hides nothing from the object of his affections. The chief matter of His communications are the sweet mysteries of His incarnation, the ways and means of redemption, which is one of the highest works of God, and so is the soul one of the sweetest" (*Spiritual Canticle,* stanza xxiii., p. 301).

This is exemplified in the life of St. Francis of Sales. One day when he was preparing to go up to the altar, absorbed in meditation to the point of forgetting the usual hour for his Mass, one of his chaplains came to tell him that they were waiting for him. Rising joyfully to his feet, he exclaimed: "Oh, I am about to receive Him, this Divine Saviour! I am about to receive Him!" And he robed himself in the sacred vestments, manifesting an extraordinary joyousness. Questioned afterwards by his confessor as to the reason of this gladness, he replied: "Because God has given me wonderful lights concerning the Incarnation and the Holy Eucharist, and has flooded my soul with such an abundance of graces, that the interior joy was reflected outwardly" *(Vie,* by M. Hamon, vi. 8).

268. Speaking of the graces granted to heroic souls, we said that those appertaining to the extraordinary way are not bestowed upon all alike. This, as the reader will have understood, is also applicable to the Saints; for the light communicated by intellectual visions and the Divine manifestations or declarations which God makes of that close union with Him called mystical marriage, and the absence of sorrows or inner sufferings, are not essential to the transforming union, the soul being able to attain to it without these favours. What does, however, seem essential to this union, as a consummation of the work of grace in the soul such as generous hearts may desire and ask Our Lord for, are those vivid illuminations concerning God, that intense and sublime love, that full dominion of grace throughout all the powers of the soul, accompanied by the perpetual peace and entire self-mastery which ensue.

§ 7. *The wonderful Virtues of the Great Saints—their Charity— their Influence with God.*

269. "Some persons believe that souls raised to this degree are confirmed in grace. It is certain that they perform acts of virtue of such purity and perfection that they honour God and increase the merit of their souls to an inconceivable extent."

Thus speaks Father Lallemant. St. John of the Cross is one of those who think that souls in this degree of love are confirmed in grace *(Spiritual Canticle*, stanza xxii.). Could Jesus, the faithful Bridegroom, permit a soul with which He had contracted such a close alliance to be lost? He told St. Veronica Juliani, as we have already seen, that He was about to contract a perpetual and indissoluble union with her. St. Teresa, on the other hand, seems to recognize the possibility of grave faults in these souls.[8]

As for venial faults of frailty, every one allows that they still commit them. "Do not suppose," says St. Teresa, "however great may be their desire and however firm their resolve not to be guilty of the least imperfection for all that the world contains, that these souls are exempt from such frailties. They do not fail to commit many such, and even actual sins, but not of set purpose." "I am truly a great sinner," said Venerable Mary of the Incarnation, "and commit meannesses without number, endless puerilities, weaknesses beyond measure" *(Vie,* iv, i, p. 606). In the case of these avowals we must doubtless put a good deal down to humility, but neither must we forget that impeccability is not for this world. It is true that we cannot understand how souls can ever sin who are the recipients of such powerful and continual graces, who are habitually conscious of the promptings of the Holy Spirit, who possess God in their innermost centres, in a region where storms and temptations do not penetrate, and, yet more, who even in their lower natures are subject only to very faint stirrings of the human passions. But were Adam and Eve less highly favoured? The angels before their fall, especially those of higher degree, and more particularly Lucifer, were they not loaded with the most precious graces and exempted from all concupiscence? And yet they were guilty of grave unfaithfulness, so that it is not surprising that these holy souls, notwithstanding all their favours, should remain liable to slight infidelities.

270. This is where the mystic writers place that heroic disinterestedness which has given rise to so much discussion,

---

[8] She does not express herself clearly. "From mortal sins of which they are cognizant," she says, "these souls are exempt. But they are not secure from them, for they may be guilty of them without knowing it, and this is no small torment to them" *(Seventh Mansion,* chap. iv.).

and which, two centuries ago, was the subject of a lively controversy between two illustrious prelates.

In order to elucidate this delicate matter and to show the point of perfection to which these great souls are raised by charity, let us listen to St. Francis of Sales who treats this difficult subject with his usual charm.

"Superior to all these souls is one, very specially unique, the most loving, the most amiable, the best beloved of all the friends of the Divine Bridegroom. One who not merely loves God above all things and in all things, but loves God alone in all things. So that it loves not many things, but one thing, which is God. And because it is God only which it loves in all that it loves, it loves Him in all things equally, according to His good pleasure, outside all things and without all things. . . . If I love my Saviour only, why should I not love Mount Calvary as much as Tabor, since He is as truly in the one as in the other? . . . So this holy bride does not love the King of the whole Universe more than if He were alone without any Universe, because all that is outside of God and not God is as nothing to her. Her soul is of such purity that she has no love even for Paradise except that the Bridegroom is loved therein ; but so sovereign is her love for the Bridegroom of the Paradise that were He to have no Paradise to offer He would be none the less desirable, none the less loved by this valorous bride, who does not know how to love the Bridegroom's Paradise, but only the Bridegroom of the Paradise, and who holds no less closely to the Calvary where her Beloved is crucified than to heaven, where He is glorified" (*Love of God,* x. 5).

271. Thus the love of God attains to such lengths in these holy souls that, absorbed in their love and mindful only of His interests, they habitually forget themselves.

"It is not surprising," says St. John of the Cross, "that the soul, intoxicated by the Divine love, is in no wise occupied with the glory which God shall give it, but yields itself to Him exclusively by an immense love, without a thought of its own advantage" *(Spiritual Canticle*, stanza xxxviii.).

It is thus that the dwellers on the ninth rock are described.

"*Jesus Christ.* They are so confirmed in faith that they no longer desire to know anything but Jesus crucified, and their humility is so profound that they judge themselves unworthy of all God's marvellous favours and heavenly consolations. And for this reason they never desire or ask for them.

"*Henry.* What, then, do they ask of God in their prayers, if they desire nothing either on earth or in heaven?

"*Jesus Christ.* They ask that in themselves and in all other creatures everything may conduce to the glory of the God whom they adore, desire, and seek after in all ways. They are so lost in Him that all that happens to them or to others seems a most precious blessing. If God accords them His grace they bless Him. If He withdraws it they bless Him still. They desire naught upon earth, only they prefer bitterness to consolation, because of their great love for the Cross.

"*Henry.* If they love nothing, do they fear anything?

"*Jesus Christ.* They are afraid of neither Hell nor Purgatory, nor the devil, nor life, nor death. They are emancipated from all servile fear. They dread one thing only, that they may not imitate the example of Jesus Christ as they desire. Such is their humility that they despise themselves and all their actions, and they abase themselves at the feet of all other creatures, never venturing to compare themselves with any. They love all men equally in God, and attach themselves with a great affection to all who are dear to Him. They live as though dead and buried to the world, and the world is dead and lost unto them. Those intellectual operations in which man finds it hardest to give up his own will are overcome and destroyed. They never seek themselves, they desire neither honour nor pleasure. They have renounced all created things for time and for eternity. They live in a sublime ignorance, knowing nothing beyond Jesus crucified."

272. In the fire of charity in which these souls are consumed there is therefore a forgetfulness and abstraction from self, not continuously, as is obvious, but very frequently.

And is there not more than this? Love is jealous. Ravished by God's perfections, the soul may even at times, in the impetuosity of its devotion, go to the lengths of intentionally rejecting everything which is not God, as being as nothing in comparison with Him, and all that is not for God as being unworthy of its affections and desires. Even its own beatitude, in so far as it affords satisfaction to its humanity, or, in other words, the satisfaction which nature might take in its eternal rest, may it not hold even this lightly, may it not even in the transports of its affection go so far as to declare that it counts its own self as nothing in the presence of its God, and that such is its love that it would not be affected even by the deprivation of that happiness? This act of charity is not in any way impossible. It is to be found in heroic souls, especially during their trial, and therefore *a fortiori* and more frequently in Saints of the supreme degree.

273. Is this act so frequently repeated by these souls as to become their *habitual* disposition? To maintain this would be to fall into the error condemned by the Brief of Pope Innocent III. In fact, the first proposition from Fénelon's *Book of Maxims of the Saints* runs thus: "There is a state of the love of God *which is habitual;* it is one of pure charity, and with no admixture of any motive of self-interest. Neither fear of punishment nor desire of reward has any longer a part in this love. Nor is God loved for the sake of the merit or perfection or happiness which loving Him must bring."

We must therefore allow that amongst the Saints of whom we are now speaking, and as they themselves testify, acts of heroic disinterestedness, such as those described above, are to be found, but also acts of simple hope, by which the soul desires the possession of God as its supreme good and, especially and most frequently, that act of perfect love in the sense already explained (No. 102).

We have said that perfect love is not merely the love of benevolence that seeks God's glory without any thought of personal advantage, but it is also the love of complacency by which the soul, entranced by the Divine perfection, tends spontaneously towards Him, desiring instinctively and by the very force of this love to become one with Him, to know Him better, to love Him, to possess Him, without in any way considering the reflex satisfaction which nature will find in becoming one with God.

274. Such, it appears to us, is the right doctrine in this delicate matter, and we think that St. Teresa's teaching will be found to tally exactly with the above description. But the reader may judge for himself.

"The most surprising thing," she says, "is that the sorrow and distress which such souls felt because they could not die and enjoy Our Lord's presence is now exchanged for a fervent desire of serving and praising Him, and helping others to the utmost of their power. Not only have they ceased to hope for death, but they wish for a long life and heavy crosses, if such would bring ever so little honour to Our Lord. Thus, if they knew for certain that immediately on quitting their bodies their souls would enjoy God, it would make no difference to them, *nor do they think of the glory enjoyed by the Saints, and long to share it.* These souls hold that their glory consists in helping, in any way, Him who was crucified, especially as they see how men offend against Him, and how few, detached from all else, care for His honour alone. It is true people in this state forget this at times, and are seized with a tender longing to enjoy God and to leave this land of exile, especially as they see how little they can serve Him. Then, however, they return to themselves, reflecting how they possess Him continually in their souls, and so they are satisfied, offering to His Majesty their willingness to live as the most costly oblation they can make Him" (*Seventh Mansion,* chap, iii., pp. 273, 274).

275. But even so we cannot fully realize the depth, the calm strength and extraordinary intensity of the acts of love made by these saintly souls.

"Alas!" said St. Catharine of Genoa one day, "if only I could tell all the emotions of my heart, which is all burnt up and consumed." "Tell us something of it," her spiritual children replied. She answered: "I can find no words with which to express such a love, and all that 1 could say would be so far from the reality that it would be almost an insult. But know only this, that if one drop of the love which fills my heart were to fall into Hell, Hell would be changed into Paradise, for so great would then be the love and unity that the devils would become angels and the pains would become consolations. Hell could not coexist with the love of God."[9]

St. John of the Cross (*Spiritual Canticle,* stanza xxxviii.) compares this love of the soul for God with that of God for the soul, the first-named being a very close participation of that act whereby God loves His own Self, with which act the soul is, as it were, associated. "Thus the soul loves God with the will and strength of God Himself, being made one with that very strength of love wherewith itself is loved by God. . . . For God not only teaches the soul to love Himself purely, with a disinterested love, as He hath loved us, but He also enables it to love Him with that strength with which He loves the soul, transforming it in His love, wherein He bestows upon it His own power, so that it may love Him. It is as if He put an instrument in its hand, taught it the use thereof, and played upon it together with the soul. This is showing the soul how it is to love, and at the same time endowing it with the capacity of loving" *(Spiritual Canticle,* stanza xxxviii., p.388).

The same writer says, a little later on: "This is a certain faculty which God will then give the soul in the communication of the Holy Ghost, who, like one breathing, raises the soul by His Divine aspiration, informs it, strengthens it, so that it too may breathe in God with the same aspiration of love which the Father breathes with the Son, and the Son with the Father, which is the Holy Ghost Himself, who is breathed

---

[9] Quoted by the Abbé Brinquant: *"La Béatitude Suprême de l'Intelligence et du Coeur dans le ciel"* p. 386.

into the soul in the Father and the Son in that transformation so as to unite it to Himself, for the transformation will not be true and perfect if the soul is not transformed in the Three Persons of the Most Holy Trinity in a clear, manifest degree. This breathing of the Holy Ghost in the soul, whereby God transforms it in Himself, is to the soul a joy so deep, so exquisite, and so grand, that no mortal tongue can describe it, no human understanding, as such, conceive it in any degree; for even that which passes in the soul with respect to the communication which takes place in its transformation wrought in this life cannot be described, because the soul united with God and transformed in Him breathes in God that very Divine aspiration which God breathes Himself in the soul when transformed in Him" *(Spiritual Canticle,* stanza xxxix., p. 394),

In *The* Living *Flame of Love,* in which he is led on to the same subject, the holy author declines to treat of it. "I would not speak," he says, "of this breathing of God, neither do I wish to do so, because I am certain that 1 cannot; and, indeed, were I to speak of it, it would seem then to be something less than what it is in reality. This breathing of God is in the soul, in which, in the awakening of the deep knowledge of the Divinity, He breathes the Holy Ghost according to the measure of that knowledge which absorbs it most profoundly, which inspires it most tenderly with love according to what it saw. This breathing is full of grace and glory, and therefore the Holy Ghost fills the soul with goodness and glory, whereby He inspires it with the love of Himself, transcending all glory and all understanding. This is the reason why I say no more" *(Living Flame,* stanza iv., p. 507).

We will imitate the Saint's reserve, and with sufficient reason, contenting ourselves by saying that in these perfect souls the perfection of charity and of all their other virtues passes everything that we can imagine.

But even at these sublime heights of perfection there are doubtless many mansions—*mansiones multae sunt*— different degrees of sanctity, we mean. We may apply to the transforming union what St. John of the Cross *(supra,* No. 101) says of the Divine union in general: *"The union of love admits of many degrees, which vary according to the capacity of the soul and the measure of grace that the Lord bestows upon each one."* But it is none the less true that the lowest degree of the transforming union communicates marvellous treasures to the soul and raiders it infinitely dear to God.

276. And if this transforming union, even in its least degree, gives such a high value to the soul, how must we regard those who receive it in full measure and are giants in sanctity? We must not be surprised by what writers tell us of these great friends of God, and of the influence over the heart of their Sovereign Master which is attributed to them. "Were such beings known for what they are—they are rare in this world," says St. Catharine of Genoa—"they would be adored even here upon earth. But God keeps them hidden, alike from themselves and from others, until the hour of their death, when the true is distinguished from the false."

"When God," says Father Lallemant, "gives to a soul the grace of elevation to the highest degree of sanctity, He refuses it nothing; it obtains, as a rule, all that it asks. If we beg such a one to ask any favour from God, then, as soon as it sets itself to lay its request before Him, it is aware that the Spirit of God transports it into secret places of such beauty that it loses itself, forgetting the subject of its prayers and no longer having any recollection of what it desired to ask. And yet God grants these desires, and its wishes have effect without its thinking of them. One soul at this point of perfection can alone uphold, by its prayers and its credit with God, a whole religious Order, an entire kingdom."

The Saints of the ninth rock are "so dear to God and enjoy such favour in His sight that if but one amongst them preferred a request and all the rest of the Christian world opposed it, God would hear its prayer and give it the preference. The grace which they possess is so great that but a fraction of it can appear outwardly, they themselves being ignorant of it and not wishing to know it. If they are few in number they are considerable in point of merit, and they are, as it were, the solid columns upon which God supports His Church. Without them Christianity would perish and the devil would capture the whole world in his nets. Formerly these beloved servants were more numerous in the Church."

In the *Life of St. Gertrude* (Book IV., chap, xix.) we read that the Saint, having a revelation of the pitiable state of a soul in Purgatory, implored God to have mercy upon it. "O Lord," she said, "wilt Thou not yield to my supplication, and pardon this soul?" To which Our Lord, with the utmost sweetness and, as it were, caressingly, replied: "For love of thee I will have compassion, not on this soul only, but also on a thousand others besides."

Oh, did we but understand the Saints, the greatness of their influence with God, the wondrousness of their power even when they remain unknown unto men, our most ardent desire would be that of seeing such souls multiplied in the Church. We should then call on God with tears to grant to the world (which, especially in our days, is in such sore need of them) these burning and shining lights which shall dispel the darkness, rekindle faith, and turn lukewarmness into zeal; these perfect servants who know how to do God's work, and who labour with such marvellous success for their Master's glory and the salvation of the brethren. *"Lord, Lord, give us Saints."*[10]

---

[10] Lacordaire.

APPENDICES

I

PREPARATION FOR FIRST COMMUNION[1]

Rule.

1. So that I may make a good preparation for my first Communion I will say my prayers regularly and always attentively.

2. I will commend my first Communion to Mary, my good Mother, and 1 will pray to her for this constantly.

3. I will force myself to practise the Christian virtues of Obedience, Industry, Patience, and the spirit of Self- sacrifice, and will always fight against my faults.

4. Since the surest way to get to heaven is by receiving Our Lord constantly, I will ask God from this time forth to permit me to communicate frequently after my first Communion.

	Sunday.	Monday.	Tuesday.	Wednesday	Thursday	Friday	Saturday
1. Morning and evening prayers well said?							
2. Decades of the Rosary							
3. Acts of obedience							
4. Industry in work							
5. Acts of patience							
6. Small sacrifices and victories over faults							
7. Other good actions							

The examen to be made every evening, and marks given (figures or noughts) how each point of the rule has been kept.

---

[1] Vol. I., No, 60.

APPENDICES

II

ALL FOR JESUS—TREASURY OF THE SACRED HEART[2]

	Sunday.	Monday.	Tuesday.	Wednesday	Thursday	Friday	Saturday
1. Offering of work to God							
2. Sufferings, contradictions, annoyances patiently endured							
3. Small acts of self-sacrifice							
4. Half-hours of silence							
5. Spiritual readings							
6. Visits to the Blessed sacrament							
7. Decades of the Rosary							
8. Acts of obedience							
9. Acts of charity and kindness							
10. Good actions, good advice, example, etc.							
11. Evil avoided: bad words, fault-finding, disobedience, etc.							

III

RULE OF LIFE FOR ASSOCIATES OF THE SACRED HEART [1]

"WHAT shall it profit a man if he gain the whole world, and lose his own soul?"

Being fully determined to become and to remain all my life long a steadfast and generous Christian, and resolving to put the great work of my salvation before every other thing, and being desirous of labouring courageously for the sanctification of my soul, I resolve to observe the following rule:

---

[2] Vol. I., No. 100

1. RISING.—On waking my first act will be to give my heart to God and to ask for grace to pass the entire day without committing even the slightest fault. I will offer Him all the day's actions. I will rise immediately, never giving way to sloth, say my prayers attentively, after having placed myself in God's presence. I will then recite a decade of the Rosary for the intentions of the Association, to draw God's grace down on myself and my companions, and afterwards read two or three pages of some spiritual book.

Study.—In class I will be very attentive at prayers. I will offer my work to God, remembering that only work done for Him has any reward. I will say, "It is God Himself who commands me to work, and in working well I am sure of pleasing Him."

2. VIRTUES TO BE PRACTISED—*Obedience.*—This shall be my favourite virtue. I will obey, promptly and without questioning, all orders given to me, either by parents or masters, and ever remember that all orders from Superiors are commands from God Himself.

Patience and Gentleness.—To keep myself from giving way to anger and impatience I will remember what Jesus has suffered for me, and I will bear uncomplainingly, for the love of Him and in expiation of my own sins, everything which might annoy me.

Charity and Zeal.—I propose every day to perform some act of this beautiful virtue of charity, by deeds of kindness, and especially by striving to do good to my companions.

Christian Mortification.—Every day I will make at least one act of self-sacrifice which I will offer to the Sacred Heart.

Purity.—I will constantly pray to Mary to guard in me this beautiful virtue, so dear to the Heart of God, and in order to preserve it intact I will drive every bad thought from my heart, and abstain from any words which are in the least dangerous; above all, I will fly from bad company as though it were the plague.

3. BEDTIME.—Every evening, if I have not already done so, I will write up my tables of the Sacred Heart. I will recite a decade of the Rosary for the same intentions as in the morning. If I have omitted my spiritual reading, I will do it now without fail before going to bed. I will omit neither my evening prayers nor my examen of conscience.

4. DEVOTION TO THE BLESSED VIRGIN.—I will have a great devotion for the Blessed Virgin, and put great trust in her. I will scrupulously observe the month of Mary and that of the Holy Rosary. Whenever I require any grace, or am in any trouble, I will address myself to the Blessed Virgin as to a dear Mother who is worthy of my fullest confidence.

5. SACRAMENTS.—I will prepare myself for them with the utmost care. I will never go to Confession without having prayed devoutly, nor without real contrition, always remembering, before entering the confessional, how our dear Lord has suffered for my sins. I will prepare myself for my Communions by earnest prayers and offerings, setting myself, with this intention, to be obedient, patient, and industrious. I will commend them always to Mary, and after my Communions I will make a fervent act of thanksgiving.

I will read over this rule every Sunday for the first two months, then on the first Sunday in the month, and examine myself whether I have kept it faithfully.

IV

ACTS OF PENANCE FOR SPENDING THE HOLY SEASON OF LENT LIKE A TRUE CHRISTIAN MAN[3]

"IF any man will come after Me," our Lord Jesus Christ has said, "let him deny himself, and take up his cross and follow Me." "He that loveth .his life shall lose it, and he that hateth his life in this world keepeth it unto life eternal." "I chastise my body," says St. Paul, "and bring it unto subjection, lest . . . I should become a castaway." This is the foundation of the evangelical teaching, this is the practice of real Christians. In fact, he alone is a true Christian who does not shrink from a little suffering for the sake of the God who has suffered so much for us; he who strives to expiate his sins by penance, and who knows how to gain the mastery over himself and not to yield to all his own caprices, checks his faults, and ends by triumphing over them; while he who always follows his own will becomes the most unhappy and the most vicious of men.

1. I will do what I have to do at once, instead of putting it off. For example, if I receive any order, instead of saying "Presently," to obey instantly. If I have some tiresome duty or occupation, to set about it first, instead of beginning with what I like best.

2. To keep silence every day for a given time.

3. At meals to accept what comes, instead of grumbling, and even, for the sake of being like Our Lord, who on the Cross was ready to slake His thirst with vinegar and gall, to choose what I like least.

4. At the hour for rising, to leave my bed without a

---

[3] Vol. I,, No. III.

moment's delay.

5. To give way readily to others instead of being obstinate and arguing; to do their will rather than my own.

6. To mortify the eyes, and not to stop needlessly in the streets to look at everything that I meet.

7. To abstain for a fixed time from raising the eyes in class, and particularly in church ; to give all my thoughts to my work and my prayers, instead of looking about to see what is going on.

8. If I am very anxious to say some unnecessary thing, not to say it.

9. For the greater detestation of my sins, and for the sake of acquiring more courage with which to fight against my faults, I will meditate from time to time on Our Lord's Passion and all that He has suffered on account of sin.

V

ACTS OF PENANCE FOR SPENDING THE HOLY SEASON OF LENT LIKE A TRUE CHRISTIAN WOMAN

"IF any man will come after Me," said Our Lord Jesus Christ, "let him deny himself, and take up his cross and follow Me." "He that loveth his life shall lose it," He has said again, "and he that hateth his life in this world keepeth it unto life eternal."

"You will make no progress in virtue," says the *Imitation,* "unless you do violence unto yourself."

This is, in fact, the foundation of the Gospel teaching. It is the doctrine which the Church brings before all Christians, particularly at this holy time of the year. We should mortify ourselves for the love of Jesus, happy to suffer something for the God who has suffered so much for us. We should mortify ourselves in expiation of our sins, in order to learn to conquer our own selves and to be victorious over our faults; to draw God's blessings down upon us and those dear to us; to obtain the conversion of so many unhappy sinners and to prevent their falling into hell; to assuage the grievous sufferings of the souls in Purgatory. For the better understanding and practice of this great and beautiful virtue of penance I will read over, from time to time, the following list of the various mortifications which I could easily practise, and, without thinking myself bound to perform them all, I could adopt now one, now another:

1. Instead of putting off anything that I may have to do, to do it at once. For instance, if I receive any orders, instead of saying "Presently," to obey immediately. If I have a tiresome duty or occupation to perform, to take this first, instead of beginning with what I like best.

2. To keep silence every day for a given time.

3. When I am inclined to plunge eagerly into any business, or to give myself up to some occupation, because it is to my taste rather than for its real utility, to sacrifice it, or at least to make myself wait awhile.

4. If I am slightly indisposed, or am feeling sad or vexed, to force myself all the same to seem cheerful and to be generally pleasant.

5. At meals, instead of grumbling about the dishes, to accept whatever comes, and even, for the sake of imitating Jesus, who on His Cross desired to quench His thirst with vinegar and gall, choose the things which I like least.

6. Not to try to know everything; to mortify my curiosity by

paying no heed to useless things and those which do not concern me.

7. To rise from my bed at the proper hour without a moment's delay.

8. To accept discomforts and the being deprived of small indulgences uncomplainingly, and even at times to forego superfluities and things which merely gratify my nature.

9. To set myself, in accordance with the counsel of the *Imitation,* to do the will of others rather than my own.

10. In the streets occasionally to make the sacrifice of not looking at everything that I meet.

11. To refrain for a certain time from raising my eyes in class. Not to look round if anything occurs which attracts attention or excites curiosity.

12. If I wish particularly to tell some story, or to make some needless remark, to keep silence or to speak of something else.

13. The better to conform myself to true Christian charity, to seek out especially those of my companions for whom I feel the least sympathy, and to be very friendly towards them.

14. If I desire anything particularly, and long for it to the point of having my head so full of it that it interferes with my duties and occupations, to condemn myself not to think of it any more, and to drive the thought out of my mind.

15. To make a practice sometimes during the day of exciting in my mind lively feelings of contrition. To do this at fixed times. For instance, when the clock strikes, to place myself in spirit at the side of Jesus suffering; to represent Him to myself in His agony or His scourging, or on Calvary; to remember that my sins were the cause of His torments, and to ask His pardon devoutly.

VI

TABLE FOR THE USE OF BEGINNERS IN THE EXERCISE OF MENTAL PRAYER[4]

I.—THE PRESENCE OF GOD.

1. GOD, Who is *present everywhere,* sees me.
2. God is *within my heart*
3. Jesus Christ *looks down* upon me from heaven.
4. To think of Jesus Christ as *close to me.*

N.B.—Dwell for some time on one or other of these thoughts. If in church, choose the last for preference, as we are then really close to Our Lord.

Prostrate yourself before God and adore Him. Ask His pardon (Act of Contrition or *Confiteor*).

Ask His aid in your prayers. Invoke Mary or your guardian angel.

II.—CONSIDERATIONS.
Object.

Some great truth, such as Death, Heaven, Hell.

Some virtue or failing.

Some mystery of our Blessed Lord's Nativity or Passion.

Some spiritual reading, meditating upon each passage.

Method.

Consider the truth which you have selected.

Call to mind the circumstances of the mystery in question.

Say to yourself that to follow virtue and to flee vice is—

1. *Right,* because not honesty only, but gratitude towards such a merciful God, makes it a duty.

---

[4] Vol 1., No, 138.

2. Advantageous, both for this life and especially for the next.

3. Easy, because so many others succeed with the aid of grace.

III.—ENTER INTO YOURSELF.

Call to mind your needs, your faults, your sins.

Consider how far you are from virtue, although you have admitted the importance of it.

IV —PETITIONS.
General Rule.

Speak to Jesus Christ as to a benefactor, a father, a friend.

Special Rule

Remind Our Lord of His many promises to hear all prayers offered in faith.

Tell Him that your weakness can accomplish everything with the aid of His grace.

Assure Him that you do not trust in your own qualities or merits, that you rely solely upon His merits and sufferings.

Invoke Mary, your good angel, your patron Saint.

V.—RESOLUTIONS.
Protestation.

I will prove the sincerity of my prayer.

Promise.

To-day in such circumstances I will perform such an act of virtue, I will avoid such a wrong action.

Perseverance.

I have often made these resolutions. If necessary, I will renew them again and again without ever losing heart.

Pater, Ave.

Another method consists in taking a prayer—*Paternoster, Salve Regina, Memorare,* etc.—and reciting it, pausing after each sentence, or even word, to meditate upon it.

Those who find it really impossible to set apart some time for meditation can make it while they are at work. Choose the moment least liable to interruption, and begin by placing yourself in God's presence. If alone, it will be better to interrupt your work and kneel for a moment, then continue your occupation, letting your mind dwell on some pious thoughts and communings with Our Lord. Conclude always by making some resolutions.

Should it be possible while at work to keep the foregoing table before your eyes, it would be a great help.

Mental prayer thus understood is possible for every one, no matter how fully occupied they may be, and it is of the greatest service.

"Without prayer," says St. Francis of Assisi, "no one can advance in virtue." "I know of no better way of salvation than mental prayer," said St. John Baptist de Rossi; "on the day when we have not meditated let us beware lest we fall into sin." "Whatever the faults of those who are beginning to pray, they must not give it up," says St. Teresa ; "if they persevere they will end by correcting them." "Nothing is of more service than prayer," she says again; "it is a necessity even in the case of those who offend God instead of serving Him." "Many fast," says St. Alphonsus, "recite the Rosary, and the Office of the Blessed Virgin, and yet remain sinners; but it is impossible for one who is faithful in prayer to continue to live in sin."

APPENDICES

OBJECTIONS OFFERED WITH REGARD TO THE PRACTICE OP MEDITATION

1. *"I have no time"*—You have plenty of leisure to eat, you manage to devote sufficient time to the satisfaction of your bodily needs. Is your soul of less value to you?

2. *"I try, but all my prayer resolves itself into efforts which end in nothing. It is time lost."*—Your time is being very well spent: your efforts are full of merit; your prayer is good and more fruitful than you think.

3. *"I have tried so often that I have lost heart"*—Say to God that you do this only to please Him, and not for your own satisfaction. Tell Him also that, as your attempts to meditate are pleasing to Him, you will continue them, although for a long time to come you should experience only failure and difficulties. In the path of prayer perseverance is especially needed. It is only, as a rule, after a long time and repeated efforts that prayer becomes an easy and pleasant thing. But why fear the trouble? Are not whole years required for the attainment of the least of human knowledge? A child does not learn to read or cipher, nor does an apprentice become a clever workman, in a week or a month. When we realize the importance of prayer we shall not allow ourselves to be put off by difficulties at the outset.

4. *"I make my meditation tolerably well as a ride, but just now I am too much worried, and have too many cares and distractions. I cannot fix my attention upon pious subjects. Always, in spite of myself, I come back to my preoccupations."*—If they are legitimate cares, if it is a question of some important affair, the thought of which is as tenacious as you say, speak of it to Our Lord, open your heart to Him, tell Him your anxieties, and entreat Him to direct the

307

matter in accordance with His interests, His glory, and the greatest good of your soul.

5. *"I find no difficulty in placing myself in the presence of God, and I turn to Him naturally and easily, opening all the desires of my heart and my resolutions to Him. But l go astray in my considerations."*—In this case do not dwell on the considerations; since you can hold communion with Our Lord, your prayer is excellent.

VII
ACTS OF MORTIFICATION[5]

"IF any man will come after Me," said Our Lord Jesus Christ, "let him deny himself, and take up his cross and follow Me." "He that loveth his life shall lose it," He says again, "and he that hateth his life in this world keepeth it unto life eternal." "I chastise my body," says St. Paul, "and bring it unto subjection, lest ... I should become a castaway." "You will make no progress in virtue," says the *Imitation*, "unless you do violence to yourselves."

I am therefore resolved to do penance and to mortify myself. I will mortify myself for love of Jesus, that I may suffer a little for my God, who has suffered so much for me. I will mortify myself in expiation of my sins; to learn to conquer myself, and to overcome my faults; to draw down God's blessings on me and all those dear to me; to obtain the conversion of so many unhappy sinners; to assuage the grievous sufferings of the souls in Purgatory. These are the various penances which I will oblige myself to perform, and carefully examine myself with regard to them.

---

[5] Vol I., No. 204.

APPENDICES

I

First, those which I will make a part of my daily life, practising them whenever the opportunity offers.

1. A generous acceptance, accompanied by an inner act of thanksgiving to God, for everything that is contrary to my will, whether in my work or other occupations, or on the part of my superiors or equals.

2. To renounce *instantly* everything which is opposed to the duties of my state, to my particular rule, or the virtue which I ought specially to strive to acquire.

3. To keep silence for a given time every day.

4. Not to complain of anything whatsoever—weather, heat or cold, men or things.

5. To recite all, even the least, of my prayers—such, for example, as the *Benedicite* and Grace—slowly.

(I will take these five resolutions especially on Monday mornings, and examine myself at least twice during the day as to how I have observed them.)

6. I will impose a short delay upon myself before reading a letter, and generally, when I am inclined to fall eagerly upon something which gratifies my nature, I will keep myself waiting for a time.

7. When I feel sad I will compel myself to appear cheerful and always pleasant.

8. Never to say to anyone that I am suffering because of this or that, when it is some slight cause which does not require any attention.

9. To eat quickly, and without stopping to taste them, the dishes that I like best, and to accept readily these which I dislike.

(These four articles will be the subject of my resolution and examen on Tuesdays.)

10. At meals to choose what I like least.

11. Not to try to know all the latest news; to mortify my curiosity by giving no heed to useless things which do not concern me.

12. To rise each morning at the first signal, as if the house were on fire.

13. To discontinue *without the least delay* any occupations in which I am taking pleasure when duty, my rule, charity, or any other virtue, calls me elsewhere.

(These points will be the matter of my resolutions and examen on Wednesdays.)

14. If others do not agree with me in matters of slight importance, to keep silence and not press my opinion.

15. To grant everything that anyone asks of me, not hesitating to put myself out for the sake of obliging others, and if compelled to refuse I will try to make my refusal acceptable by my pleasant words.

16. Only to make use of the conveniences and luxuries of life when necessary—for example, to go away from the fire or to take my feet from the foot-warmer as soon as I am warm enough. To prefer, as a rule, to be a little inconvenienced, taking as a maxim these words of St. Francis of Sales: "I am never so well off as when I am badly off."

17. Whenever I awake in the night to raise my heart to God, and repeat ten times "My Jesus, mercy" for the holy souls in Purgatory.

18. To resolve to try always to please others instead of myself.

(I will practise these acts of mortification particularly on Thursdays, and offer them to God in view of my next confession, that I may obtain a lively contrition for my faults.)

II

The following penances I can perform from time to time: First, on Friday—

19. For some minutes together to adopt an uncomfortable posture—not leaning back, for instance, or not changing my position when seated.

20. If alone and sure of not being observed, to recite one or more decades of the Rosary or the *Miserere*, with arms extended in the form of a cross.

21. Not to look to the right or the left when out walking.

22. To refrain from raising my eyes for a certain time when at work, and more particularly in church; not to turn my head if something occurs which attracts attention or excites curiosity,

23. Whenever a clock strikes, to put myself in spirit at the feet of Jesus suffering (His agony, scourging, crowning with thorns, crucifixion, etc.), and remind myself of the part which I have had in His torments by my sins, and ask His pardon earnestly.

24. To kiss the ground in expiation of my sins of the tongue, and trace a cross on the ground.

On Saturdays the following acts of mortification may be offered in preparation for Sunday's Communion:

25. To eat your bread dry at meals if you can do so unperceived.

26. To bear any little inconveniences or small pains patiently, without trying to get rid of them.

27. To substitute another remark for one which I am particularly anxious to make, and deny myself the pleasure of telling some piece of news.

28. For the space of half an hour to drive from my mind everything that does not relate to God, and occupy myself with pious thoughts, or to commune with God for the same length of time.

On Sundays I will select the following mortifications, and offer them in thanksgiving for the morning's communion:

29. Seek out those persons who attract me the least, and make myself very pleasant to them.

30. Give up for to-day some part of my dress which pleases me particularly, and choose another that I do not like so well.

31. When anything appeals to me very strongly, and I am specially anxious to have it, to banish the thought of it from my mind.

32. Not to excuse myself when blamed, whether by my superiors or equals.

33. To strike or hurt myself in some other way, whenever I have been guilty of any fault.

THE END

88271318R00179